# CENTRAL ILLINOIS CHRONICLES

## Volume 3

*Helen Cox Tregillis*

HERITAGE BOOKS
2019

## HERITAGE BOOKS
*AN IMPRINT OF HERITAGE BOOKS, INC.*

### Books, CDs, and more—Worldwide

For our listing of thousands of titles see our website
at
www.HeritageBooks.com

Published 2019 by
HERITAGE BOOKS, INC.
Publishing Division
5810 Ruatan Street
Berwyn Heights, Md. 20740

Copyright © 1998 Helen Cox Tregillis

Heritage Books by the author:

*Ancestors: A Teaching Story Using the Families of Cox, Hayes, Hulse,
Range, Worley and Others with Suggested Lessons*

*Central Illinois Chronicles, Volumes 1-3*

*Illinois, the 14th Colony: French Period*

*Indians of Illinois*

*People and Rural Schools of Shelby County, Illinois*

*River Roads to Freedom: Fugitive Slave Notices and Sheriff Notices Found in Illinois Sources*

*The Native Tribes of Ohio*

All rights reserved. No part of this book may be reproduced or transmitted in any form or by any means, electronic or mechanical, including photocopying, recording or by any information storage and retrieval system without written permission from the author, except for the inclusion of brief quotations in a review.

International Standard Book Numbers
Paperbound: 978-0-7884-4944-4
Clothbound: 978-0-7884-8196-3

CONTENTS

Volume III, Number I..........................................................................1
   Boone Co., Cass Co., Champaign Co., Christian Co., Clark Co., Crawford
      Co., Edgar Co., Fayette Co., Gallatin Co., Hamilton Co., Illinois,
      Monroe Co., Pope Co., Richland Co., Shelby Co., Washington Co., Wayne
      Co., White Co., Whiteside Co., Searching Illinois Ancestors.

Volume III, Number II........................................................................30
   Christian Co., Clay Co., Clinton Co., Coles Co., Cook Co., Edgar Co.,
      Fayette Co., Hamilton Co., Hancock Co., Illinois, McDonough Co., Saline
      Co., Shelby Co., Union Co., Vermilion Co., Wabash Co., Warren Co.,
      Searching Illinois Ancestors.

Volume III, Number III.......................................................................57
   Christian Co., Crawford Co., Cumberland Co., DeKalb Co., DeWitt Co., Edgar
      Co., Fayette Co., Franklin Co., Hamilton Co., Illiinois., Shelby Co.,
      Stark Co., St.Clair Co., Stephenson Co., Tazewell Co., Searching
      Illinois Ancestors, Index.

Volume III, Number IV........................................................................83
   Alexander Co., Christian Co., Clark Co., Coles Co., Cumberland Co.,
      Douglas Co., DuPage Co., Edgar Co., Edwards Co., Ford Co., Franklin Co.,
      Jackson Co., Jefferson Co., Moultrie Co., Perry Co., Union Co., Shelby
      Co., Pedigree Chart, Searching Illinois Ancestors, Index.

Volume III, Number V........................................................................103
   Book Reviews, Christian Co., Cumberland Co., Edgar Co., Fulton Co.,
      Gallatin Co., Jackson Co., Lawrence Co., Macon Co., Moultrie Co., Peoria
      Co., Putnam Co., Randolph Co., Richland Co., Rock Island Co., Shelby
      Co., Searching Illinois Ancestors, Index.

Volume III, Number VI.......................................................................120
   Christian Co., Clay Co., Clinton Co., Coles Co., Effingham Co., Fayette
      Co., Gallatin Co., Greene Co., Illinois Biographies, 1910, Illinois
      Mounted Volunteer Regiment, Black Hawk War, Illinois Mounted Regiment,
      War of 1812, Johnson Co., Lawrence Co., Perry Co., Shelby Co.,
      Williamson Co, Searching Illinois Ancestors Queries, Index.

SEARCHING ILLLINOIS ANCESTORS

VOLUME III NO. I

November December 1986

INDEXED IN GENEALOGICAL PERIODICAL INDEX

Issued bi-monthly by Helen Cox Tregillis. Publication and advertising offices: Box 392, Shelbyville, IL 62565. Current single copy price, $2 plus 69 cents postage. Yearly subscription, $12. Send check or money order payable to: Helen Cox Tregillis, Box 392, Shelbyville, IL 62565. Surnames, articles appearing in publication are indexed in GENEALOGICAL PERIODICAL INDEX. Postage paid at Shelbyville, IL. Send address changes, queries, advertising to above address.

ISSN 0886 - 7763
PAYMENT MUST ACCOMPANY SUBSCRIPTION, QUERY AND ADVERTISING

## TABLE OF CONTENTS, VOLUME III NO. I

| | |
|---|---|
| Boone County | |
|     Genealogical Sources, Help | 2 |
|     Marriage Records | 2 |
| Cass County | |
|     Genealogical Sources, Help | 3 |
| Champaign County | |
|     Genealogical Sources, Help | 3 |
| Christian County | |
|     Genealogical Sources, Help | 4 |
|     Marriages | 5 |
| Clark County | |
|     Genealogical Sources, Help | 6 |
| Crawford County | |
|     Genealogical Sources, Help | 6 |
|     1883, Biographical Surnames | 7 |
| Edgar County | |
|     Genealogical Sources, Help | 8 |
|     Marriages | 8 |
| Fayette County | |
|     Genealogical Sources, Help | 9 |
|     Newspaper Abstracts | 9 |
| Gallatin County | |
|     Genealogical Sources, Help | 13 |
|     1887, Biographical Surnames | 14 |
| Hamilton County | |
|     Genealogical Sources, Help | 14 |
|     Newspaper Abstracts | 14 |
|     Black War Regiment | 15 |
| Illinois: War of 1812 Regiments | 16 |
| Monroe County | |
|     Genealogical Sources, Help | 16 |
|     Delinquent Taxes of 1833 | 17 |
| Pope County | |
|     Genealogical Sources, Help | 17 |
|     Newspaper Abstracts | 18 |
| Richland County | |
|     Genealogical Sources, Help | 19 |
| Shelby County | |
|     Genealogical Sources, Help | 20 |
|     Early Divorces | 20 |
|     Miscellaneous Records | 21 |
| Washington County | |
|     Genealogical Sources, Help | 22 |
|     Delinquent Taxes of 1833 | 23 |
| Wayne County | |
|     Genealogical Sources, Help | 23 |
|     Black Hawk War Regiment | 23 |
| White County | |
|     Genealogical Sources, Help | 24 |
|     Black Hawk War Regiment | 24 |
| Whiteside County | |
|     Genealogical Sources, Help | 24 |
| SEARCHING ILLINOIS ANCESTORS | 1,11,12,13,25,26 |

## SEARCHING ILLINOIS ANCESTORS
## COUNTY, SURNAME, PERSON SEARCHING

SHELBY: Kilgore, Jones, Austin, Reed
    Jim Lattit, Box 213, Columbia, IL 62236
SHELBY: Kirchner
    Ray Kruse, 9736 S. Broadway, St. Louis, MO 63125
SHELBY: Marshall
    Mrs. Jerome F. Parenteau, 2 Club Drive, Sunnybrook, Phoenix, MD 21131
CHRISTIAN: Drake, Short
    Doris D. Haugen, 16 W. 600 N. Main, Farmington, UT 84025
CHAMPAIGN, VERMILION: Hillsberry, Brakes; COUNTY UNKNOWN: Ragsdale; PERRY: Arterberry, Atterberry
    Nova Lemons, 12206 Brisbane, Dallas, TX 75234
CLAY CITY, ILL.: Markland
    Cleora Craw, 1409 Meadowwear Dr., Austin, TX 78753
WHITE: Jones, Pearce
    Florence Morrison, 3309 Santa Rosa Ave. 29, Santa Rosa, CA 95407
MENARD: Alsbury
    Nancy Smith, 1141 East Meadowmere, Springfield, MO 65807
WILL: Theiler, Scheidt, Wanner
    Laura Barthelme, 6901 Blaisdell Ave., Richfield, MN 55423
WASHINGTON: Ragland, Maxwell
    Ruth D. Gregory, 3436 Surry Place, Fremont, CA 94536
COOK: Mrs. A.D. Cope, 1123 Alexander, Winfield, KS 67156
ALTON, ILL: Smith, Leonard
    Patricia J. Bugher, 418 Indiana St., Park Forest, IL 60466
MORGAN: Carlisle, Stott, Hoopes; LIVINGSTON: Hummel
    Linda E. Bivenour, 1002 Piermont St., Philadelphia, PA 19116
FULTON: Gossett, Shaw; KNOX: Gossett, Shaw; EDGAR: Laswell, Dellague, Rickords, Ryason; MERCER: Higgins, Moriarty, Conway, Ayers
    Letha L.M. Trebbe, 3801 W. 13th St., No. 906, Wichita, KS 67203
FAYETTE: Bee, Erickson, Keen, Long; FORD, LIVINGSTON: Bennett, Steward/t; LOGAN/PEORIA: Brockett, Hunn, Lake, Merritt
    Beulah S. Weaver, 535 Cornelia, apt. 1104, Chicago, IL 60657
MADISON: Dorman
    Kathleen Hontz Jeanneret, 700 North 16th Street, Kansas City, KS 66102
FRANKLIN: Webb, Taylor, Neal, Phillips, Washburn, Sims
    Ethelyn M. Crawford, 1230 W. Battlement Pkwy K-203, Parachute, CO 81635
WILLIAMSON: Hornbeck/Hornback, Baker, Wood, Brown, Smith
    Shirley McClean Hornbeck, P.O. Box 5061, Hac. Hts., CA 91745
COOK: Londergan, O'Connor
    Mrs. Judy M. Smith, 9117 Chaney Ave., Downey, CA 90240
CHRISTIAN: Armstrong, Henderson, Hutchison
    Fred L. Venaas, P.O. Box 81, Springfield, IL 62705

## BOONE COUNTY, ILLINOIS
## GENEALOGICAL SOURCES, HELP

Boone County created 4 March 1837 from parent county Winnebago. Named for Daniel Boone. County seat at Belvidere, IL 61008 has vital, land records (county clerk, 815-544-3103) and court records (circuit clerk, 815-544-0371). Court house hours: Monday through Friday, 8:30 to 5. Boone county located on north boundary line of state between Winnebago and McHenry. Illinois genealogical society that covers this county and others is North Central Illinois Genealogical Society, P.O. Box 1071, Rockford, IL 61105. Society had a bi-monthly as of 1983.

### SOURCES

1892, PORTRAIT AND BIOGRAPHICAL RECORD OF WINNEBAGO AND BOONE COUNTIES, by Biographical Publishing Co.

1850 Boone County, Illinois Census by Harley Haskin.

Cemetery Inscriptions of Flora and Manchester twps., 1971, Hazel Hyde and Taylor Decker.

1877, PAST AND PRESENT OF BOONE COUNTY, ILLINOIS by H.F. Kett & Co.

BOONE COUNTY RECORDS by Mrs. Harlin B. Taylor, 1972.

COMBINED ATLASES OF WINNEBAGO AND BOONE CO. by North Central Ill. Gen. Soc., 1984. Indexed.

Check with the society for other genealogical aids.

## BOONE COUNTY, ILLINOIS
## MARRIAGE RECORDS, COUNTY CLERK

Sept. 4, 1851 J.B. WATKINS and Ann E.J. TANNER
Aug. 25, 1851 Richard HEWIT and Mrs. Clarissa STORY
Aug. 23, 1851 Samuel E. STEVENSON and Sarah E. WILLARD
Sept. 1, 1851 A.J. BUCK and Nancy D. HOYT
Sept. 12, 1851 Folney LEWIS and Rosalia HAWLEY
Sept. 25, 1851 Otis OSBORNE and Ann CRANE
Oct. 16, 1851 John M. ADAMS and Caroline JOHNSON
Oct. 16, 1851 Spencer JOHNSON and Augusta FOSTER
Oct. 8, 1851 Nathan BECKER and Angelia SPENCER
Oct. 4, 1851 Ole JOHNSON and Ann JOHNSON
Nov. 5, 1851 Hitam HAWLEY and Arvilla FARRAND
Nov. 8, 1851 Erastus BURROUGHS and Mary WEBSTER
Oct. 18, 1851 William McCARTY and Mrs. Nancy GIBBS
Nov. 17, 1851 John E. EMERY and Abagail CONWELL
Oct. 20, 1851 John INMAN and Susan E. HUBBARD
Nov. 23, 1851 Jacob HOUDESBELL and Emily YOUNG
Nov. 10, 1851 Alman HULL and Nancy SMITH
Nov. 22, 1851 Thorr OLESON and Margaret Tostem DATTER
Nov. 27, 1851 Trustom DODGSTO and Adeline HARVEY
Oct. 22, 1851 Ole ELLENSON and Sarah NELSON
Nov. 18, 1851 George W. AVERY and Ann SHATTUCK
Dec. 7, 1851 Thomas DEAN and Healthy WITTER
Nov. 20, 1851 Thomas GOUGH and Harriett CAPERZ

Dec. 14, 1851 Sereno CHANDLER and Laura TILLOTSON
Nov. 18, 1851 H.H. LAND and Lucinda D. PERRY
Dec. 18, 1851 Yates V. BEBEE and Julia A. WINKLER
Dec. 17, 1851 Michael HERRINGTON and Rachel WARD
Dec. 16, 1851 Joseph NORTON and Mary E. BROCKWAY
Dec. 3, 1851 Thomas CUNHAM and Nancy HALE
Dec. 31, 1851 Franklin L. FULLER and Mary Ann HIGGINS

---

## CASS COUNTY, ILLINOIS
## GENEALOGICAL SOURCES, HELP

Cass County created 3 March 1837 from parent county Morgan. Named for Gen. Lewis Cass. County seat at Virginia, IL 62691 has vital, land records (county clerk, 217-452-7217) and court records (circuit clerk, 217-452-7225). Court house hours: Monday through Friday, 8:30 to 4:30. Cass county located on east side of Illinois River, between Morgan and Menard. Illinois genealogical society that covers this county and others is Jacksonville Area Genealogical and Historical Society, P.O. Box 21, Jacksonville, IL 62651.

### SOURCES

1840 Census Index, Adams through DuPage Co., Ill. Vol. 1 by Wormer, 1973.

1850 Census of Cass County by Fox, 1970.

CASS COUNTY SESQUINCENTENNIAL by Dowell, 1968.

CASS COUNTY, ILLINOIS by Perrin, reprinted 1968. Index only.

County board minutes, 1837 to 1843; 1849 to 1878 at State of Illinois Archives, Springfield, Ill.

1855 State Census Index by Linda Allison and Violet Taylor.

1915, HISTORY OF CASS COUNTY, Vol. 2 by Newton Bateman, editor.

1892, BIOGRAPHICAL REVIEW OF CASS, SCHUYLER AND BROWN COUNTIES.

1874, Illustrated Atlas Map of Cass County by W.R. Brink & Co.

OLD CEMETERIES OF CASS COUNTY by Arthur Crumrin, 1978.

BURIALS GAR CEMETERY, HOMER, 1971, by Decatur Genealogical Society.

1873, EARLY HISTORY OF THE SANGAMON COUNTRY.

1882, HISTORY OF CASS COUNTY by William Henry Perrin.

CASS COUNTY, ILL. MARRIAGES by Mrs. Edna Renner and Mrs. Mary Ann Bell, 1980.

TO MAKE A HOME IN PIONEER CASS COUNTY by Marjorie C. Taylor, 1979.

Check with the society for other genealogical aids.

---

## CHAMPAIGN COUNTY, ILLINOIS
## GENEALOGICAL SOURCES, HELP

Champaign County created 20 Feb. 1833 from parent county Vermilion. Named for county in Ohio. County seat at Urbana, IL 61801 has vital, land records (county clerk, 217-384-3720) and court records (circuit clerk, 217-384-3725). Court house hours: Monday through Friday, 8 to 4:30. Champaign county located in central eastern portion of Illinois between Vermilion and Piatt. Illinois genealogical society that covers this county is Champaign County Genealogical Society, Urbana Free Library, Archives Room, 201 S. Race, Urbana, IL 61801.

## SOURCES

1840 Census Index Adams through DuPage Co., Ill. by Wormer, 1973.

Champaign County Board Minutes 1833-1849; 1859-1867 at State of Illinois Archives, Springfield, Ill.

1905, HISTORY OF CHAMPAIGN COUNTY, Vol. 2 by Newton Bateman, editor.

1900, BIOGRAPHICAL RECORD OF CHAMPAIGN COUNTY, ILL.

1878, HISTORY OF CHAMPAIGN COUNTY, ILLINOIS.

1871, CHAMPAIGN COUNTY DIRECTORY by J. Lothrop.

EARLY HISTORY AND PIONEERS OF CHAMPAIGN CO., 1886 by Milton W. Mathews.

Plat book of Champaign County, 1893, by George Ogle & Co.

Cemeteries of Champaign Co., a Location Guide by Fonda D. Baselt and Josephine F. Moeller, 1984.

1887, PORTRAIT AND BIOGRAPHICAL ALBUM OF CHAMPAIGN COUNTY by Chapman Brothers.

THE 125TH REGIMENT, ILL. VOL. INF., CIVIL WAR by Robert M. Rogers, 1984 reprint of 1882.

Check with the society for other genealogical aids.

-----------

## CHRISTIAN COUNTY, ILLINOIS
## GENEALOGICAL SOURCES, HELP

Christian County created 15 Feb. 1839 from parent counties, Sangamon and Shelby. First called Dane county till 1840, then named Christian for county in Kentucky. County seat at Taylorville, IL 62568 has vital, land records (county clerk, 217-824-4969) and court records (circuit clerk, 217-824-4966). Court house hours: Monday through Friday, 8 to 4. Christian county is located central Illinois between Shelby and Sangamon. Illinois genealogical society that covers this county is Christian County Genealogical Society, P.O. Box 174, Taylorville, IL 62568.

## SOURCES

1840 Census Index of Adams through DuPage Counties, Ill., Vol. 1 by Wormer, 1973.

1850 Census of Christian Co., Ill. by Puckett and Shellhammer, 1971.

County Board Minutes 1839 to 1911 at Illinois State Archives, Springfield, Ill.

1918, HISTORY OF CHRISTIAN COUNTY, vol. 2 by Newton Bateman, editor.

Cemetery Inscriptions, four volumes by Decatur Genealogical Society.

1840 Christian County, Ill. Census by Decatur Genealogical Society, 1975.

1893, PORTRAIT AND BIOGRAPHICAL RECORD OF CHRISTIAN COUNTY.

1904, PORTAIT AND BIOGRAPHICAL RECORD OF CHRISTIAN COUNTY.

Check with the society for other genealogical aids.

CHRISTIAN COUNTY, ILL.
MARRIAGES, COUNTY CLERK
1839-1866, Book I

Robert HAYWARD and Amelia J. LEIGH, page 2
Justus HINKLE and Hannah MILLER, page 4
West HARRIS and Wenny Ann ESTUS, page 6
George HANING and Sarah MILLER, page 9
William HOLDFORD and Susan HUTCHEN, page 10
Burgess HARRIS and Mary Ann SHARROCK, page 10
William F. HALL and Gloriana JACOBS, page 13
Franklin HAINES and Mary HENDRICKS, page 13
George W. HOOVER and Nancy ADAMS, page 17
James H. HILL and Nancy RALSTON, page 18
Jacob HANSON and Lucinda HALIN, page 18
William R. HARPER and Mary Ellen SANDERS, page 19
George R. HONNOLD and Ann PORTER, page 21
Isaac HARRIS and Sally GOODEN, page ??
Lucian HIGBEE and Lura A. LILLIE, page 23
John HAMLIN and Mary DYSON, page 25
Jaber HALL and Melinda J. WATKINS, page 26
Thomas J. HARDIN and Harriet BEARDEN, page 27
Justus HINKLE and Susan BRADLEY, page 27
William HARGIS and Nancy B. HALFORD, page 27
Jesse HANON and Missouri Ann MINNIS, page 28
Adison HUMMER and Rebecca A. LANGLEY, page 34
Christopher HARRIS and Louisa WESTBROOK, page 39
William HAYS and Louisa TAYLOR, page 41
William HALFORD and Arrenda BANKSON, page 41
Edwin HARRIS and Ann DUGG, page 42
Tippo HARRIS and Mary Jane HARKER, page 42
Silas HARRIS and Hannah GOODE, page 42
James HERRON and Louisa OVERTON, page 43
Cornelius HARKER and Mary HARKER, page 43
John E. HENRICKS and Sarah A. MORRIS, page 43
Benjamin HARRIS and Nancy R. WELCH, page 43
Joseph HAYWARD and Sarah Ann SMITH, page 44
Edward F. HARDIN and Nancy BELL, page 46
William H. HALFORD and Nancy SPINDLE, page 46
Hardy HINTON and Cinilla KELLER, page 48
Woodson B. HAILEY and Marilda MAUPIN, page 48
Lucian W. HUMMER and Elizabeth COURTNEY, page 49
John HOLLEY and Elizabeth McCAY, page 49
Benj. F. HAILEY and Fanny HILL, page 51
P.B. HAIGHT and Lucinda SKINNER, page 52
Fletcher HAINES and Lydia Ann ANDERSON, page 54
John B. HARRIS and Julia A. KELLER, page 54
Richard HI?VER and Amelia S. CAY, page 55
Hardy HINTON and Delany COX, page 56
John T. HILL and Emily NUCKOLLS, page 57
Isaac HOOVER and Sophia COFFEE, page 57

## CLARK COUNTY, ILLINOIS
## GENEALOGICAL SOURCES, HELP

Clark County created 22 March 1819 from parent county Crawford. Named for George Rogers Clark. County seat at Marshall, IL 62441 has vital, land records (county clerk, 217-826-8311) and court records (circuit clerk, 217-826-2811). Court house hours: Monday through Friday, 8 to 4. Clark County located on the Indiana border between Edgar and Crawford. Illinois genealogical society that covers this county is Clark County Genealogical Society and Library, P.O. Box 153, Marshall, IL 62441.

### SOURCES

1840 Census Index of Adams through DuPage Counties, Vol. I by Wormer, 1973.

County board minutes, 1833 to 1869, State of Illinois Archives, Springfield, Ill.

1907, Historical Encyclopedia of Illinois and History of Clark County, Ill. by Newton Bateman, editor.

1892, Plat book of Clark County, Ill. by George A. Ogle & Co.

1883, History of Crawford and Clark Counties, by William Henry Perrin, editor.

Church records of Martinsville First Baptist Church, 1879-1909.

Roll of Honor, Deceased Ex-service Men and Women in Illinois, 1929, Springfield, Ill.

Check with the society for other genealogical aids.

## CRAWFORD COUNTY, ILLINOIS
## GENEALOGICAL SOURCES, HELP

Crawford County created 31 Dec. 1816 from parent county Edwards. Named for William H. Crawford. County seat at Robinson, IL 62454 has vital, land records (county clerk, 618-546-1212) and court records (circuit clerk, 618-544-3512). Court house hours: Monday through Friday, 8 to 4. Crawford County located Indiana border between Clark and Lawrence Counties. Illinois genealogical society that covers this county is Crawford County Genealogical Society, P.O. Box 110, Robinson, IL 62454.

### SOURCES

1840 Census Index of Adams through DuPage Counties, Ill., Vol. I by Wormer, 1973.

Roll of Honor, Deceased Ex-Service Men and Women in Illinois, 2 volumes, Springfield, Ill., 1929.

1860 Census of Crawford County, Ill. by Deanna McNeely, 1981.

1850 Federal Census of Crawford Co., Ill. by Decatur Genealogical Society, 1970.

Our Crawford County, Ill. Heritage by Donna Gowin Johnston, 1983.

Quaker Lane and Other Upper Crawford Co., Ill. Placenames by William P. Medlin, 1984.

1883, History of Crawford and Clark Counties by W. H. Perrin.

Check with the society for other genealogical aids.

HISTORY OF CRAWFORD AND CLARK COUNTIES, ILL.
1883: Chicago: O.I. Baskin & Co.
Surnames of Biographies Only

Crawford County, Robinson Twp.

Adams, Alexander, Allen, Bales, Barlow, Bishop, Bradbury, Browning, Brubaker, Bull, Callahan, Carey, Collins, Cooper, Cox, Crowley, Davis, Eagleton, Firebaugh, Guinnip, Harper, Hill, Hiser, Huston, Johnson, Jones, Kessler, Kirk, King, Lamb, Lewis, Lindsay, Lowe, Lutes, Mail, Marbry, Maxwell, Meserve, Meyer, Midkiff, Mills, Murphy, Myers, Olwin, Otey, Parker, Price, Reinohl, Robb, Ruddell, Shipman, Short, Steel, St. Clergy, Stephenson, Stephens, Talbot, Walker, Walters, Watkins, Wilkin, Willis, Wilkin, Wilson, Wiseman, Woodworth.

" " , Hutsonville Twp.

Adams, Athey, Bennett, Boyd, Bradbury, Buckner, Chambers, Colliflower, Correll, Cox, Draper, Eaton, Everingham, Fitch, Flesher, Furry, Golden, Green, Hand, Harness, Hill, Holaday, Holmes, Horning, Hurst, Keys, Lindley, McNutt, Megeath, Mount, Musgrave, Newlin, Newton, Olwin, Pearce, Prevo, Rackery, Rains, Rausch, Reynolds, Rogers, Rush, Voorheis.

" " , LaMotte Twp.

Alexander, Andrew, Apple, Boker, Beecher, Cunningham, Daugherty, Decker, Dewitt, Donnell, Emmons, Erfft, Ferguson, Fox, Freeman, Fulling, Gogin, Goodwin, Gordon, Harper, Haskett, Hill, Hughes, Iliff, Johnson, Kitchell, Lackey, Leaverton, Magill, Mail, Malone, Martin, Maxwell, McGahey, Mills, Patton, Paull, Pearce, Pifer, Plunkett, Rafferty, Raney, Richey, Salesberry, Stoner, Swearingen, Sweet, Vane, Walker, Westner, Wilson, Woodworth.

" " , Montgomery Twp.

Adams, Crews, Fox, Fuller, Goodwin, Higgins, Highsmith, Hope, Ingles, Kent, Kincaid, Lindsay, Lynch, MacHatton, McCoy, Mickey, Montgomery, Palmateer, Parker, Reavill, Ross, Seaney, Shaw, Waters, Wesner, Wheeler, Young.

" " , Oblong Twp.

Beeman, Boofter, Dale, Foff, Good, Hale, Henry, Hooper, Ikemier, Kendall, Kibbie, Kirtland, Lackey, Leach, Lefever, Lively, Marshall, McLain, Mitchell, Newbold, Rafferty, Reed, Sears, Siler, Sheets, Snyder, Wilkin, Williams, Winters, Wirt, Wood.

" " , Martin & Southwest Twps.

Carlton, Cortelyon, Donnell, Ducommon, Due, Fristoe, Goff, Haskin, Hicks, Martin, Price, Prier, Richart, Shipman, Siler, Spillman, Weirick, Wilson.

" " , Honey Creek Twp.

Highsmith, Jones, Weger, Parker, Shaw, Thompson, Tohill.

" " , Licking Twp.

Aathey, Lincoln, Vance, Wiman.

" " , Addn. bios.

Crews, Hill, Moers, Pifer, Smith.

## EDGAR COUNTY, ILLINOIS
## GENEALOGICAL SOURCES, HELP

Edgar County created 3 Jan. 1823 from parent county Clark. Named for John Edgar. County seat at Paris, IL 61944 has vital, land records (county clerk, 217-465-4151) and court records (circuit clerk, 217-465-4107). Courthouse hours: Monday through Friday, 8 to 4. Illinois genealogical society that covers this county and others is Clark County Genealogical Society, P.O. Box 153, Marshall, IL 62441.

### SOURCES

County Board Minutes 1823 to 1884 at State of Illinois Archives, Springfield, Ill.

1894, Plat Book of Edgar County, Ill. American Atlas Company.

1905, HISTORICAL ENCYCLOPEDIA OF ILLINOIS AND EDGAR COUNTY. Newton Bateman, editor.

1892, SOUVENIR HISTORY OF EDGAR COUNTY by U.O. Colson.

1879, HISTORY OF EDGAR COUNTY.

1889, PORTRAIT AND BIOGRAPHICAL ALBUM OF VERMILION AND EDGAR COUNTIES.

1830 Federal Census Index of Edgar, etal. Heritage House, Danville, Ill.

Check with the society for other genealogical aids.

## EDGAR COUNTY, ILLINOIS
## MARRIAGE RECORDS, COUNTY CLERK

Sept. 27, 1824 Hiram M. CUREY and Rachel WHITAKER
Jan. 4, 1825 Rezin CRIST and Sophia CLAPP
Jan. 26, 1825 Isaiah CLAYTON and Jane HELPHENSTINE
Nov. 29, 1825 Hezekiah CUMMINGHAM and Mary ALEXANDER
Feb. 25, 1826 Rezin CRIST and Eve ASTIN
Feb. 25, 1826 Levi CLAPP and Polly BURRISS
Oct. 7, 1826 Thomas COX and Jan VANHOUTEN
Nov. 9, 1826 Joseph CLAPP and Lydia HANDLEY
Dec. 14, 1826 John COZAD and Betsy BURR
April 17, 1828 John COX and Margaret BRIGHT
Aug. 20, 1828 Samuel COZAD and Ruhema REDMON
Oct. 25, 1828 John CLAPP and Elizabeth BIDDLECUM
June 20, 1829 James COWAN and Mary J. CRATZER
Dec. 23, 1829 Eli CROAGO and Experience JONES
Jan. 19, 1830 Sandford CLEMENTS and Lavina WEAVER
Feb. 23, 1830 Isaac CRIST and Jane ROGERS
Feb. 27, 1830 Luther C. CONERY and Helen WYATT
April 17, 1830 John CONERY and Nancy LOWRY
Aug. 5, 1830 Geo. T. COLOM and Catharine R. CHINOWITH
April 4, 1831 James CHASTAIN and Cordilia CONREY
April 9, 1831 Isaac CRAIG and Katharine HENSON
June 29, 1831 James F. CRAFTON and Sinai CASADAY
Nov. 22, 1831 Alexander CUNNINGHAM and Elizabeth JAMES
Jan. 13, 1832 Jackson CHANEY and Eveline DONICA

Feb. 20, 1832 Young COHO and Sarah ALLIN
Dec. 9, 1832 John CALDWELL and Mary Ann HINSON
March 27, 1833 George W. CUPPS and Judyam HAYS
May 13, 1833 James CHATMAN and Nancy TERHUNE
June 1, 1833 David CALVIN and Jane STEPHENSON
Abisha CAMP and Louisa H. STUMP
Oct. 31, 1833 Elliot J. CHASTAIN and Aditha DAVIS
Nov. 21, 1833 Edward COOMBS and Elizabeth NEWCOMB
Jan. 15, 1834 William CALVIN and Rachel PAYNE
Nov. 21, 1834 John K. CUMMINGS and Katharine SMITH
Feb. 3, 1835 Phineas CAREY and Amarilla HORTON
May 27, 1835 George CLAPP and Eliza WHITE
June 17, 1835 Benjamin S. CLEMMONS and Malinda RIPPLE
July 16, 1835 Adam CHRONIC and Susan LOVEL
Aug. 22, 1835 B.H. COVINGTON and Sarah CONREY
Aug. 25, 1835 Stephen B. CONNER and Mary REDMON
Sept. 24, 1835 James M. CONDUIT and Lydia DUNN

---

## FAYETTE COUNTY, ILLINOIS
## GENEALOGICAL SOURCES, HELP

Fayette County created 14 Feb. 1821 from parent counties of Bond, Wayne, Clark and Jefferson. County named for Marquis De La Fayette. County seat at Vandalia, IL 62471 has vital, land records (county clerk, 618-283-0394) and court records (circuit clerk, 618-283-0309). Courthouse hours Monday through Friday, 8 to 4. Illinois genealogical society that covers this county is Fayette County Genealogical Society, Box 177, Vandalia, IL 62471.

### SOURCES

1881, Plat Book of Fayette County, Ill. Adlen, Ogle and Co.
1910, HISTORY OF FAYETTE COUNTY, Vol. 2 by Newton Bateman, ed.
Cemetery Inscriptions, Vol. I by Decatur Genealogical Society, 1975.
1830 Federal Census, Decatur Genealogical Society, 1969.
1840 Federal Census, Decatur Genealogical Society, 1968.
1850 Federal Census, Decatur Genealogical Society, 1976.
1821-1874 Marriage Index, 1979.
1878, HISTORY OF FAYETTE COUNTY, ILL.
1820 to 1860 Federal Censuses, Fayette County Genealogical Society.
1870, 1880 Federal Censuses, Fayette County Genealogical Society.

Check with the society for other genealogical aids. The society publishes a quarterly.

---

## NEWSPAPER ABSTRACTS
## ILLINOIS ADVOCATE AND STATE REGISTER
## VANDALIA, ILLINOIS
## MICROFILM

April 27, 1833
At Cold Spring, in Shelby County, on the 18th inst., Mr. Thomas Williams of that county to Miss Julia Prentice, daughter of John O. Prentice, Esq. of that place.

In Springfield, on the 9th inst., Seth M. Tinsley, of the firm of Bill Tinsley, to Miss Hannah Taylor, daughter of John Taylor, Esq.

On the 16th inst. by Guy Beck, Esq., Mr. James Tawlbee, to Miss Sidney Harris, both of this county.

May 4, 1833

In Edwardsville, on the 30th ult., Mrs. Adams, wife of John Adams, Esq., aged 36, after a long and painful illness, which she bore with christian fortitude and resignation, in full faith of a blessed immortality.

Franklin Co., Ill. 1833 April Court Term, Mary Nelson vs. Robert C. Nelson, divorce. Margaret Youngblood vs. Jonathon Youngblood, divorce.

Taken up by Ormsby VanWinkle, living 22 miles north of Vandalia, Fayette Co., a brown bay mare, 14 hands high, supposed to be 8 years old, white spot on her right side, and some white hairs on her right thigh, appraised to $40, by Andrew Harris and William Hatfield, before me, this 13th April 1833. Guy Beck, J.P. Jas. W. Berry, Clerk.

Estray mare, taken up by John McKinzie, living on the Flat Branch, one sorrel mare, about 15 hands, 1 inch high, 6 years old, a natural trotter, a small blaze on her forehead, three white feet, marked with the genar, appraised in $47.50 before Aaron McKinzie, Esq., 25th April 1833. Joseph Oliver, Clerk, Shelby County, Ill. May 4.

John M'Kee lately removed from Paris, Kentucky announces wool carding business in Shelbyville, Ill.

Clinton Co., Ill., April Term, 1833, court term, Henry Curtis vs. James J. Ryan, etal. for chancery.

Jefferson Co., Ill., March Term, 1833, court term, Levi Robertson vs. Elizabeth Robertson, divorce.

Washington Co., PA, Sept. 1827, William and Jane Kelly, his wife vs. heirs of law of William Buckingham, deceased. Isaac Buckingham in Illinois to answer summons.

May 18, 1833, Saturday

By yesterday's mail, we learn from gentlemen who left St. Louis yesterday morning, that the cholera was still raging in that place but we are unable to learn the extent of the pestilence. Report says it is more mortal than it was last year. We do not learn that it has yet extended into the country; it however behooves every one to be careful of their diet and the premonitory symptoms.

Married--

In this place, Mr. Abraham Viles to Miss Rachel Douglas.

In this county, on the 12th inst., Mr. Hez. B. Thompson to Miss Mary Lewellen.

In this county, on the 16th inst., Mr. Zenas Brines to Miss Nancy Haley.

Died--

At his residence in Bond Co., Ill., on Sunday last, Williamson Plant, Esq., of the cholera. We learn that Mr. Plant had been at St. Louis, and returned home on Saturday, and was taken that same evening, and died the next morning at 12 o'clock.

Feb. 23, 1893, page 1

Mrs. Sarah Dayhuff, of Sefton Twp., wife of Phillip Dayhuff, a well known farmer, died at her home last Monday, aged about 68 years. The funeral service was held at Liberty Church Tuesday afternoon and was largely attended. The husband is at present lying seriously ill at his home.

Sefton Column: Mr. and Mrs. Phillip Dayhuff are very sick at this writing. Dr. Martin attending.

Vandalia Union, Vandalia, Illinois--microfilm

March 2, 1893

Sefton column: William Dayhuff and family will soon start for Oklahoma, where they expect to make their future home.

Those of the sick list are William Flowers, Phillip Dayhuff, Albert Wilson, Carrie Camp, Mrs. Wm. Buchanan and Mrs. Spruell.

Vandalia Union, Vandalia, Illinois--microfilm

March 16, 1893

Wilberton twp. James Monroe Manlon, born Allen Co., KY, Nov. 18, 1824, married Margaret Day, 5 June 1845; she died Feb. 17, 1866; children: Mary A. Shelton, wife of J. B. Shelton; Richard F. Manlon; George C. Manlon; Emily O. Duncan; William O. Manlon, living; and the following dead: Jas. M., Martha J., Caroline, Eubert, John Logan and one infant; married second, May 1868, Amanda V. Day; children, all living, Margaret, Hezekiah, Robert, Charles, Chester, Rolla and Birt; the father James Manlon died 20 Feb. 1893

Vandalia Union, Vandalia, Illinois--microfilm

May 4, 1893

S.D. Perry, born Nashville, Tenn., 4 June 1817, came to Ill. 1824, living at Springfield, then moved to Shonbonier; died April 9, 1893; funeral services conducted by Rev. G.C. Sheppard, pastor of the M.E. Church, assisted by D.W. Baker, writer of this article.

Vandalia Union, Vandalia, Illinois--microfilm

May 25, 1893

Anna M. Shroad McElhaney, born 8 Feb. 1842 Lancaster Co., Pa.; marrieed Samuel McElhaney, 31 Aug. 1862; moved to Indiana, 1865; then to Ill. 1872; settled Sefton Twp.; died 21 April 1893; burial in Forbus Cemetery; left husband, two sons, three daughters.

Vandalia Union, Vandalia, Illinois--microfilm

---

## SEARCHING ILLINOIS ANCESTORS
### ADDITIONAL QUERIES, FREE

COUNTY UNKNOWN, SOUTHERN AREA: Thompson
Marjorie Dougan, 210 S. Railroad Ave., Moweaqua, IL 62550

COUNTY UNKNOWN: Crow
Rochelle Clipston, Macon St., Moweaqua, IL 62550

CHRISTIAN: Lawrence, Ziegler
Evelyn Wooters, R.R. 2, Box 220, Moweaqua, IL 62550

LASALLE: Moffatt, Alward: LOGAN: Young
Patricia Dobson, R.r. 1, Box 8, Moweaqua, IL 62550

COUNTY UNKNOWN: White originating from Eastern Tenn.
Sue Gregory, 102 N. Macon, Moweaqua, IL 62550

SHELBY: Stump, Davis, Starter
Eleanor Hight, 326 E. Main, Moweaqua, IL 62550

MACON: Kirk
    Eila Kirk, 313 East Wall St., Moweaqua, IL 62550
COUNTY NOT GIVEN: Perry, Rogers
    Norma Schorfheide, 220 South East, Moweaqua, IL 62550
WASHINGTON: Schorfheide, Doelling, Ahrens, Isringhaus, Eckert
    Fred Schorfheide, 220 South East, Moweaqua, IL 62550
FULTON: Smith, Martin
    Robert Smith, 328 E. Locust, Moweaqua, IL 62550
CHRISTIAN: Adams; ST CLAIR: Lowe, Phillips
    Sherry Wempen, 108 Ponting, Moweaqua, IL 62550
COUNTY NOT GIVEN: Weidenhammer, Hart, Willard, Nelson
    Maxine Bear Roberts, 5048 J Parkway, Sacramento, CA 95823
SHELBY COUNTY?: Bauer, Von Behren, Sponeman
    Edna Casey, 4040 S. 42nd St., Omaha, NE 68107
ZIEGLER, ILL.: Miklich
    Ruth Zurga, Rt. 8, Box 114, Harrison, AR 72601
CRAWFORD: Lankston; FULTON: Compton, Taylor, Lindey, Hodson, Humphrey; KNOX: Cunningham; MCDONOUGH: Goodsell
    Carol M. Lankston, 3475 St. Catherine Street, Florissant, MO 63033
BOND, CARROLL, CHAMPAIGN, CLARK, COLES, COOK, DEWITT, DUPAGE, EDWARDS, EFFINGHAM, FAYETTE, FULTON, GREENE, HARDIN, HENRY, IROQUOIS, JO DAVIES, JACKSON, KANKAKEE, KNOX, LAKE, LOGAN, MADISON, MCLEAN, MCHENRY, MONROE, MONTGOMERY, OGLE, PEORIA, POPE, PULASKI, ROCK ISLAND, SALINE, SHELBY, STARK, STEPHENSON, UNION, VERMILION, WABASH, WHITESIDE, WINNEBAGO, WHITE: Geer, most all spellings; BOND: Hobbs; CARROLL: Peden, Haynes; CHAMPAIGN: Heller, Clark, Higgins, Cady, Russell, Perry, Catron, Davis, Dare, Crissey, Marvin, Biddlecomb, Lincoln, Lee, Wright, Thompson, Cooper, Radebaugh, Lochrie, Murphey; CLARK: Lee; COLES: Roberts; COOK: Schryver, Baltz, Bowen, Mason, Blythe, Goudy, Welch; DUPAGE: Stofft; FULTON: Goudy, Vaughn; HENRY: Bassett, Brady, Heath, Pardee; IROQUOIS: Gallup; JoDAVIESS: Gilbert, Farrar; KANKAKEE: Edmundson; KNOX: Addis, Crane, Cartwright, Grim, Ferguson, Hunt, Murphy, Prentiss, Toothe; LOGAN: Larrison; LAKE: Welch; PEORIA: Burnham, Foster, Moore; STARK: Hempstead, Peterson, Stockner, Murphy, Foster, Smith; VERMILION: Bliven, Reynolds; WHITESIDE: Meyer; WINNEBAGO: Bowen.
    Cities of Goshen, Geer, all spellings; city of Darwin, Geer, all spellings, Clark, Higgins, Cady, Russell, Perry, Catron, Davis, Dare, Crissey, Marvin, Biddlecomb, Thompson, Heller; city of Tete des Morts, Geer, all spellings
    Ginger M. August, 32 Stetson Way, Princeton, NJ 08540
LAWRENCE: John William born NC
    Leva Joy Brantley, R. 1, Box 1440, Fletcher, OK 73541
CHAMPAIGN, DOUGLAS, PEORIA, LANCASTER, TAZEWELL: Hobble, BAndy, Nelson, Boggs; MCHENRY: Mattocks; IROQUOIS: Jones
    Maxine Hobble, 902 Wayne, Topeka, KS 66606
SHELBY, CUMBERLAND: Becker; SCHUYLER: Swisher, Trimble, Strong
    Diane Delbridge, 2804 Durango Circle, Yukon, OK 73099
SHELBY: Hoyer, Spurgeon, McDaniel, Price
    Joe V. Jones, P.O. Box 185, Blytheville, AR 72316

RICHLAND: Harrell or Harrold
    Karen Flannery, 122 Spruce, Niles, MI 49120
SHELBY: Griffith
    Margaret L. Griffith, 1221 Grant St., Danville, IL 61832
HANCOCK: Spiker
    Beverly S. Davis, 1252 Slaughter Road, Madison, OK 35758
PUTNAM: Hiltabrand, Gunn, Hailey, Kreider; LASALLE: Hiltabrand, Stillwell, Osgood, Kreider; FULTON: Kreider; FAYETTE: Carson, Pasley, Barker; LAWRENCE: Barnes, Carson; JASPER: Pierce, Fulk, Barker
    Phyllis Gadbury, R.R. 1, Box 341, Monticello, IL 61856
CHRISTIAN: Hunt, Gasham
    Mrs. Cecil Schultz, 2717 Larchmont, Ponca City, OK 74604
COUNTY NOT GIVEN: Compton, Taylor, Lankston, Goodsell
    Carol M. Lankston, 3475 St. Catherine St., Florissant, MO 63033
DEKALB: Myers-George and Naomi
    Louise Farrington, 1961 Goodhaven, Memphis, TN 38116
COUNTY NOT GIVEN: Weidenhammer, Hart, Willard, Nelson
    Maxine Bear Roberts, 5048 J Parkway, Sacramento, CA 95823

----------------

## GALLATIN COUNTY
### GENEALOGICAL SOURCES, HELP

Created Sept. 14, 1812 from Randolph Co., Ill. Named for Albert Gallatin. County seat at Shawneetown, IL 62984 has vital, land records (county clerk, 618-269-3025) and court records (circuit clerk, 618-269-3140). Courthouse hours, Monday through Friday, 8 to 4.

Illinois genealocial society that covers this county and others is Southern Illinois Genealogical Society, 607 N. Logan St., Marion, IL 62959 or Genealogical Society of Southern Illinois, care of John A. Logan College, Carterville, IL 62918. The latter publishes a quarterly.

### SOURCES

County board minutes, 1807-1829; 1840-1846; 1860-1941 at State of Illinois Archives, Springfield, Ill.

Gallatin Co. Marriage Bonds 1803-1821, Illinois State Society Quarterly, Vol. 5, No. 2, 1973.

Gallatin Co. Marriage Bonds 1822-1829, Illinois State Society Quarterly, Vol. 5, no. 4, 1973.

History of Gallatin, Saline, Hamilton, Franklin and Williamson Co., Ill. 1887.

Miscellany Gallatin Co., Ill. State Genealogical Society, Vol. 8, no. 1, 1976.

1850 Federal Census of Gallatin Co., Ill., 1972.

Index to Goodspeed's 1887 History of Gallatin, Saline, Hamilton, Franklin and Williamson Co., Ill., 1973.

1860 U.S. Census by John V. Murphy, 1982.

1920, Prairie Farmers Directory of Saline and Gallatin Co., Ill.

Check with the societies for other genealogical aids.

## GALLATIN COUNTY, ILLINOIS
### SOME SURNAMES FROM HISTORY OF GALLATIN, SALINE, HAMILTON, FRANKLIN AND WILLIAMSON CO., ILL.
### Chicago: Goodspeed Pub. Co., 1887

Gallatin County

Barger, Barnett, Bishop, Boyd, Burroughs, Caldwell, Combs, Colvard, Cook, Crawford, Davenport, Davis, Drone, Dupier, Duval, Earnshaw, Eddy, Edwards, Fillingin, Gates. Gatewood, Gill, Gross, Harrington, Hargrave, Harsha, Hemphill, Hill, Jones, Kanady, Karcher, Kimsall, Lamb, Lemen, Logsdon, Loomis, McBane, Mills, Millspaugh, McGehee, McIlrath, McLain, Meesman, Moore, Moxley, McMurchy, Nolen, Peeples, Phillips, Pool, Potter, Rensmann, Rich, Richeson, Ridgway, Roedell, Sellers, Speer, Stiles, Strickland, Townshend, Tromly, Vineyard, Wathen, Wilson, White, Wiseheart, Youngblood, Zinn.

---

## HAMILTON COUNTY, ILLINOIS
### GENEALOGICAL SOURCES, AIDS

Created 8 Feb. 1821 from parent county of White. Named for Alexander Hamilton. County seat at McLeansboro, IL 62859 has vital, land records (county clerk, 618-643-2721) and court records (county clerk, 618-643-3224). Courthouse hours, Monday through Friday, 8 to 4:30. Illinois genealogical society that covers this county and others is Southern Illinois Genealogical Society, 607 N. Logan St., Marion, IL 62959 or Genealogical Society of Southern Illinois, care of John A. Logan College, Carterville, IL 62918. The latter publishes a quarterly.

### SOURCES

County board minutes, 1821-1876; 1886-1934 at Illinois State Archives, Springfield, Ill.

Cemetery Inscriptions, Volume I, Decatur Genealogical Society, 1969. Reprinted 1979.

Illinois, Hamilton Marriage Records, 1981.

History of Gallatin, Saline, etal. Goodspeed, 1887.

McLeansboro, Blooming Grove Baptist Church, 1850-1968.

---

### HAMILTON CO. HERALD NEWSPAPER ABSTRACTS
### McLeansboro, Illinois

5 March 1885

Died--Monday, March 2nd, 1885, at 10:30 a.m. little Roy, son of J.K. and L.R. Irwin, aged 4 years 7 months 10 days

Died--Friday, Feb. 20, 1885, little Effie May Sneed, daughter and only child of Mark and Lizze Sneed, aged 2 years 6 months

Robert H. Johnson died at the home of his son, Samuel Johnson, two miles south of town, last Thursday (Feb. 19) aged about 78. He was the father of Mrs. Wilson Thompson and had been a pioneer of Hamilton County. Mt. Vernon News.

12 Feb. 1885

Marriages--James C. Hall, 30, to Millie A. Spain, 20, both of Flannigan Precinct

Enoch R. McMahon, 18, to Eliza Ray, 23, both of Lasater Prec.

Ezekiel Sneed, 21, to Harriet Harrelson, 18, both of Knights Prairie Prec.

Hinston Hynes, 27, to Emmaline Oglesby, 36, both of Flannigan Prec.

William Wheeler, 23, to Lucy Wheeler, 21, both of Lasater Prec.

Lewis S. Calvert, 18, to Samantha Pott, 21, both of Shelton Prec.

Mr. Richard Munsell, an old and well respected farmer residing two miles E of town, died last Friday night at 11 o'clock, and was buried at Concord Church, Sunday 10 a.m.

Mrs. Louisa J. Snover, grandmother of Mrs. R. R. Barnett, of this place, died at her son-in-law's, Timothy Davis, who resides in the NW corner of Franklin Co., died at a good old age, Tuesday, Feb. 3, 1885, of paralysis.

Obituary--Richard Munsell, age 63 years old, native of NY, came when quite young with father to Illinois, married 1847 Malison Proctor and moved to Hamilton Co. from Enfield, Ill.

November 22, 1884

Died--at 12:00 Monday night, Nov. 17, 1884, Travis Daniel, at his son-in-law's, Thos. Beard's residence, of consumption aged 66 years. Funeral services were held at the Baptist Church at 2 p.m.

Mrs. Virginia Duff, living near Benton, was instantly killed Friday of last week by the falling of a chimney. She had just rented and moved onto a farm belong to Mr. McGruire, about 4 miles N of that place, where the fatal accident occurred.

Married--Geo. H. Stich, 27, to Julia Reubenaker, 21, both of Crouch Prec.

James L. Sinks, 17, to Sarah O. Hart, 21, both of Shelton Prec.

Moses Robinson, 48, of McLeansboro Prec., to Malinda M. Clark, 29, of Knight Prairie Prec.

John L. Lay, 24, to Georgeann Lucas, 23, both of McLeansboro.

William L. Lowry, 36, to Emma T. Rudsell, 20, both of Shelton Prec.

---

HAMILTON COUNTY, ILLINOIS
Captain James Hall's Company
Black Hawk War, May 15, 1832 to Aug. 13, 1832, enrollment
ILLINOIS ADJUDANT GENERAL

Captain, James Hall; First Lt., John Burton; 2nd Lt. John Townsend; Sgts, Milton Carpenter, Robert Witt, John M. Smith, Alfred Moore; Corps, John Heard, Charles Heard, Keling T. Maulding, Willis Atkinson; Bugleman, Clinton Hopkins; Privates, Philip Adair, Elisha Bond, John Burnett, Shearwood Brown, Elijah Burness, Thomas Coffee, Samuel Cannimore, Martin Coons, James Davenport, John Fouch, Charles Hungate, Joseph Hall, Sanford Hutson, Thomas Hall, Thomas J. Hanks, Jesse Johnston, Charles Krisel, John Krisel, Louis Lane, Levin Lane, Frederick Meredith, Samuel Monday, Azabel McBroom, William McLaughlin, William Morris, Ambrose Maulding, Rhebin Oglesby, Adam Overturf, Charles Phelps, Alexander Pauley, William Perry, Willie Prigmore, Jonathon Kedrick, John Rich, Jeremiah Reynolds, Moses

Shearly, James Schoolcraft, Martin Sims, Hiram Townsend, Elijah Tramel, Snead White, Wiley Williams, Samuel Ward.

---

### Capt. Dudley William's Co.
### of the 4th Regiment Militia
Mounted Riflemen, Oct. 14th to Nov. 5th, 1812
ILLINOIS ADJUDANT GENERAL

Capt. Dudley Williams; Lt. David Moore; Ensign, Reuben Linn; Cornet, Alfred Linsey; Sgts., Joseph Ferguson, John Reed, Henry Griffin, James Moor; Corps, Wm. Megee, James Brown, Thomas Armstrong, John Jarrat; Privates, Henry Fuel, John Walker, Asher Davis, John Neal, John Hallin, Daniel Calhoun, Allen Barnes, Furnas Harrison, Hiram Dikerson, Matthew Thomas, Thomas Futral, Andrew Hallin, John Show, Isaac Davis, Micajab Fort, Jesse Rascow, William Cravens, Elijah Ladd, Thomas Casten, Samuel Reas, Redden Wolf, Wilbourn Furial, Joseph Bridges, Samuel Walker, William Mathias, Ezekiel Stevens, Robert Cain, Jeremiah Mitchell, James Woolf, Hiram Griffith, Samuel Jennings, John Matthews, Richard Clark, Daniel Coshler, Joseph Williams, John Ferguson, Charles Brownfield, James Blasingham, William Armstrong, John Mabury, James Randolph, James Cook, Harvey Brumlett, Thomas White.

### Capt. James B. Moore's 3d Co.
April 17, 1813, War of 1812
ILLINOIS ADJUDANT GENERAL

Capt. James B. Moore; 1st Lt. David Robinson; 2nd Lt. Arthur Morgan; Ensign John Duitt; Sgts. Thomas Jordan, Jacob Young, Benjamin Marney, James Hutton; Corps, Isaac Basey, James Talbott, Henry Randleman, John Crawford; Pvts., Enoch Moore, Jesse Miller, Joseph Miller, David Miller, Abraham Miller, John Enoch, Jonathon Knox, Anthony B. Conner, Samuel McFarland, George Lary, Thomas Johnston, Hugh Roylston, Marcus Pelham, Peter Wills, Thomas Marney, Solomon Strong, Amos Shook, Francis Pelham, Fielding Porter, John Ryan, Stephen Lacy, Elihu Axely, William Ryan, John Stallings, David Porter, John Waddle, John Briscoe, John Moore, Jacob Clark, John Clover, William Harrington, David Moore, Thomas J. Mattingly, Willy Harrington, Felix Clark, Stephen Rector, Joshua Vaughn, Charles Gilham, George Richardson, William Griffin, Pleasant Going, William Ferguson, Hiram Huitt, Joseph Ferguson, Ornan Beman, John Finley, Fleming Cox, Aaron Whitney, Martin Wood, Bennett Nowlin, Henry Mace, Isaac Smith, Daniel Winn, Roland Huitt, Edward Crouch, Isaac Carmack, William Going, Elisha Taylor, Andrew Robinson, William Hogan, Prior Hogan, Bartley Cox, Richard Windsor, Alexander Biron, Jude Converse, George Hawk, John Hogan, Eli Langford, William Chance, Jacob Luntzford, Josiah Langford, John Marney, John Collins, Thomas Marney, Daniel Converse, John Ferguson, Robert Hawke, Benjamin Edwards, James Marney, Jesse Harrison.

---

### MONROE COUNTY, ILLINOIS
### GENEALOGICAL SOURCES, AIDS

Created 6 Jan. 1816 from parent counties of Randolph and St. Clair. Named for James Monroe. County seat at Waterloo, IL 62298 has vital, land records (county clerk, 618-939-8681) and court records (circuit clerk, 618-939-8681). Courthouse hours, Monday through Friday, 8 to 4:30.

## SOURCES

County Board Minutes, 1816 to 1936, Illinois State Archives, Springfield, Ill.

1883, Combined History of Randolph, Monroe and Perry Counties, Ill.

1901, Standard Atlas of Monroe County, Ill. Ogle & Co.

1850 Census of Monroe Co., Ill. by Maxine Wormer, 1979.

1894, Portrait and Biographical Record of Randolph, Monroe, Perry and Jackson Co., Ill. Biographical Publ. Co.

New Design--Bethel Baptist Church, 1866-1951. History included.

------------

## MONROE COUNTY, ILLINOIS DELINQUENT TAXES 1833
Abstracted from Illinois Advocate & State Register
Vandalia, Illinois: Newspaper microfilm

Nov. 2, 1833, issue of newspaper

Monroe Co., Ill. Delinquent taxes due and unpaid on first day of Sept. 1833.

Samuel M'Kee, Lydia Moore, Williard M'Clintic, Enoch Moore, Thomas M. Hamilton, A.W. Snyder, Franklin E. Owen, Theron Brownfield, James B. Moore, Jesse Waddle, E. M. Hempstead, Seth Converse, Heirs of Sol. Guise, William Rector, Seth Converse (in here twice), Porter, Glasgow and Nevin, James Morrison, William M'Intosh, Thomas Hill, Chequier and Holmes, Joseph Morrison, William M'Intosh (in here twice), Raphael Drury, N. Hull's heirs, Joseph Hennet, Tobias Brashiers, William Hamilton, Benjamin Ryan, J. Ogle & G. Atchinson, Francis Belew & Son, George Atchinson, J. Scott. Daniel Converse, county court clerk commissioner.

------------

## POPE COUNTY, ILLINOIS
### GENEALOGICAL SOURCES, AIDS

Created 10 Jan. 1816 from parent counties of Gallatin and Johnson Co., Ill. Named for Nathaniel Pope. County seat at Golconda, IL 62938 has vital, land records (county clerk, 618-683-4466) and court records (circuit clerk, 618-683-3941). Courthouse hours, Monday through Friday, 8 to 4. Illinois genealogical society that covers this county and others is Genealogical Society of Southern Illinois, care of John Logan College, Carterville, IL 62918.

## SOURCES

County board minutes, 1816 to 1905, Illinois State Archives, Springfield, Ill.

1893, Biographical Review of Johnson, Massac, Pope and Hardin Co., Ill.

Pope County Marriages, 1816 to 1839 by Janet Schonert, 1972.

1850 Census of Pope County, Ill. by Maxine Wormer, 1972.

Early landowners of Pope Co., Ill. 1900's, by Ronald Nelson, 1979.

Rosebud, Antioch, Missionary Baptist Church Records, 28 May 1864-March 1972.

## POPE COUNTY, ILLINOIS
### Newspaper Abstracts from Illinois Gazette, microfilm
### Shawneetown, Illinois

**2 March 1820**

$50 reward. Ranaway from the subscriber, some time about the 1st of January last, from the United States Saline, hired to Timothy Card, Esq., a negro man named Jacob, very black, about 38 years of age, five feet four or five inches high, chunky for his height, somewhat inclined to be bowlegged, has a fierce look when spoken to. AS he had been at work at the Lick, it is difficult to describe his clothing. He had been accustomed to a variety of work such as on a farm, on the river, at the Lick, etc. Being an artful, cunning fellow, he may procure forged papers, and attempt to pass as a free man, perhaps may call his name Jacob Herral. The above reward will be given for the delivery of him to the subscribers. Morgantown, Kentucky, or to Timothy Card, Esq., United States Saline, or for securing him in jail so that I get him again. James A. Porter & Co., Shawneetown, Ill. March 2, 1820

**May 6, 1820**

Died at this place, on Monday morning last, Col. John Waggoner, much lamented by all who knew him. It can be truly said of him that he knew no guile, and if an honest man is the noblest work of God, he was one.

Take Notice: That on the first Monday in June next, the subscriber will attend the commissioners court to settle the accounts of John Herod, deceased. All persons interested are hereby requested to attend said court. Nancy Herod, administratrix. Shawneetown, May 6, 1820.

State of Illinois, Pope County vs. Toseph Lewsey, a non-resident of said state.

Notice: At the suit of Abram Hawkins, and Abram Hawkins, administrator of Peter Lewis, deceased, and George Wilcoxon, tenants in common, and not joint tenants, etc.

State of Illinois, Gallatin Co., Notice to Samuel L. White, Sarah White seeking divorce.

State of Illinois, Pope Co., John W. Joiner, plff. vs. Betsy Joiner, deft. Libel for divorce.

**May 13, 1820**

Married at Albion, Ill. on the 28th March last, Hugh Ronalds, Esq. to Miss Mary Katherine, second daughter of Richard Flower, Esq. of that place.

Notice, that on the first Monday in June next, the subscriber will attend the commissioners court to settle the estate of Alexander Wilson, deceased. All persons interested are hereby requested to attend said court. H. Wilson, Adminstrator. Shawneetown, May 11th, 1820.

**May 20, 1820**

State of Illinois, Crawford County, Commissioners Court, April 1820. Whereas, J.B. McCall, one of the administrators of the estate of Thomas McCall, deceased, having produced vouchers to the satisfaction of the court, etc. May 20, 1820.

## RICHLAND COUNTY, ILLINOIS
## GENEALOGICAL SOURCES, HELP

Created 24 Feb. 1841 from parent counties of Clay and Lawrence. County seat at Olney, IL 62450 has vital, land records (county clerk, 618-392-3111) and court records (circuit clerk, 618-392-2151). Court house hours, Monday through Friday, 8 to 4. Illinois genealogical society that covers this county is Richland County, Ill. Genealogical Society, Box 202, Olney, IL 62450.

### SOURCES

County board minutes, 1841-1917, Illinois State Archives, Springfield, Ill.

1909, Biographical and Reminiscent History of Richland, Clay and Marion Counties, Ill.

1884, Counties of Cumberland, Jasper and Richland.

1901, Standard Atlas of Richland County, Ill. by Ogle & Co.

1893, Portrait and Biographical Record of Effingham, Jasper, and Richland Co., Ill. Lake City Pub. Co.

1850, 1860, 1870, 1880, 1900, 1910 Federal census of Richland County, Ill. Richland County, Ill. Genealogical and Historical Society.

Check with the society for other genealogical aids.

---

## AGRICULTURAL CENSUS
## STATE OF ILLINOIS ARCHIVES
## SPRINGFIELD, ILLINOIS

EDITOR'S NOTE: The state of Illinois also recorded agricultural census every ten years to coincide with the federal census. Each of Illinois' 102 counties is on microfilm at the Archives in Springfield, Illinois. Considering the year 1850:

All kinds of information was recorded for each land owner in a particular county. These items included: name of owner, agent or manager of farm, improved or unimproved acres, cash value of land, value of farming tools, no. of horses, asses and mules, milch cows, working oxen, other cattle, sheep, swine, value of livestock, bushels of wheat, bushels of rye, bushels of indian corn, bushels of oats, bushels of rice, bushels of tobacco, bales of ginned cotton, lbs. of wool, bushels of peas and beans, bushels of sweet potatoes, bushels of irish potatoes, bushels of barley, bushels of buckwheat, value of orchard products, gallons of wine, value of produce and market goods, lbs. of butter, lbs. of cheese, tons of hay, bushels of clover seed, lbs. of grass seeds, lbs. of hops, lbs. of rotted dew, tons of water rotted, lbs. of flax, bushels of flaxseed, lbs. of silk cocoons, lbs. of maple sugar, lbs. of cane sugar, gallons of molasses, lbs. of beeswax and honey, value of homestead manufactures, value of animals slaughtered, making a total of 46 different items for each individual.

U.S. Agricultural Census Roll no. 31-4 contains the counties of Richland through Woodford. Caution: Most of the handwriting on the names is scratchy and faint. The quill originally did not contain enough ink in most cases.

## SHELBY COUNTY, ILLINOIS
## GENEALOGICAL SOURCES, HELP

County created 23 Jan. 1827 from parent county of Fayette. Named for Governor Isaac Shelby, first governor of Kentucky. County seat at Shelbyville, IL 62565 has vital, land records (county clerk, 217-774-4421) and court records (circuit clerk, 217-774-4212). Courthouse hours, Monday through Friday, 8 to 4. Illinois genealogical society that covers this county is Shelby County Historical and Genealogical Society, Box No., Shelbyville, IL 62565. Check with the society or editor for genealogical sources, help.

-----------

## SHELBY COUNTY, ILLINOIS
## EARLY DIVORCES, CIRCUIT CLERK
## Part II

From File Box 2

Oct. term 1843 of court, Peter Neil vs. Ruth Neil. Married 11 July 1841, Ruth Harmon in Shelby County, Ill. She left him Sept. 1841.

May term 1847 of court, Margaret A. Ferguson vs. Dobson Ferguson. Married as Margaret A. Smith, 5 April 1842 Coles Co., Ill. He left fall 1844.

May term 1847 of court, Isaac Corbin vs. Mary Ann Corbin. Married 4 Jan. 1842 Mary Ann Ladon, Shelby Co., Ill. She left Oct. 1844.

Oct. term 1844 of court, Martin C. Couch vs. Mary Ann Couch. Married Mary Ann Hoke, June 1837 in Limestone Co., Alabama. She left Oct. 1837.

Oct. term 1842 of court, Hiram Welton vs. Jane Welton. Married Jane Belnap, Feb. 1837, Crawford Co., Pa. Both now residents of Shelby Co., Ill.

May term 1844 of court, George W. Hunter vs. Marinda Hunter. Married M. Neal, 7 Oct. 1841 Shelby Co., Ill. Both residents of Shelby Co., Ill.

May term 1842 of court, Levina Eastern vs. Hiram Eastern. Married 13 Nov. 1836 at Marshall, Clark Co., Ill. He a habitual drunkard; lived together until fall 1841.

July term 1843 of court, Elizabeth Tune vs. John F. Tune. Married 12 Oct. 1837 Marion Co., Ill. Lived in Ill. and Mississippi for 2 years. He left in Ill. March 1843.

Jan. term 1843 of court, Albert Doyle vs. Caroline Doyle. Married June 1834, Caroline Holder, White Co., Tenn. File incudes testimony of Reuben Webster, Jonathon Nichols, Sr. and Louis Doyle, all of White Co., Tenn.

### FILE BOX THREE

Nov. term 1849 of court, Nancy A. Preston vs. Jesse Preston. 15 Feb. 1846 Nancy A. Stanley married Jesse Preston, Shelby Co., Ill. He left 26 July 1846.

May term 1848 of court, Archibald C. Moore vs. Caroline Moore. Married 8 Dec. 1845 Fayette Co., Ill. She left 8 Jan. 1846.

May term 1848 of court, William S. Clair vs. Jane Clair.

Married Jane Spalding, 20 Nov. 1842, Effingham Co., Ill. She left after 18 months of marriage.

May term 1848 of court, David Kilgore vs. Elizabeth Kilgore. Married July 1839 Stark Co., Ohio. She left Sept. 19, 1847 after they were in Shelby Co., Ill. a few years.

Dec. term 1850 of court, Elizabeth Ball vs. Lewis Ball. Married 23 Jan. 1848 Morgan Co., Ill. He left 1 Sept. 1848.

Dec. term 1850 of court, Mary Thomason vs. John Thomason. Married 25 Dec. 1835 Fountain Co., Ind. He left residence in Shelby Co., Oct. 1850, leaving her with two children: David, aged 14, and Eliza, aged 11.

---

## SHELBY COUNTY, ILLINOIS
## MISCELLANEOUS RECORDS

Mason, Noah
    Heirs of 1885 Sangamon Co., Ill. MRB 189, page 583.

Mathew, James W.
    Will and estate of Moultrie co., Ill., died 21 Dec. 1915. MRB 234, pps. 420-421.

Mathew, Martha
    Heirs of, died 9 Aug. 1915. MRB 193, page 642.

Mather, Thomas S.
    Of Sangamon Co., Ill. Land no. ?, 1857. MRB 143, page 636.

Mathers, Mary E.
    Estate of Moultrie Co., Ill. MRB 178, page 248-250.

Mathias, Joseph F.
    Heirs of Moultrie Co., Ill., died 2 Jan. 1919. MRB 215, p. 570. Also on pages 191-202.

Mayhew, Calvin
    Heirs of Coles Co., Ill. MRB 157, pps. 265-289.

Melcher, Samuel B.
    Heirs, died 5 Dec. 1927. MRB 234, page 372.

Merrick, Jacob B.
    Heirs of, d. 1863 Hampden Co., Mass. MRB 172, page 43.

Merrick Family History,
    History of family to 1793. MRB 178, page 538.

Messer, Harrison
    Heirs of, aff. by Amos H. Messer. MRB 172, pps. 35-36;584.

Messer, Amos H.
    Deceased of Coles Co., Ill. 1912. MRB 178, pps. 617-621.

Messer, Amos H.
    Will, estate of, Coles Co., Ill. MRB 178, pps. 20-26;404-405.

Messer, Daniel
    Will of Erie Co., Ohio, 27 July 1860. MRB 172, pps. 88-90;101.

Messer, Harrison
    Heirs of, Coles Co., Ill. MRB 189, pps. 385-386.

Messer, Harrison
    Heirs of. MRB 157, pps. 454-455.

Middlesworth, Abraham
    Of Fairfield Co., Ohio. Land no. 258, 8948 (1840), MRB 236, pps. 88-89.

Middlesworth, James G.
    Heirs of Fayette Co., Ill. MRB 189, pps. 527-528.
Middlesworth, John
    Heirs of, d. 19 Dec. 1862. MRB 193, p. 450.
Middlesworth, Josiah
    Heirs of, Wapello, Iowa, 1915. MRB 200, pps. 188-190.
Middleton, John
    Heirs of, d. 1855. MRB 189, p. 532.
Miller, Catherine
    Will of Monmouth Co., NJ, 1912. MRB 189, p. 160.
Miller, Christopher P.
    Heirs of, died 1 Feb. 1893. MRB 236, p. 161.
Miller, Cyrus L.
    Heirs of, d. 1884. MRB 178, p. 627.
Miller, G.C.
    Affadavit, heirs of Catherine Roessler. MRB 178, p. 16.
Miller, Milcah
    Widow of Mathew Miller, War of 1812, Capt. Perry's Co., Md. militia. MRB 200, p. 106-107.
Miller, William C.
    Estate of Macon Co., Ill. 1911. MRB 189, p. 1-2.
Miller, William H.
    Heirs of. MRB 143, p. 65.
Milliken, George
    Heirs of 1875. MRB 200, p. 119.
Milliken, Louisa Hobson
    Heirs of. MRB 143, p. 426.
Minor, Henry and Myrtle
    Divorce, Denver Co., Colorado. MRB 178, p. 18-19.
Minor, Lucian
    Of Albemarle Co., Va. Land no. 4616,5868 (1838) MRB 157, pp. 575-576.

---------------

## WASHINGTON COUNTY, ILLINOIS
## GENEALOGICAL SOURCES, HELP

Created Jan. 2, 1818 from parent county of St. Clair. Named for George Washington. County seat at Nashville, IL 62263 had vital, land records (county clerk, 618-327-8314) and court records (circuit clerk, 618-327-3383). Courthouse hours, Monday through Friday, 8 to 4 p.m. Illinois genealogical society that covers this county is Winnetka Public Library, 768 Oak St., Winnetka, IL 60093.

### SOURCES

County board minutes 1818-1835; 1846-1880 at Illinois State Archives, Springfield, Ill.

1850 Census Transcription by Maxine Wormer, 1973.

Index to 1879 Persons in Brink, McDonough's History. Winnetka Genealogical Projects Committee.

Index to 1884 Portrait and Biographical Record of Clinton, Washington, Marion and Jefferson Co., Ill.

1879 History of Washington Co., Ill.

1906, Atlas of Washington Co., Ill. by Ogle Publications.

WASHINGTON CO., ILLINOIS
ABSTRACT FROM ILLINOIS ADVOCATE AND STATE REGISTER
Newspaper on Microfilm

Issue of Nov. 9, 1833

Washington Co., Ill. List of taxes due and unpaid on 1st day of Nov. 1833

William Kinney, Lowry Morrison, Phillips & Bennett, David Payan, Morrison and Conway, J. Phillips & S. Morrison, William Bennett, Willis Wilkinson, Abner Nash, exec. of C.F. Nash, deceased, John Evans. Orceneth Fisher, clerk.

------------

WAYNE COUNTY, ILLINOIS
GENEALOGICAL SOURCES, HELP

Created 26 March 1819 from parent county of Edwards. Named for Gen. Anthony Wayne. County seat at Fairfield, IL 62837 has vital, land records (county clerk, 618-842-5182) and court records (circuit clerk, 618-847-4701). Courthouse hours, Monday through Friday, 8 to 4:30 p.m. Check with the societies for southern Illinois.

SOURCES

County board minutes 1886-1941 at Illinois State Archives, Springfield, Ill.

Illinois Cemetery Inscriptions, Vols. I-IV, VI-VIII by Doris Ellen Witter Bland.

1850 Federal Census, Decatur Gen. Soc., 1969. Rept. 1974.

1881, Atlas of Wayne Co., Ill. B.N. Griffing.

1884, History of Wayne Co., Ill.

1910, Standard Atlas of Wayne Co., Ill. by Ogle & Co.

1830, 1840, 1860, 1870 Federal censuses by Betty Ann Beeson.

Wayne Co., Ill. Marriages, Part I by Betty Ann Beeson.

Wayne Co., Ill. Newspaper gleanings 1855-1875. By Doris Ellen W. Bland. 1974.

Fairfield, Pleasant Grove Missionary Baptist Church, 1853-1958.

------------

Capt. James N. Clark's Co.
Wayne Co., Ill.
Black Hawk War, Illinois Adjudant General

Capt. James N. Clark, 1st Lt. David Ray, 2nd Lt. Jesse Laird, Sgts. Daniel Sumpter, William A. Howard, Henry Oley, Isaac Street. Corps. Joseph Walker, John A. McWhartens, Lewis Watkins, Nathan E. Roberts. Privates: Harris Austin, James B. Austin, David Alexander, Robert Bain, Greenup Bradshaw, Asa Bullard, Joseph M. Campbell, James Clark, William Clark, Younger H. Dickerson, George Dolton, Andrew C. Dolton, George Farleigh, John F. Fitzgerald, Joseph L. Garrison, James Garrison, William Graham, Jeremiah Hargrave, William Harland, Alfred Haws, Benjamin Haws, John Hanson, Samuel James, Peter Kenshalow, David Martin, Nathan Martin, Andrew Mays, James Mays, William McCullam, Joseph Morris, Chesley Ray, Asa Ray, Jacob Rister, Fenton Sanders, Richard Sessions, David D. Slocumb, David Smith, James Trotter, Johalen Tyler, George Walker, Greenbury Walker, Jefferson Warrick, James K. Warrick, Joohn g. Widdus, John L. White, Arthur Bradsahw. (This unit mustered into service June 16, 1832.)

## WHITE COUNTY, ILLINOIS
### GENEALOGICAL SOURCES, HELP

Created 9 Dec. 1815 from parent county of Gallatin. Named for Capt. Leonard White. County seat at Carmi, IL 62821 has vital, land records (county clerk, 618-382-4776) and court records (circuit clerk, 618-382-5451). Courthouse hours, Monday through Friday, 8 to 4 p.m. Check with the genealogical societies that cover southern Illinois.

### SOURCES

1850 Census of White Co., Ill. Decatur Gen. Society, 1972.

County board minutes, 1816-1913, at Illinois State Archives, Springfield, Ill.

1883, History of White County, Ill.

White Co., Ill. Marriages 1816-1840 by Emogene Tindall, 1983.

1901, Atlas of White Co., Ill. Keller & Fuller.

------------

### Capt. John McCann's Co.
### White Co., Ill. Adjudant General
### Black Hawk War, Mustered into service, 19 June 1832

Capt. John McCann, 1st Lt. Samuel Slocumb, 2nd Lt. Walter Burress, Sgts. William Garrison, Solomon Garrison, Noah Staley, James Keneda. Corps., Levi Wells, William Stephens, William Daniels, Henry McCann. Privates: George Berry, Alfred Bailey, Joseph M. Brittain, John Blackledge, James C. Blackwell, James Cann, Willis Council, John Campbell, John Crowder, Thomas Coonts, Ambrose Edwards, Jonathon Evans, Martin Farley, John Farley, John George, Francis George, James Goodman, Allen Hood, Anderson Hood, William Hilyard, Demsey Holderly, Daniel Heasty, John Hunt, William S. Hamilton, Thomas J. Lindsey, Thomas Lowe, Wilkerson McMullin, Wm. G. Nevett, James Neslar, Wilson Parker, Michael Robinson, Nicht's A. Robinson, Burress Rippstoo, Aaron Robinson, Thomas W. Stone, Slade Smith, George Staley, Rodolphus M. Sutler, Silas Smith, Christopher Wilson, Hardy Williams.

------------

## WHITESIDE COUNTY, ILLINOIS
### GENEALOGICAL SOURCES, HELP

Created 16 Jan. 1836 from parent counties of Jo Daviess and Henry. County seat at Morrison, IL 61270 has land, vital records (county clerk, 815-772-7201) and court records (circuit clerk, 815-772-7201). Courthouse hours, Monday through Friday, 8 to 4 p.m. Illinois genealogical society that covers this county is Whiteside Co. Genealogists, Box 145, Sterling, IL 61081.

### SOURCES

1877, History of Whiteside County by Charles Bent.

1900, Biographical Record of Whiteside Co., Ill.

1907, two volumes, History of Whiteside Co., Ill. by Wm. H. Davis.

1893, Plat book of Whiteside Co., Ill. by Ogle & Co.

1885, Portrait & Biographical Record Album of Whiteside Co., Ill.

1850 Census Whiteside by Dora Wilson Smith, 1979.

1872, Atlas of Whiteside Co., Warner & Beers.

PAID QUERIES   PAID QUERIES   PAID QUERIES   PAID QUERIES   PAID QUERIES

STEWARD: Isaac Harris Steward, b. 1812 CT m. 1836 Huron Co., OH Maria Moore. d. 1888 Cabery, Ford Co., IL In Will Co., IL, 1850 census, hotelkeeper. Ch: SAnford M. b.c. 1837 OH; Lucas W. b. Oct. 1839 OH in 1900 Kendall Co., IL census; Aurealia b. Apr 1842 OH, m. Wm. W. Hiddleson lived Ford Co.; Mary b.c. 1844 IL; Harwick b. 1850 IL Granddaughter Relia Steward. Want info. on this family or any of their descendants.
B.S. Weaver, 535 Cornelia Apt. 1104, Chicago, IL 60657

---

Need parents, siblings of James HAMLETT b. 1795 Warren Co., NC d. May 1887, age 92 Clarksville, Montgomery Co., TN; to this county age 10, 1805. His parents were said to have been James and Mary. James and wife Mary Bedford were in Lunenburg Co., VA 1782. His parents?
Mrs. Clara Hamlett Robertson, 303 West Bank Apt. 2, Salisbury, NC 28144

Need parents, sibs of John ROBINSON/ROBERSON/ROBERTSON (wife Francky Watts-Huckstep) Albemarle Co., VA 1785 tax list; son Archelaus Jonathon (1st) m. Polly Carver 1799; sons Colby and Cosby Minor R. (1st) m. Susan Browning; son A.J. (2nd) m. Annis Woodson 1848; son Elisha Wm. m. Alberta Rothwell 1878.
Mrs. Judson Hall Robertson, 303 West Bank Apt. 2, Salisbury, NC 28144

Need grandparents of Claiborne ROTHWELL b. 1741; d. 1828 Albemarle Co., VA; his father Thomas Rathwell/Rauthwell/ Louisa Col, VA "deserted" the family and Claiborne was bound out to Nathan Watson, planter with consent of his mother Eliza Rothwell in 1747. Claiborne served as Pvt. in Wm. Phillips rangers 1773.
Mrs. Judson Hall Robertson, 303 West Bank Apt. 2, Salisbury, NC 28144

---

Freeman--Woolard--Beck--Lucas--Ward

Wish to correspond with descendants of Thomas R. and Edah Woolard Freeman. They had children: Henry who married Sarah A. Williams; James who married Rhoebe Jane Casey; Nancy who married John Kay; William Beck who married Anna B. Gwinn; Mary who married John Lewis; Thomas Richard who married Margaret Woolard.

Thomas Freeman came to Shelby Co., IL 1833 and died there 1875. He was son of Richard Freeman who died 1837 in Montgomery Co., IL His mother or stepmother said to be Eleanor Yates.

Allied families of Richard Freeman's (1837) were Beck, Lucas, Ward.

Edith Freeman Affatato, 8706 W. Sample Road, Apt. 4, Coral Springs, FL 33065

## ADDITIONAL FREE QUERIES

COUNTY UNKNOWN: Benjamin Craven Harrison
    Mrs. Hugh Harrison, 3808 Overland Dr., DEl City, OK 73115

COUNTY UNKNOWN: Nora E. Haskell
    Betty Maher, 3899 Green Valley Rd. Sirsun City, CA 94585

FRANKLIN: Smothers, Neal/Parents of Priscilla Smothers?
    Ethelyn M. Crawford, 1230 W. Battlement Pkwy, Willow Park
      Apts. K-203, Parachute, CO 81635

PIKE: Vaughn
    Beverly Truesdale, 2105 N. Buena Vista, Burbank, CA 91504

HANCOCK: Duckworth, Howard
    Marguerite S. McCurry, 17730 Minnow Way, Penn Valley, CA 95946

CUMBERLAND: Wright, Felther; CRAWFORD: Maddox, Reynolds; COLES: Wright, Maddox, Asher; EDGAR: Gallaty, Wright, Ewell; VERMILION: Wright, Maddox, Asher
    Mrs. H.O. Sims, 6773 Washington, Groves, TX 77619

COUNTY NOT GIVEN: Smith
    Sims publishing, M.Sims, P.O. Box 9576, Sacramento, CA 95823

---

## INDEX TO VOLUME III, NUMBER I
### SEARCHING ILLINOIS ANCESTORS

PLEASE NOTE: Page 7, Hamilton Co. Black Hawk War, p. 15;16 of 1812 regiments, and Black Hawk War regiment, p. 23; White Co. Black Hawk War Regiment, p. 24 are NOT included in this index.

Adair, 15
Adams, 5,2,10,12
Addis, 12
Agricultural Census, 19
Ahrens, 12
Alexander, 8
Allin, 9
Alsbury, 1
Alward, 11
Anderson, 5
Armstrong, 1
Astin, 8
Atchinson, 17
Atkinson, 15
Atterberry, 1
Austin, 1
Avery, 2
Ayers, 1
Baker, 1,11
Ball, 21
Bandy, 12
Barkson, 5
Barker, 13
Barnes, 13
Barret, 15
Bassett, 12
Bauer, 12
Beard, 15
Bearden, 5
Bebee, 3
Beck, 10
Becker, 2,12
Bee, 1
Belew, 17
Bell, 5
Belrap, 20
Bennett, 1,23
Berry, 10
Biddlecum, 8,12
Bliven, 12
Blythe, 12
Boggs, 12
Bord, 15
Boone Co., 2
Bradley, 5
Brady, 12
Brakes, 1
Brashiers, 17
Bright, 8
Brines, 10
Brockett, 1
Brockway, 3
Brown, 1,3 15
Brownfield, 17
Buchanan, 11
Buckingham, 10
Buck, 2
Bugg, 5
Burress, 15
Burrett, 15
Burnham, 12
Burr, 8
Burriss, 3
Burroughs, 2
Burton, 15
Cady, 12
Caldwell, 9
Calvin, 9
Camp, 9,11
Cannimore, 15
Caperz, 2
Card, 18
Carey, 9
CArlisle, 1

Carpenter, 15
Cartwright, 12
Cassaday, 8
Cass Co., 3
Catron, 12
Cay, 5
Champaign Co., 3
Chandler, 3
Charey, 8
Chastain, 8,9
Chatman, 9
Chequier, 17
Chinowith, 8
Christian Co., 4,5
Chrojnic, 9
Clair, 20
Clapp, 8,9
Clark, 12,15
Clark, Capt. James, 23
Clark Co., 6
Carson, 13
Clayton, 8
Clements, 8
Clemmons, 9
Coffee, 5,15
Chho, 9
Colon, 8
Combs, 9
Compton, 12,13
Conduit, 9
Conery, 8,9
Conner, 9
Converse, 17
Conway, 1,23
Conwell, 2
Coors, 15
Cooper, 12
Corbin, 20
Couch, 20
Courtney, 5
Covington, 9
Cowan, 8
Cozad, 8
Cox, 5,8
Crafton, 8
Craig, 8
Crane, 2,12
Cratzer, 8
Crawford Co., 6,7
Crissey, 12
Crist, 8
Croago, 8

Cunningham, 12
Crow, 11
Cummings, 9
Curhan, 3
Cunningham, 8
Cupps, 9
Curey, 8
Curtis, 10
Daniel, 15
Dare, 12
Datter, 2
Davenport, 15
Davis, 9,12,15
Day, 11
Dayhuff, 11
Dean, 2
Dehague, 1
Dodgsto, 2
Doelling, 12
Donica, 8
Dorman, 1
Douglas, 10
Doyle, 20
Drake, 1
Drury, 17
Dudley, Capt. Wm., 16
Duff, 15
Duncan, 11
Dunn, 9
Dyson, 5
Eastern, 20
Eckert, 12
Edgar Co., 8
Edmundson, 12
Ellenson, 2
Emery, 2
Erickson, 1
Estus, 5
Evans, 23
Farrar, 12
Ferguson, 20
Fisher, 23
Farrand, 2
Fayette, Co., 9
Ferguson, 12
Flower, 18
Flowers, 11
Foster, 2,12
Fouch, 15
Fulk, 13
Fuller, 3
Gallatin Co,, 13,14
Gallup, 12

Gasham, 13
Geer, 12
George, 13
Gibbs, 2
Gilbert, 12
Glasgow, 17
Goode, 5
Gooden, 5
Goodsell, 12,13
Gossett, 1
Goudy, 12
Gough, 2
Griffith, 13
Grim, 12
Guise, 17
Gunn, 13
Haight, 5
Hailey, 5,13
Haines, 5
Hale, 3
Haley, 10
Halford, 5
Hall, 5,14,15
Hamilton, 17
Hamilton Co., 14
Hamlin, 5
Hardley, 8
Haring, 5
Harks, 15
Harmon, 5
Harson, 5
Hardin, 5
Hargis, 5
Harker, 5
Harmon, 20
Harper, 5
Harrell, 13
Harris, 5,10
Hart, 12,13,15
Harvey, 12
Hawkins, 18
Hawley, 2
Haynes, 12
Hayes, 5,9
Hayward, 5
Heard, 15
Heath, 12
Heller, 12
Helphenstine, 8
Hempstead, 12,17
Henderson, 1
Hendricks, 5

Hemet, 17
Henson, 8
Herod, 18
Herrington, 3
Herron, 5
Hewit, 2
Highbee, 5
Higgins, 1,3,12
Hill, 5,17
Hillsberry, 1
Hiltabrand, 13
Hinkle, 5
Hinson, 9
Hinton, 5
Hobble, 12
Hobbs, 12
Hobson, 22
Hodson, 12
Hoke, 20
Holder, 20
Holdford, 5
Holley, 5
Holmes, 17
Honrold, 5
Hooper, 1
Hoover, 5
Hopkins, 15
Hornbeck, 1
Horton, 9
Houdesball, 2
Hoyer, 12
Hoyt, 2
Hubbard, 2
Hull, 2,17
Hummel, 1
Hummer, 5
Humphrey, 12
Hungate, 15
Hunn, 1
Hurt, 12,13
Hurter, 20
Hutchen, 5
Hutchison, 1
Hutson, 15
InmAN, 2
Irwin, 14
Isringhaus, 12
Jacobs, 5
James, 8
Johnson, 2,14
Johnston, 15

Joiner, 13
Jones, 1,3,12
Kedricks, 15
Keen, 1
Keller, 5
Kelly, 10
Kilgore, 1,21
Kinney, 23
Kircher, 1
Kirk, 12
Kreider, 13
Krisel, 15
Ladon, 20
Lake, 1
Laird, 3
Lare, 15
Largley, 5
Larkston, 12,13
Larrison, 12
Laswell, 1
Lay, 15
Lawrence, 11
Lee, 12
Leight, 5
Leonard, 1
Lewellen, 10
Lewis, 2,18
Lewsey, 18
Lillie, 5
Lincoln, 12
Lindey, 12
Lochrie, 12
Logan, 11
Lonergan, 1
Long, 1
Lovel, 9
Lowe, 12
Lowry, 8,15
Lucas, 125
M'Clintic, 17
M'Intosh, 17
M'Kee, 17
McBroom, 15
McCall, 18
McCann, Capt. John, 24
McCarty, 2
McCay, 5
McDaniel, 12
McElharey, 11
McRuire, 85
McKee, 10

McKinzie, 10
McLaughlin, 15
Malin, 5
Manlon, 11
Markland, 1
Marshall, 1
Mattin, 12
Mason, 21
Mather, 21
Mathew, 21
Mathias, 21
Matocks, 12
Maulding, 15
Maupin, 5
Maxwell, 1
Mayhew, 21
Melcher, 21
Meredith, 15
Merrick, 21
Merritt, 1
Messer, 21
Meyer, 12
Middlesworth, 21,22
Miklich, 12
Miller, 5,22
Milliken, 22
Minnis, 5
Minor, 22
Moffatt, 11
Monday, 15
Monroe Co., 16,17
Moore, 12,15,17,20
Moore, Capt. James, 16
Moriarity, 1
Morris, 5,15
Morrison, 17,23
Murhpy, 12
Myers, 13
Naomi, 13
Nash, 23
Neal, 1,20
Neil, 20
Nelson, 2,10,12,13
Nevin, 17
Newcomb, 9
Nichols, 20
Noresby, 5
Nuckolls, 5
O'Connor, 1
Ogle, 17
OLeson, 2
Olgesby, 15

Oliver, 10
Osborne, 2
Osgood, 13
Overton, 5
Overturf, 15
Owen, 17
Pardee, 12
Pasley, 13
Pauley, 15
Payan, 23
Payne, 9
Pearce, 1
Peden, 12
Perry, 3,11,12,15,22
Peterson, 12
Phelps, 15
Phillips, 12
Pierce, 13
Phillips, 23
Plant, 10
Pope Co., 17
Porter, 5,17,18
Prentice, 9
Prentiss, 12
Preston, 20
Price, 12
Prigmore, 15
Proctor, 15
Queries, 1,11,12,25,26
Radebaugh, 12
RAglard, 1
Ragsdale, 1
Ralston, 5
Rector, 17
Redmon, 8,9
Reed, 1
Reubemaker, 15
REynolds, 12,15
Rich, 15
Richland, Co., 19
Rickords, 1
Ripple, 9
Robertsson, 10
Robinson, 15
Roessler, 22
Rogers, 8,12
Ronalds, 18
Rudsell, 15
Russell, 12
Ryan, 10,17

Ryason, 1
Sanders, 5
Scheidt, 1
Schoolcraft, 16
Schorfheide, 12
Scott, 17
Sharock, 5
Shattuck, 2
Shaw, 1
Shearly, 16
Shelby Co., 20
Shelton, 11
Sheppard, 11
Shoot, 1
Shroad, 11
Sims, 1,16
Skinner, 5
Smith, 1,2,5,9,12,15,20
Sneed, 14
Snyder, 17
Spain, 14
Spalding, 21
Spencer, 12
Spiker, 13
Spindle, 5
Sporeman, 12
Spruell, 11
Spurgeon, 12
STanley, 20
Starter, 11
STephenson, 9
Stevenson, 2
Stewart, 1
Stich, 15
Stillwell, 13
Stockler, 12
Stofft, 12
Story, 2
Stott, 1
STrong, 12
Stupp, 9,11
Swisher, 12
Tanner, 2
Tawlbee, 10
Taylor, 1,5,10,12,13
Terhune, 9
Theiler, 1
Thomason, 21
Thompson, 10,11,12,14
Tillotson, 3
Tinsley, 10
Toothe, 12

Townserd, 15,16
Tramel, 16
Trimble, 12
Ture, 20
VArhouten, 8
Von Behren, 12
VAn Wickle, 10
Vaughn, 12
Viles, 10
Waddle, 17
Waggoner, 18
Wanrer, 1
War of 1812, 16
Ward, 3,16
Washburn, 1
Washington Co., 222
Wakkins, 2,5
Wayne, Co., 23
Weaver, 8
Webb, 1
Webster, 2,20
Weiderhammer, 12,13
Welch, 5,12
Welton, 20
Westbrook, 5
Whitaker, 8
White, 11,9,16,18
White Co., 24
Whiteside Co., 24
Wilcoxson, 18
Wilkinson, 23
Willard, 2,12,13
William, 12
Williams, 9,16
Wilson, 11,18
Winkler, 3
Witt, 15
Witter, 2
Wood, 1
Wright, 12
Wyatt, 8
Young, 2,11
YOungblood, 10
Ziegler, 11

---

County, surname queries
  published free.
$5 for maximum of 50
  word queries.
Check with the publisher
for advertising rates.

SEARCHING ILLLINOIS ANCESTORS

VOLUME III NO. II

January February 1987

INDEXED IN GENEALOGICAL PERIODICAL INDEX

Issued bi-monthly by Helen Cox Tregillis. Publication and advertising offices: Box 392, Shelbyville, IL 62565. Current single copy price, $2 plus 69 cents postage. Yearly subscription, $12. Send check or money order payable to: Helen Cox Tregillis, Box 392, Shelbyville, IL 62565. Surnames, articles appearing in publication are indexed in GENEALOGICAL PERIODICAL INDEX. Postage paid at Shelbyville, IL. Send address changes, queries, advertising to above address.

ISSN 0886 - 7763

PAYMENT MUST ACCOMPANY SUBSCRIPTION, QUERY AND ADVERTISING

NO BACK ISSUES AVAILABLE

## TABLE OF CONTENTS, VOL. III, NO. II

| | | |
|---|---|---|
| Christian County, Marriage Records | 30 | |
| Clay County, Genealogical Sources | 31 | |
|     Capt. John Onslott's Co. | | 31 |
| Clinton County, Genealogical Sources | 32 | |
|     22nd. Ill. Infantry | | 32 |
| Coles County, Genealogical Sources | 33 | |
|     25th Ill. Infantry | | 33 |
| Cook County, Genealogical Sources | 34 | |
|     Capt. Seission's Unit | | 34 |
|     Capt. Napier's Unit, Black Hawk War | | 35 |
| Edgar County, Marriage Records | 35 | |
| Fayette County, Newspaper Abstracts | 36 | |
| Hamilton County, Newspaper Abstracts | 37 | |
| Hancock County, Genealogical Sources | 39 | |
|     Nauvoo Newspaper Abstracts | | 39 |
| Illinois, Capt. Wm. Jones Co., War of 1812 | 40 | |
| McDonough County, Genealogical Sources | 41 | |
|     Newspaper Abstracts | | 41 |
| Saline County, 1887 Biog. Surnames | 42 | |
| Shelby County, Newspaper Abstracts | 42 | |
|     Miscellaneous Records | | 44 |
| Union County, Genealogical Sources | 45 | |
|     Capt. Craig's Unit, Black Hawk War | | 45 |
| Vermilion County, Genealogical Sources | 45 | |
|     25th Ill. Infantry, Co. A | | 46 |
| Wabash County, Genealogical Sources | 46 | |
|     Capt. Arnold's Co., Black Hawk War | | 46 |
|     Capt. Jordan's Co., Black Hawk War | | 47 |
| Warren County, Genealogical Sources | 47 | |
|     Burials of Soldiers of 1812 War | | 47 |
| SEARCHING ILLINOIS ANCESTORS | 47 | |

CHRISTIAN COUNTY, ILLINOIS
MARRIAGES, BOOK I, 1839-1866

Harris BRITON and Nancy WESTBROOK, page 58
James M. HAINES and Myren O. RICKS, page 58
Cumberland HUFFORD and Mary Jane ADAMS, page 60
Green B. HILL and Sarah Ann CURRY, page 61
William L. HUMMER and Isabel M. EAST, page 61
Christopher HARRIS and Nancy A. EDWARDS, page 61
Ransom HURGES and Lavina ALEXANDER, page 63
James HARPER and Elizabeth VERMILLION, page 64
David C. HALL and Julia N. MOORE, page 65
James B. HALFORD and Mary Jane LANGLEY, page 66
James HATCHETT and Emma WALLIS, page 66
John HINTON and Eveline GALLOWAY, page 68
Chriistian HUTCHINS and Martha A. HELMICK, page 69
Terry HILL and Mary Jane LAMB, page 74
Joseph HANON and Mary A. F. MINNIS, page 77
Robert J. HANNA and Sarah BUSH, page 78
James HENDSON and Frances E. DAVIDSON, page 80
John HOLSTON and Mary J. WATERS, page 82
John H. HATFIELD and Margaret CARBILL, page 82
William F. HAYS and Elizabeth RICHARDSON, page 87
Charles HUMPHREYS and Mary WILCOX, page 87
John W. HUNTER and Martha VERMILLION, page 90
William M. HARRIS and Barbara M. HULLFORD, page 101
Timothy HOOVER and Mary M. WADDLE, page 103
William H. HILL and Amanda J. MATHEWS, page 104
Thomas HAMMON and America HATCHETT, page 104
John HARDEN and Mary Ann PAINTER, page 104
David HUMPHREYS and Mary A. CHAPMAN, page 105
James H. HUDSON and Jemima BARNS, page 112
Isaac HENSHI and Sarah J. BLANKENSHIP, page 113
Andrew M. HALFORD and Emily BLOUNT, page 115
Andrew HAYWARD and Mary LOCKARD, page 116
Alfred HOLLINGSWORTH and Sarah OSBURN, page 117
Anlos HUDDLESTON and Celia A. HUNTER, page 118
Rodney P. HILL and Ellen REESE, page 118
William M. HULEN and Harriet M. WILSON, page 118
Tipo HARRIS and Mary Jane WELLER, page 119
Robert HAYWARD and Elizabeth CHUMLEY, page 120
James HONSANAN and Roda SARGENT, page 122
Oskar HURST and Elizabeth RUSSELL, page 124
Joseph HARRIS and Mariah SEABON, page 124
George H. HILLABRANT and Virginia G. HOWARD, page 125
H. L. HOUSLEY and Ruth J. HURST, page 125
William L. HURST and Mary D. HUNTER, page 125
Jacob HARROD and Catharine HAWKINS, page 125
James M. HARDIN and Martha J. ADAMS, page 128
Charles C. HARREL and Sarah J. BOST, page 129
Richard L. HALL and Abby J. HILL, page 130

William C. HAINES and Lucy E. YOUNG, pag 133
James HOGAN and Harriet J. NISERWANER, page 134
John HILL and Nancy E. BRENTS, page 135
Wm. T. HESKET and Casander MAXWELL, page 135
Next marriage unclear
Robert W. HOPPER and Catharine COWGILL, page 221
Wm. HUNTER and Martha BARTLETT, page 222
Rrichard HEWITT and Mary A. BRAGG, page 224
John H. HATFIELD and Clara M. JOY, page 224
George M. HOPKINS and Emma DEMOT, page 226
Thomas T. HARRIS and Martha A. HARRIS, page 227
George N. HUDDLESTON and Sarah A. WOODSIDES, page 228
James H. HOLDEN and Amanda KEMMERER, page 229
William HAMEL and Julia F. DICKSON, page 232
William W. HAINES and Mary L. LEIGH, page 233
Wm. H. HOOVER and Sally F. READING, page 234

------------------

## CLAY COUNTY, ILLINOIS
### GENEALOGICAL SOURCES, HELP

County created 23 Dec. 1824 from parent counties of Wayne, Lawrence, Fayette. Named for Henry Clay. County seat of Louisville, IL 62858 has vital, land records (county clerk, 618-665-3526) and court records (circuit clerk, 618-665-3523). Courthouse hours, Monday through Friday, 8 to 4.

### SOURCES

1909, Biographical and Reminiscent History of Richland, Clay and Marion Counties. B.F. Bowen & Co.

Important Surnames Researched. Anthony Jones, Peter Schaun, 1981.

Cemetery Inscriptions of Clay County, Ill. 509 pages. John W. Tanner.

1850 Census Transcription, 1973. Maxine Wormer.

------------------

Capt. John Onslott's Company
Black Hawk War, Mustered out Aug. 15, 1832
Clay County, Illinois
Page 17 of ILLINOIS ADJUDANT GENERALS's RECORDS, volume I

Capt. John Onslott; 1st Lt. Trussey P. Hanson; 2nd Lt. Alfred J. Moore; Sgts. Cyrus Wright, Elisha Bashford, Arch. T. Patterson, James Tompkins; Corps. Samuel Whiteley, Strother B. Walker, Joseph Whiteley, Francis Herman; Pvts. James T. Ano, Jefferson Creek, James Cook, Sol. B. Carbaugh, Young Chamberlin, Augur Campbell, Levi Daniels, A.S. Fitzgerald, Joseph Lethcoe, Russell Logan, Hugh McDaniel, Robert McDaniel, John McGrew, James McKenney, Bennett W. Moseley, Perkey Mortin, John G. Nicholson, James Nelson, Isaac Rogers, Thomas Rogers, Jesse Skief, Abram Songer, Lockhard Stallings, David Sincoe, John Sutton, John Speaker, Frederick Tarter, James Van Cleave, Isaac Walker, Jas. L. Wickersham, Martin Whiteley.

## CLINTON COUNTY, ILLINOIS
## GENEALOGICAL SOURCES, HELP

County created 27 Dec. 1824 from parent counties of Washington, Bond, Fayette, and Crawford. Named for DeWitt Clinton. County seat at Carlyle, IL 62231 has vital, land records (county clerk, 618-594-2464) and court records (618-594-2415). Illinois genealogical society that covers this county is Clinton County Historical Society, Box 82, Aviston, IL 62216. Courthouse hours, Monday through Friday, 8 to 4.

The society publishes a quarterly.

### SOURCES

1877-1899 Clinton County Recorded Death Records, Clinton County Historical Society.

Clinton County Marriages, Book No. 1, 1857-1872. Clinton County Historical Society.

Clinton County Marriages, Book No. 2, 1856-1872. Clinton County Historical Society.

1850 Census of Clinton County. Decatur Genealogical Society.

1850 Census of Clinton County. Maxine Wormer, 1973.

---

## CLINTON COUNTY, ILLINOIS
### 22nd infantry regiment, Company A
### Illinois Adjutant General's Records
### Civil War

Capts: Samuel Johnson, Samuel T. Malehorn, Franklin A. Smalley

1st Lts. Theodore Wiseman, Samuel T. Malehorn, William S. Ford, Franklin A. Smalley, John W. Koone

2nd Lts. William S. Ford, William Roper, William H.H. Ireland

1st Sgt. Samuel T. Malehorn

Sgts. William N. Bailey, William Roper, Franklin Smalley

Corps: Frank Murray, Oliver Maddux, George S. Perry, Charles L. Smiley, William M. Austin, John Bluthardt, Obed Fink, John Garber

Musician: William Mace

Wagoner: James S. Parker

Pvts.: Casper Ackerman, Adam Arend, Burrell J. Blanton, William T. Bright, Thomas J. Borin, Charles Behler, Michael Burkhardt, John D. Blackwell, Michael Branger, Henry Bohnhoff, Joseph Bousman, Thomas Clayton, Anton Claus, H.H. Christopher, John Chinnery, John B. Coverdale, Frederick Dumbeck, John Dumbeck, Samuel Dyalie, Thomas C. Darneal, John Deriker, John Diffenour, William P. Daly, Joseph Easington, Lorenzo D. Epperly, Jacob Engle, Peter Florin, Clark Gaddis, Frederick Grob, Joseph Hahnn, Robert F. Hacker, Frederick Habler, William Hesse, Anslem Huss, Frederick Harter, John M. Irwin, Samuel Jackson, George T. Kirkham, Frank Millink, Thomas J. Maddux, Simeon W. Maddux, Robert McDonald, James McFarlin, George A. Niernan, John C. Parks, Jacob Preashel, Jonathon Pickering, John Roper, Louis Rader, John Robinson, George Robbason, Andrew Reeder, Aarron Suber, John S. Sager, Lafayette Smith, Samuel Smith, John Scenn, Jacob Scharlier, Mathias Swartz, Frederick Schepfur, Alexander H. Sharp, William P. Sharp, Lewis Sharp, Cyrus Sharp, Julius Schlenker, John Shoemaker, Ernest Schram, Francis Tieling, William Umbarger, George

Vita, George Walker, John B. Weber, Gotlieb Waldhaber, Joseph White.
Veterans: Franklin A. Smally, John S. Robinson.
Recruits: Frank Adams, Geroge Altermont, William Carter, Mark S. Clay, Fernando J. Erwin, George W. Engler, Charles Elling, John H. Grote, William Y. Gilmore, John A. Glasgow, Gustav Gredding, Cornel's B. Lockwood, John S. Lander, Conrad Melk, Albert Mace, Benjamin Roper, Howard B. Woodward, Henry F. Wilton, Charles Wiseman.

------------

## COLES COUNTY, ILLINOIS
## GENEALOGICAL SOURCES, HELP

County created 25 Dec. 1830 from parent counties of Clark and Edgar. Named for Gov. Edward Coles. County seat at Charleston, IL 61920 has vital, land records (county clerk, 217-348-0501) and court records (circuit clerk, 217-345-0516). Court house hours: Monday through Friday, 8:30 to 4:30. Illinois genealogical society that covers this county is Coles County Genealogical Society, P.O. Box 225, Charleston, IL 61920.

### SOURCES

Coles County Early Marriages: 1830-1850; 1850-1870. Coles County, Ill. Genealogical Society.
1840, 1850, 1860 Coles County, Ill. Censuses. Coles County, Ill. Genealogical Society.
Historical Plat Maps of Coles County, Ill. Coles County, Ill. Genealogical Society.
Cemetery Inscriptions. Check for volumes with the society.
Cemetery Inscriptions. Check with the Decatur Genealogical Society, Decatur, Ill.
1879, History of Coles County, Ill. William LeBaron, Jr. and Co.

------------

## COLES COUNTY, ILLINOIS
## 25TH ILL. INFANTRY, CO. E
## CIVIL WAR
## ILLINOIS ADJUTANT GENERAL'S REPORT

**Captains** Westford Taggert, William J. Sallie

**First Lts.** William J. Sallie, Thomas W. Brazleton

**Second Lt.** Thomas W. Brazleton

**First Sergeant** Benjamin F. Lamb

**Sergeants** Henry Beevers, Bergus Fitzpatrick, Joseph B. Spence, Joshua Rickets

**Corporals** John West, William Beevers, William K. Morris, E.B. Bradley, William Woods, Sam'l F. McCannaba, Redrick Cartwright, James Lake

**Musicians** Michael Myers, Isaiah D. Moore

**Wagoner** Thomas A. Mayes

**Privates** Philip Andrews, Robert Bare, Thomas Benseley, Zachariah Campbell, James S. Cartwright, Isaac N. Coffin, Michael Caton, Thomas Devick, Thornton B. Easton, John W. Ferbroche, Robert A. Goodrich, James C. Gilbert, Asahel Griffin, Shannon Hart, Levi H. Harrington, Miles Higgins, Joseph Ingle, Hammon Knock, Joseph Merritt, John Malone, Daniel McMahon, Peter McImoy,

Henry Mallen, Eli J. Nelson, Charles B. Prather, Isaiah Paskal, Eliash Prather, John R. Quick, Charles Quest, Andrew A. Rickets, Joseph Riggs, Martin Shaffer, William R. Smith, Jacob T. Salmons, Thomas Temple, James Temple, John G. Titus, James Umphries, William P. Walker, James Wallace, Andrew J. West, William West, James Waldrop, Charles Westley, William White

Recruits John Ashby, Jacob L. Bruner, George Bertine, W. Brandenberg, Benjamin N. Baker, Henry Coope, Nanthaniel Cheek, Peter Drury, David C. Davis, Enoch A. Frost, William C. Goodrich, Aaron Hatmaker, Jordan B. Haddock, John C. Hawkins, William H. Halbrooks, Daniel Hogan, Peter Hogan, Stephen Jester, Samuel T. Larkin, Samuel H. Merritt, Benjamin F. Mowell, Tyre M. Myers, Calvin Mallicoat, Thomas McLain, Anthony Nabeck, David Smith, Zachariah Scott, Francis M. Scott, Robert Strickland, Henry Shultz, Samuel Von, Justis G. Williams, Luke Waltrip, Michael Waltrip, Charles Wilson

------------

## COOK COUNTY, ILLINOIS
## GENEALOGICAL SOURCES, HELP

County created 15 Jan. 1831 from parent county of Putnam. Named for Daniel P. Cook. County seat at Chicago, IL 60600 has vital records (county clerk, 312-443-5656); land records, (recorder, 312-443-5055) and court records (circuit clerk, 312-443-5030). Court house hours: Monday through Friday, 9 to 4:30. Illinois genealogical societies that cover this county are: Chicago Genealogical Society, P.O. Box 1160, Chicago, IL 60646 and North Suburban Genealogical Society, care of Winnetka Public Library, 768 Oak St., Winnetka, IL 60093.

Both societies have extensive collections of publications. Check with them for help.

------------

## COOK COUNTY, ILLINOIS
## BLACK HAWK WAR, 1832
## ILLINOIS ADJUTANT GENERAL'S RECORDS
### Odd Battalions

Captain Holden Seission

First Lt. Robert Stephens

Second Lt. William H. Bradford

Sergeants James Sayres, Uriah Wentworth, John Cooper, Abraham Franciss

Corporals Armstead Runyan, Thomas Coons, Edward Poor, Corneli's C. VanHorn

Privates William Barlow, Joseph Cox, Timothy B. Clarke, Barrett Clarke, William Clarke, William Chapman, David Crandell, Alva Crandell, Enoch Darling, Samuel Fleming, Patterson Frame, Thomas Franciss, John Friend, Aaron Friend, William Gougar, John Gougar, Nicholas Gougar, Daniel Gougar, Daniel Haight, Silas Henderson, Alfred Johnson, Joseph Johnson, James Johnson, Peter Lampseed, Peter Lemsis, Selah Lamfear, Aaron More, David Maggard, James Mathews, Joseph Norman, George Pettijohn,

Anderson Poor, Calvin Rowley, William Rodgers, Rufus Rice, Daniel Robb, William H. Scott, Lucius Scott, David Smith, Oren Stephens, O.I. Turner, Abraham Van Horne, Simon C. Van Horne, Aaron Wares, John Wilson.

## Capt. Joseph Napier's Co.
## Black Hawk War, 1832
## Cook County, Ill.

Captain: Joseph Napier
First Lt. Alanson Sweet
Second Lt. Sherman King
Sgts. S.M. Salisbury, John Manning, Walter Showell, John Napier
Corps. T.E. Parsons, Lyman Butterfield, J.P. Bladget, Nelson Murray
Privates Anson Ament, Calvin Ament, William Barter, Dennis Clark, George Fox, Caleb Foster, John Fox, William Gault, Josiah H. Gebblens, Peres Hawley, Edmund Harrison, Bailey Hobson, Daniel Langdon, P.F.W. Peck, T. Parsons, Uriah Paine, Christopher Paine, John Stevens, John Stevens, Jr., Williard Scott, Augustine Stowell, Galvin M. Stowell, Richard M. Sweet, Seth Waistcoat, Henry T. Wilson, Peter Wicoffe.

---

## EDGAR COUNTY, ILLINOIS
## MARRIAGE RECORDS

1836, Joseph CAMERRER and Judea STEEL
31 March 1836 James B. CRAWFORD and Mary Jane SHAW
1836, Willard CENTER and Eliza HOWELL
28 May 1836 Perry CALVIN and Priscilla CONERY
11 June 1836 Thomas B. CARR and Mariah OLMSTEAD
16 July 1836 James COX and Lucinda TACKETT
27 Dec. 1836 Daniel COY and Mary EVANS
7 Feb. 1837 Preston M. CRAIG and Elizabeth JAMES
22 Feb. 1837 Josiah CALLUMS and Levina WALLER
14 March 1837 Spencer COLLINS and Elizabeth HOGAN
14 Oct. 1837 Joel COOPER and Elizabeth CALLAWAY
2 Nov. 1837 Harvey COOPER and Holley WILSON
12 Feb. 1838 James A. CUSICK and Martha BENNETT
15 Feb. 1838 Samuel CRAIG and Jane HEAD
27 Feb. 1838 Burges CORNWELL and Sarah DOING
6 March 1838 H.A. CANKEY and Jane KEYES
20 April 1838 Joshua COOK and Sarah ALEXANDER
9 July 1838 James CUMMINS and Nancy CANUTE
6 Sept. 1838 Joseph CHAPMAN and Caroline WILSON
16 Oct. 1838 Argaleso N. CLARK and Sarah KEARN
26 Dec. 1838 Enoch CHATMAN and Juliann BERRY
1 Jan. 1839 Isaiah CALLAWAY and Susannah QUICK
27 Feb. 1839 Moses CONNER and Margaret GOODMAN
18 April 1839 Hesekiah COAMER and Amanda LAUGHLIN
13 July 1839 George CULVER and Mary VARLEY
24 Aug. 1839 William CANADY and Elizabeth BOOTH
12 Sept. 1839 Morris CENTER and Mary MAPES
24 Oct. 1839 John CHILDRESS and Catharine HOGUE

15 Nov. 1839 Robert CHAPMAN and Ruth HURST
9 Jan. 1840 James C. CLARK and Margaret CAMERER
9 Jan. 1840 Allen CARNES and Rebeccah RAMSEY
6 April 1840 William CUSTER and Isabel Jane NEWCOMB
14 Sept. 1840 Timothy D. CALVIN and Mary MIDDLETON
2 Nov. 1840 Jacob P. COMES and Rebecca KERAN
2 March 1841 James CHATMAN and Margaret BERRY
13 March 1841 Robert H. COWAN and Luisa W. CAMERER
22 April 1841 Walter H. CROSS and Mariah L. SMITH
7 Aug. 1841 Michael CHISM and Delila BEELEHEMER
30 Sept. 1841 William CANADY and Nancy ALLISON
21 Feb. 1842 John R. CONLEY and Caroline GORDON
14 March 1842 John COTTERAL and Paulina BOATMAN
15 Oct. 1842 Jeremiah CURNUTT and Leanuah DAVIS
25 Nov. 1842 Harvey CLOE and Elizabeth ESLINGER

---

FAYETTE COUNTY, ILLINOIS
ABSTRACTS FROM ILLINOIS INTELLIGENCER NEWSPAPER
VANDALIA, ILLINOIS
MICROFILM

Saturday, Dec. 23, 1820, page 4 from Kentucky Report

Extrodinary longevity. We published a few weeks ago, an account of the death of Col. Daniel Boone, whose name is associated with many interesting events in the history of Kentucky, and we are now informed that the last of his brothers died a few days ago, in this state, in an adjoining county. The following statement, derived from a correct source, of the longevity of the family, is the most remarkable that we have ever seen:

Ages of five brothers and three sisters:

Col. Daniel Boone     83
Samuel Boone          88
Jonathon Boone        85
Squire Boone          75
George Boone          83
Mrs. Wilcox           91
Mrs. Smith            84
Mrs. Grant            84

(Ages may be miscopied as microfilm was unclear on numbers but the names were legible.)

Tuesday, January 23, 1820

Page 3, on Motion of Mr. Calvins, the house nominated the following persons as justices of the peace:

Crawford County: Joel Phelps, Zephaniah Lewis, Joel Cheek.

Clark County: John Black, Chas. Patrick, Lewis Murphy, Thomas Foster, Elijah Austin, Jona. Mayo, Samuel Perry, Joseph Shall and Samuel Prevo.

Lawrence County: Henry Gilliam, Thomas Anderson, James Weselfall, Joseph Beard, Jonathon Parker, John Dunlap, Benjamin M'Leof, David McCord, William Dennison, Victor Bohannson, James Rawlings, George Barney, Elisha Warden and Reason Club.

Tuesday, Feb. 13, 1821
Page 3

On Saturday last, the following gentlemen were elected judges of probate of the several counties in the state, by the joint ballot of both houses of the general assembly.

Madison, Jacob W. Walker; St. Clair, Edmund P. Wilkinson; Bond, Thomas Kirkpatrick; Washington, William H. Bradsby; Monroe, Caldwell Cairns; Randolph, Curtis Coon; Jackson, Joel Manning; Union, Abner Field; Johnson, Andrew McCorkle; Pope, Joshua Scott; Franklin, John Conger; Gallatin, Joseph M. Street; White, James Ratcliff; Edwards, Jesse B. Brown; Crawford, James Wilson; Clark, Samuel Provost; Wayne, Samuel Leech; Jefferson, Joel Pace; Alexander, Alanson Powell; Lawrence, Henry M. Gilham; Hamilton, Jesse O. Lockwall; Fayette, James Jones; Montgomery, Eleazor M. Townsend; Greene, John G. Lefton; Sangamon, James Latham; Pike, Abraham Beck.

Tuesday, April 3, 1821

Page 3, List of letters remaining in post office at Vandalia, on 31st of March 1821, which if not taken out within three months, will be returned to the general post office as dead letters.

John A. Anderson, Sidney Breese, William Caldwell, Maria Davis, Jeremiah Johnson, Jacob Lough, A.L. Langham, John McLean, Ezra Owen, Col. Robertson, Cye Smith, James Turney, Raphael Widen, William Boone, John Bussing, Stephen Coe, Thomas Hambleton, James Lathatt, William Low, Harris McGregor, John McLure, Joseph Phillips, Abel Robinson, William Tilford, Nathan Weatherspoon. J. Warnock, p.m.

Tuesday, Sept. 4, 1821

Page 3: To the people of Fayette County, Ill. It may seem somewhat strange that I should trouble the paper at this time; but the wicked attack of Joseph Oliver made on me in a handbill, dated March 30th, 1821, wherein he implicated me as assisting in circulating false reports to injure his election to the office of sheriff. On the morning of the day of the election, I notified that gentlemen that I should call on him in the evening of the same day to answer me before the people, to certain parts in his handbill, which I should attempt to refute; accordingly I requested him to come forward; he totally refused or neglected to render any satisfaction whatever.

Therefore it has become necessary, in order to do justice to myself and friends, that I should lay the following affidavits before the public, to wit: (One each from William Biggs, Jr.; John Scott; Robt. Thomas; William Padfield.) Martin Jones, August 11, 1821441w.

HAMILTON COUNTY, ILLINOIS
HAMILTON COUNTY HERALD NEWSPAPER
MCLEANSBORO, ILL. MICROFILM

Nov. 8, 1884 Marriage licenses

Norris E. Deitz, 24, to Rachel G. Maulding, 20, both of McLeansboro Precinct

Thomas Malone, 23, to Samantha Price, 23, both of Lasater Precinct

Mark Hannford, 24, to Barthena Gibbs, 18, of Knights Prairie Precinct

John W. Williams, 22, to Kesihah Halley, 17, both of Delafield.

James W. Williamson, 45, to Ellen Jones, 25, both of Shelton Precinct.

William T. Guill, 18, to Mollive Long, 18, both of Knights Prairie Precinct.

## Nov. 1, 1884

John Davis, Jr., 52, to Manerva A. Fite, 26, both of Allen Precinct.

Edward E. Allen, 23, to Susie A. Walters, 19, both of Lasater Precinct.

William C. Huff, 26, to Jane York, 18, both of Beaver Precinct.

James A. Gibbs, 22, to Mannie Rogers, 13, both of Knights Prairie Precinct.

Robert M. Land, 22, of Enyfield Twp., to Lizzie Jordon, 18, Beaver Creek Precinct.

John W. Witters, 21, of Knights Prairie, to Annie H. Maberry, 15, McLeansboro

## Oct. 25, 1884

John Harrison, 23, of Beaver Precinct, to Christenia Fields, 21, of Lasater Precinct.

Adam A. Simmons, 22, to Elizabeth Harrawood, 17, both of Maberry Precinct.

Obituary.....James M. Wilson, Jr. died Oct. 13, 1884 at 3 o'clock a.m. at his residence 6 miles E of McLeansboro. Born 2 Feb. 1807 Jessamine Co., Ky.; moved with father John Wilson to territory in White County, seven mile prairie; married Jan. 1834 Sarah Roberts of White County; she died 15 years later leaving him with children: Lector Ann, John N., Mary S. and Henry M. Wilson; he married 2nd Sept. 1849/50 Mrs. Mary Jane Morrow, mother of C.B. Robinson and Martha H. Fowler; she died in 1878; they had children: Sarah, Laura, Josie, Willie and Jennie.???prev. issue, burial, Corncord burial grounds on the 14th.

## Oct. 18, 1884

Marriage licenses....

William F. White, 14, to Lucinda T. Johnson, both of Flannagan Precinct.

Willie A. Smith, 20, of Galatia Twp., to Malinda J. Galbraith, 21, of Flannigan Precinct.

Benjamin F. Drew, 33, to Hannah V. Stephenson, 19, of Twin Precinct.

Thomas P. Stevenson, 23, of Mt. Vernon, Ind., to Varah H. Neel, 23, of Thackeray.

John Mayberry, 25, of Lasater Precinct, to Sarah C. Gaultney, 18, of Mayberry Precinct.

## Sept. 27, 1884

Franz J. Frey, 22, of Crouch Precinct, to Christena Erink, 23, of Shelton Precinct.

James C. Cross, 31, to Martha Sturman, 29, both of Shelton Precinct.

David E. Vires, 25, of McLeansboro Precinct, to Nancy J. Nipper, 23, Lasater Precinct.

## HANCOCK COUNTY, ILLINOIS
## GENEALOGICAL SOURCES, HELP

County created 13 Jan. 1825 from parent county of Pike and unorganized territory. Named for John Hancock. County seat at Carthage, IL 62321 has vital, land records (county clerk, 217-357-3911) and court records (circuit clerk, 217-357-2616). Courthouse hours, Monday through Friday, 8 to 4. Illinois genealogical society that covers this county and others is Tri-County Genealogical Society, P.O. Box 355, Augusta, IL 62311.

### Sources

Pioneers of the Prairie. Wilma B. Brunenn. Indexed.
Derena DeLong Family 100 Years in America. Frank DeLong. 1982.
1880, History of Hancock County. Thomas Gregg.
1907, Biographical Review of Hancock County, Ill.
Nauvoo, 1839-46. Lyman D. Platt.
1894, Portrait and Biographical Record of Hancock, McDonough and Henderson Counties, Illinois.
1850 Federal Census of Hancock County, Ill. Tri-City Genealogical Society.
1860 Census of Hancock County, Ill. Tri-County Genealogical Society.
1829-1849 Hancock County, Ill. Marriage Index.

Check with the society for other genealogical help.

---

## TIMES AND SEASONS
## NAUVOO, ILLINOIS NEWSPAPER ABSTRACTS

### February 1842

Married in this city on the 6th inst. by the Rev. Erastus H. Derby, Mr. Gilbert H. Rolfe, to Miss Eliza Jane Bales, all of this city.

Married in this city by Pres't Hyrum Smith, Mr. J.W. Johnson to Miss Elizabeth Knight, all of this city.

Died in Schuyler Co. on the 28th of Dec. 1841, Elder Isaac W. Pierce in the 31st year of his age.

Mr. Pierce was a native of New York, born in the township of Oswegatchie, St. Lawrence on Feb. 3d, 1811.....

### March 1842

Married in this city, on Wednesday, the 23d ult. Mr. William L. Hide, to Miss Elizabeth H. Bullard.

Died in this county, near Carthage, on the 22d of Feb. last, Mrs. Emeline Leyland, wife of Benjamin Leyland, aged 14 years and 8 months....

### April 1843 and June 1843

Both issues contain lists: one of elders from various parts of the United States who attended a conference. A quorum of the TWELVE was present: Brigham Young, president; Heber C. Kimball, William Smith, Orson Hyde, Orson Pratt, Wilford Woodruff, John Taylor, George A. Smith and W. Richards. The other list contained names of elders and their Illinois counties for missions.

# WAR OF 1812 ILLINOIS REGIMENTS
## ILLINOIS ADJUTANT GENERAL RECORDS
### Campaign of 1813

Captain William Jones' Company
    May 9, 1813, to June 9th, 1813

<u>Captain</u> William Jones

<u>Lt.</u> John Springer

<u>Ensign</u> Thomas Finley

<u>Sergeants</u> Edward Reavis, John Whitley, Sr., David White, Robert Brazel

<u>Corporals</u> Solomon Pruitt, Jacob Gragg, David Smelson, Andrew Lockhart

<u>Privates</u> Simon Lindley, Sr., Simon Lindley, Jr., Joseph Lindley, Benjamin Henson, John Henson, William Stubblefield, Easley Stubblefield, John Lindley, John Green, Ephraim Cox, John Finley, James Finley, Howard Finley, Moses Finley, Fields Pruitt, Martin Jones, John Jones, William Roberts, Abraham Bateman, William Bateman, Samuel Lindley, Mills Whitley, John Whitley Jr., Randolph Whitley, Elisha Whitley, Andrew Robert, Charles Tetricks, Valentine Brazel, Abraham Tetricks, William Brazel, Jacob Tetricks, Richard Brazel, Peter Tetricks, Robert White, David S. White, John Holt, James Anderson Sr., James Anderson Jr., Abraham Howard, James Chilton, Sr., William Chilton, John Giger, William Howard, Mathias Chilton, Isaac Ferguson, John Higgins, Aquilla Dollarhide, Harmon Smeiser, Joshua Chilton, James Chilton Jr., Byrd Lockhart Sr., George Tayes, George Hutton Sr., Henry Green Sr., William Lockhart, George Hutton Jr., Henry Green Jr., John Green, Bartlett Tayes, Abraham Van Hoozer, Jacob Neely, Joseph St. John, William Davis, Henry Walker, Henry Cox.

Sergeant James N. Fox's Detachment
    From frontier of Johnson County

<u>Sergeant</u> James N. Fox

<u>Privates</u> William Edwards, James Flanery, Buckner Harris, James Buchan, George Deason, Daniel Griffin, Moss Blane, John F. Norton, Shadrack Rawlison, William Rawlison, John Davis.

Captain William Boon's Company
    From Randolph County, Illinois, mounted volunteers, 6 March 1813 to 5 day of June 1813

<u>Captain</u> William Boon

<u>First Lt.</u> John Lacy

<u>2nd Lt.</u> William Bilderback

<u>Ensign</u> John Bilderback

<u>Sergeants</u> Robeert Gaston, Louis LaChapelle, Michael Buyat, Amos Chaffin

<u>Corporals</u> Joseph French, Adam Wolrick, Zophue Brooks, Henry Barbeau

<u>Privates</u> James Lee, Charles Garner, William Tilford, David Dailey, Peter Dolin, Archibald Snodgrass, Ellis Chaffin, John Drury, Erne Godler, Joseph LaFranbris, Louis Dory, William Gaston, John Young, Adam Winghart, Stace McDonough, Greyone DeGoynle, Henry Teabeau, Charles Bilberback, William Barnett, Robert Thompson, George Cochran, Elias Roberts, Andre Roy, John

Gadier, Levi French, Samuel French, Ralph Davis, John Wooten, Isaac Glenn, Thomas Glenn, Jacob Bowerman, Francis Garner, John Robinson, George Creath, Jacob Philhart, Joel Craine, John Roberts, Daniel Bilderback, William Fisher, Robert Alexander, James Hughes, William Garner, Thomas Wadley, John Machen, Benjamin Buyat, Baptiste Gendron, Julian Bart, Francis Moutroy, Peter Pillet, Henry Conner, Peter Cossy, Isadore Godier, Antoine Barbeau, Jacob May, Archibald Steele, Jacob Honnan, James Robinson, Daniel Hull, Shadrock Lively, Alexander Clarke, John Clyne, Peslo, Levi Tamaraoa, Cola, Poscal, John Baptiste Tamaraoa, Jabez Leone, Jacob Lazadder.

---

## McDONOUGH COUNTY, ILLINOIS
### GENEALOGICAL SOURCES, HELP

County created 25 Jan. 1826 from parent county of Schuyler. Named for Com. Thomas McDonough. County seat at Macomb, IL 61455 has vital, land records (county clerk, 309-833-2474) and court records (circuit clerk, 309-837-4889). Courthouse hours, Monday through Friday, 8 to 4. Illinois genealogical society that covers this county is McDonough County Genealogical Society, P.O. Box 202, Macomb, IL 61455.

### Sources

1850-1880 Mortality Schedules of McDonough County, Ill. Margaret McKee Allen. 63 pages.
1850 Federal Census of McDonough County, Ill. Bates and Mayhugh.
1885, History of McDonough County, Ill. Continental History Company.
Mt. Auburn Cemetery, Colchester, Ill. Cordell, McMillan and Smalling. 1983.
Industry Cemetery, Industry, Ill. McDonough Co. Hist. and Gen. Society, 1984.
1864-1871 Vol. III McDonough Co. Marriages. Hartmann. 1983.
Check with the society for other publications which are numerous.

---

## McDONOUGH COUNTY, ILLINOIS
### Post Office List of Letters, 1 July 1835
### Macomb, Illinois
### From Illinois Bounty Register, Quincy, Ill.
### Newspaper Microfilm

Cavill Archer, Mr. Beattle, James Barrels, Thomas Bridges, John Bridges, Robert Bean, John Charter, James Cyrus, Enoch Cyrus, M.W. Chapman, George W. Dameron, Soloman H. Dover, Thomas Dunsworth or Augstin Lillard, James Edmonston, David Feese, Asa Farrington, Martin Fugate, Dickson Gatten, John Gibson, Ross Honck, George Hepner, George Hughes, Levi Hamilton, Rebecca Hill, George K. Jackson, Daniel Klauberg, Dutton Lane, Jon Lansdown, Samuel McGee, Samuel W. McKamy, Benjamin Matthews, John Miller, Ebenezer Nowland, Joseph Orsborn, George Palmer, Bird Pyle, George W. Palmer, Grandison Pennington, Mr. Penington, Ephraim Perkins, Tobias G. Painter, Elbert W. Scott, Jesse Seybold, Isaac G. Smith, John Vance, Joseph G. Walker, Cyrus Walker, Mr. Walker, John Woodside, David Wallace. James M. Campbell, P.M.

SALINE COUNTY, ILLINOIS
Biographies contained in
History of Gallatin, Saline, Hamilton, Franklin,
and Williamson Counties, Ill.
Chicago: Goodspeed Pub. Co., 1887

Jesse Abney, John M. Baker, Louis Baker, John Baker, William C. Baker, Dr. Joseph K. Baker, John B. Berry, John M. Berry, Rev. W.S. Blackman, Bennett L. Blackman, W.W. Bourland, Reuben Bramlett, W.K. Barnett, Joseph M. Butler, J.J. Butler, Capt. T.J. Cain, Dr. S.L. Cheaney, J.P. Chenault, A.S. Clark, William D. Clary, G.W. Clayton, John Curtner, Robert H. Davis, B.A. Durham, A.W. Durham, E.F. Dwyer, G.J. Empson, M.D. Empson, W.H. Evans, W.D. Ezell, M.M. Fox, W.P. Furlong, F.F. Gasaway, Josiah Gold, J.H. Grace, Wm. M. Gregg, James Gore, W.H. Hall, Otto Heinmann, Prof. N.B. Hodson, D.N. S. Hudson, Prof. James E. Jobe, John J. Jones, Thos. A. Jones, A. Karnes, J.G. Karnes, Rev. M.B. Kelly, William M. Kittlinger, J.S. Lewis, George Limerick, John M. Lockwood, T.W. Lusk, G.R. Mace, James Macklin, R.J. McIlrath, R.S. Marsh, J. C. Matthews, Robert Mick, Dr. J.W. Mitchell, L.D. Nolen, Col. Clinton Otey, W.H. Pankey, J.G. Porter, Hon. Boen Phillips, Francis M. Pickett, Dr. G.B. Rawlings, Dr. J.W. Renfro, Thos. Y. Reynolds, J.W. Rose, Dr. J.H. Rose, J.M. Russell, W.F. Scott, J.H. Scott, R.L. Shaw, W.H. Shook, A.J. Sisk, Col. C.P. Skaggs, James Slatten, W.H. Thornberry, J.W. Towle, W.C. Travelstead, H.L. Von Lieven, R.N. Warfield, David Westbrook, Richard Westbrook, Hon. S.F. Williford, E.T. Wills, John H. Wilson.

---

SHELBY COUNTY, ILLINOIS
OBITUARIES ABSTRACTS FROM NEWSPAPER MICROFILM

Seward, Daniel        Died 13 April 1885
  Born 7 Nov. 1809 Hamilton Co., Ohio; married first, 1 Jan. 1833 Theodocia Wolverton: 8 children, 6 deceased; children surviving, E.A. and Mrs. Lucinda Shelton, wife of Archibald; married second, 30 Sept. 1847 Sarah V. Sloan, 3 children, all deceased.
    23 April 1885 Shelbyville Democrat, Shelbyville, Il.

Sexson, Morgan        Died 27 Dec. 1887
  Born Kentucky; son of Free Sexson; married at 21 years of age to Elizabeth Williams of White Co., Ill. 10 children, 6 survives along with widow.
    5 Jan. 1888 Shelbyville Democrat, Shelbyville, Il.

Sexson, Elizabeth     Died 16 May 1890
  Born 1816 North Carolina; came to White Co., Ill. in 1826; married Morgan F. Sexson in 1838, moved to Shelby County in 1840; 10 children, five survive--four sons and one daughter; funeral at Ash Grove Cemetery on 18th.
    May 1890 Our Best Words Weekly, Shelbyville, Il.

Shelby, Anna          Died 1 Jan. 1887
  Born about 18 years ago in Jackson Co., Ind.; only child; surviving, mother; died of typhoid fever at Henton, Ill.
    13 Jan. 1887 Shelbyville Democrat, Shelbyville, Il.

Shelton, Jesse        Died 5 July 1884
   Born 87 years ago Pittsylvania Co., VA; family moved to Gallia Co., Ohio; married Margaret Blake in Ohio; 1827 moved to Indiana; 1857 moved to Shelby County, Ill.; she died in Nov. 1878; children, Arch Shelton and Mrs. Mary Davis.
      10 July 1884 Shelbyville Democrat, Shelbyville, Il.
Shelton, Margaret Blake   Died 18 Nov. 1878 Prairie Twp.
   Died of pneumonia at age 78; born 25 Oct. 1800 Virginia; mother of Arch Shelton; married Jesse Shelton.
      21 Nov. 1878 Shelbyville Democrat, Shelbyville, Il.
Shepard, Sarah        Died 16 June 1891
   Born 22 July 1804 Brackin Co., Ky., daughter of Solomon Shepard who was born 1769, moved to Kentucky 1779, married Elizabeth Baker there 1791 and moved to Clermont Co., Ohio 1809; then Franklin Co., Ind. 1814; married John Barrickman 1827; 8 children; Oct. 1845 came to county with husband who died 15 July 1886.
      25 June 1891 Shelbyville Democrat, Shelbyville, Il.
Sherburn, Harvey E.   Died 11 Oct. 1891
   Born 9 March 1871 Fairfield Co., Ohio, son of W.H. Sherburn of near Cowden, Ill. Death caused by internal injuries.
      17 Oct. 1891 Our Best Words, Shelbyville, Il.
Sims, Charles A.      Died 9 Jan. 1877 Flat Branch Twp.
   Aged two years 8 months 24 days, son of Gen. W. and E. Sims; funeral at New Presbyterian Church and preached by Quin.
      25 Jan. 1877 Shelby County Independent, Shelbyville, Il.
Sittler, Jacob and Mary Sidney Cummings, 50th anniversary
   Jacob, born 27 Dec. 1813 Westmoreland Co., Pa., and Mary Sidney Cummings, born 12 March 1820 Westmoreland Co., Pa., married 5 March 1839 Westmoreland Co., Pa.; 12 children, John M., born 2 Aug. 1840 Westmoreland Co., Pa. and died 18 Sept. 1861 at Paducah, Ky.; Simon, born 13 July 1842 Shelby Co., Ill. and died 24 Feb. 1846 Shelby County, Ill.; Alexander, born 13 March 1844 Shelby Co., Ill., married S.C. Milligan of Ohio, and died 10 June 1867; George W., born 25 Aug. 1847 Shelby Co., Ill., married 13 Oct. 1870 Lizzie Middlesworth, and died 21 Sept. 1887 Springfield, Mo.; Martha J., born 27 May 1849 Shelby Co., Ill., married 2 July 1866 W.G. Buckley of Ind.; Thomas J., born 13 Jan. 1851 Shelby County, Ill., married 3 Oct. 1872 Jane M. Venters; Mary H., born 8 Dec. 1853 Shelby County, Ill., married 23 Oct. 1870 Ab. Fear of England; H.C., born 28 July 1855, married 4 Jan. 1877 Alice Stansberry of Ohio; F.A., born 11 May 1857 Shelby County, Ill., married 29 Feb. 1880 Alonzo Hornaday of Ind.; and E.C., born 3 June 1859 Shelby County, Ill., married 13 June 1859 Shelby County, Ill., married 13 June 1880 S.L. Dove of Ohio; S.A., born 25 July 1861 Shelby County, Ill., married 13 May 1881 V.M. Dittoe of Ohio; W.B., born 10 Feb. 1863 Shelby County, Ill. and died 10 July 1863 Shelby County, Ill.
      14 March 1889 Shelbyville Democrat, Shelbyville, Il.

## SHELBY COUNTY, ILLINOIS
## MISCELLANEOUS RECORDS, COUNTY CLERK

NOTE: These usually cover more than given county, since non-residents or heirs would own property in other places or have heirs in other places.

Mitchell, James
    Heirs of, died 30 Jan. 1859, MRB 193, page 479.

Mitchell, Samuel
    Will and estate of Christian Co., Ill. Died 5 Aug. 1899. MRB 236, pages 454-459.

Moberley, Benjamin
    Land warrant no. 26741, 1854, MRB 200, page 103; warrant no. 1781, 1854, MRB 200, page 104; land no. 3240, 1838, MRB 157, page 38.

Moberly, William B.
    Heirs of, MRB 215, page 17.

Moffat, Rachel
    Deceased, estate of Clinton Co., Ill. 1905. MRB 189, pps. 48-52.

Moffat, Rachel Weakly
    Heirs of, MRB 163, page 259-260.

Moll, Daniel
    Heirs of, MRB 157, page 422.

Moore, Peyton
    Land warrant no. 5489, 1838. MRB 236, page 216.

Moore, Zachariah
    Heirs of, MRB 236, page 222.

Moran, James
    Will of Christian Co., Ill. MRB 143, page 254-259.

Morgan, Allen H.
    Will of Moultrie Co., Ill. 1893, MRB 172, pps. 78-80; 159.

Morgan, Lizzie vs. Wm. A. Morgan
    Divorce Marion Co., Ind. 1900. MRB 178, page 50-52.

Morris, John G.
    Heirs of 1865. MRB 189, page 182.

Morrison, John
    Land warrant no. 12657, 1843. MRB 163, page 147.

Morrison, John W.
    Heirs of, Christian Co., Ill., decd. 1913. MRB 200, page 1.

Morrison, Joseph
    Heirs of 1862. MRB 200, page 174-176.

Morrison, Thomas Jr.
    Land no. 10344, Pvt. Capt. Crawford's Co., 7th Reg. NC military. Assigned to John H. Wallace, 10 May 1854. MRB 193, page 606.

Morse, Enos L.
    Heirs of, MRB 215, page 376.

Mortimer, James
    Heirs of, Christian Co., Ill., decd. 1898. MRB 189, pps. 126-127.

Mort, Chamberlain
    Land no. 26879, 1855. MRB 157, page 583.

## UNION COUNTY, ILLINOIS
## GENEALOGICAL SOURCES, HELP

County created 2 Jan. 1818 from parent county of Johnson. Named for the Union. County seat at Jonesboro, IIL 62952 has vital, land records (county clerk, 618-833-5711) and court records (circuit clerk, 618-833-5913). Courthouse hours, Monday through Friday, 8 to 4. Illinois genealogical society that covers this county is Genealogical Society of Southern Illinois, care of John A. Logan College, Carterville, IL 62918.

### Sources
1820-1880 Federal Census Index of Union County, Ill. Ernest H. Jackson. 1978.
1818-1880 Marriages of Union County, Ill. 1971. Ernest H. Jackson.
1883, History of Alexander, Union and Pulaski Counties, Ill. William H. Perrin.
1850 Census of Union County, Ill. Bernice C. Richard.
1852-1983, Anna-Big Creek Baptist Church History.
1876-1973, Cobden, First Baptist Church History.
Check with the society for other genealogical help.

---

Capt. B.B Craig's Company
Black Hawk War, 1832
Union County, Illinois
Illinois Adjutant General Records

Captain B.B. Craig
First lieutenant William Craig
Second lieutenant John Newton
Sergeants Samuel Moland, Solomon David, Hezekiah Hodges, John Rendlemen
Corporals Joel Barker, Adam Cauble, Martin Ury, Jeremiah Irvine
Privates Aaron Barringer, John Barringer, John Crogan, Mathew Chester, Daniel Ellis, William Farmer, Thomas Farmer, Moses Fisher, Abraham Goodin, William G. Gavin, Hiram Gramer, William Gramer, Lot W. Hancock, Daniel P. Hill, Jackson Huntsucker, Peter Lance, Andrew Lance, John Langley, Moses Liveley, A.W. Lingle, John Murphy, P.W. McCall, John Morris, Nimrod McIntosh, John McIntosh, Solomon Miller, Thomas McElyea, James Morgan, Washington McLean, Elijah McGraw, John Penrad, John Parmer, John Quillman, W.H. Rumsey, Elijah Rumsey, Elijah Shepherd, Daniel Salmons, Preston Staten, John Vincent, Jesse Wright.

---

## VERMILION COUNTY, ILLINOIS
## GENEALOGICAL SOURCES, HELP

County created 18 Jan. 1826 from parent county of Edgar and unorganized territory. Named for Vermilion River. County seat at Danville, IL 61832 has vital, land records (county clerk, 217-442-3700) and court records (circuit clerk, 217-442-3700). Courthouse hours, Monday through Friday, 8 to 4:30. Illinois genealogical that covers this county is Illiana Genealogical and Historical Society, Box 207, Danville, IL 61832.

Society has extensive collection. Check with them for genealogical help.

---

## CIVIL WAR ILLINOIS ADJUTANT GENERAL RECORDS
### Vermilion County, Illinois
### 25 Ill. Infantry, Company A

Capt. Charles A. Clark. Surnames of men in his company.

Mitchell, West, Martin, Moore, Baldwin, Kirby, Blanchard, Dicken, Pierce, Thompson, Wangaman, Williams, Jackson, Stites, Wilcox, Carney, Scott, Ashburn, Agnus, Adams, Belle, Beechum, Bechel, Barth, Blake, Baum, Brady, Breyley, Brinkley, Barr, Conover, Cook, Crone, Cook, Canaday, Campbell, Cunningham, Duff, Downing, Frazier, Garrard, Hesler, Hilyard, Hasting, Hamilton, Judd, Jackson, Joice, Kean, Lyon, Lewis, Maxey, Manning, Mayo, Malfaffy, Moore, Macy, McNeese, Miliner, Milholland, Nunsmaker, Newlon, Osborn, Opdycke, Partridge, Payten, Payne, Patty, Ratroff, Rodgers, Richards, Ryan, Sanders, Staats, Starkey, Stratton, Solomon, Tweedy, Thompson, Wilson, Willard, West, Watts, Wilmarth, Weston, Wray, Wrightmire, White, Bellus, Livingston, Manning, Milner, McNamer, Shaffer, Adams, Parker.

---

## WABASH COUNTY, ILLINOIS
### GENEALOGICAL SOURCES, HELP

County created 27 Dec. 1824 from parent county of Edwards. Name taken from an Indian. County seat at Mt. Carmel, IL 62863 has vital, land records (county clerk, 618-262-4561) and court records (circuit clerk, 618-262-5362). Courthouse hours, Monday through Friday, 8 to 5. Check with societies at Edwards or Lawrence for any genealogical help on this area.

### Sources
1883, Combined History of Edwards, Lawrence and Wabash Counties, Ill. J.L. McDonough and Co.
1860 Federal Census of Wabash County, Ill. Geraldine Satterthwaite, 1981.

---

### Capt. John Arnold's Company
### Black Hawk War, 1832
### Illinois Adjutant General Records
### Wabash County, Illinois

<u>Captain</u> John Arnold
<u>First Lieutenant</u> George Danforth
<u>Second Lieutenant</u> Samuel Fisher
<u>Sergeants</u> Mitchel C. Minnis, Hiram Couch, Mathias Leatherland, John A. Dodds
<u>Corporals</u> Solomon Frear, John Golden, Ira Keen, Wesley Woods
<u>Privates</u> James Desley, Dolphin Bass, John W. Buchannan, Jos. O. Buchannan, Henry R. Buchannan, Jefferson Brines, Joseph M.

Dodds, John Godds, James Garner, William Golden, Philip Hull, Jonathon S. Hoyt, Henry Hobbert, Dennis Keen, Barton S. Miller, James McMillen, John Ochletree, Isaac Parmeter, Isaac Pixley, William Ridgely, Henry R. Reel, Thomas Sanford, Jacob Sanford, John O. Smith, Abner Turner, John Utter, Philip Vanderhoof, Jeremiah Woods, Thomas Wear, Harvey Wear, Warren Winders, Robert Wright.

### DETACHMENT OF CAPT. ELIAS JORDAN'S COMPANY
### Black Hawk War, 1832
### Wabash County, Illinois

First lieutenant James Kennerly
Second lieutenant John N. Barnett
Sergeant James Grayson, 4th
Corporal Zack Wilson, 2nd
Privates Benj. F. Barnett, Robt. Carlton, Robert Campbell, Patrick S. Campbell, Daniel Fortney, William Grayson, Albert Hood, Joseph Levellett, Joseph Painter, Thomas Summer, Joseph Summer.

---

### WARREN COUNTY, ILLINOIS
### GENEALOGICAL SOURCES, HELP

County created 13 Jan. 1825 from parent county of Pike. Named for General Joseph Warren. County seat at Monmouth, IL 61462 has vital, land records (county clerk, 309-734-8592) and court records (circuit clerk, 309-734-5179). Courthouse hours, Monday through Friday, 8 to 4:30. Illinois genealogical society that covers this county is Wabash County Genealogical Society, P.O. Box 240, Monmouth, IL 61462.

#### Sources

There are several published sources. Check with the society for genealogical help.

---

### WARREN COUNTY, ILLINOIS
### Some Soldiers Buried in County from
### War of 1812
### Roll of Honor: Record of Burial Places, etc.
### Springfield, Ill. 1929

Sheldon Lockwood, P. Matteson, Thomas Pierce, John Brown, D.B. Bailey, Joshua Rockwell, John Wren, Humphrey Acheson, Abigal Yeomans, Justin Parker.

---

### SEARCHING ILLINOIS ANCESTORS
### FREE QUERIES, COUNTY SURNAME, ONLY

COUNTY UNKNOWN: Parr, Ream
    Beverly Quadros, No. 15 Corte de la Canada, Martinez, CA 94553
COUNTY NOT GIVEN: Ludwick reunion, July 1987, Grants Pass, Oregon
    Trudy Belcher, P.O. Box 230285, Tigard, OR 97223
COUNTY NOT GIVEN: Ludwick, Bonneau, Goodwater, Morisette, Steptoe
    Trudy Belcher, P.O. Box 230285, Tigard, OR 97223

BUREAU: Long
    Phyllis M. Long, P.O. Box 773, Palmer, AK 99645
MCLEAN, PIATT, FORD, CHAMPAIGN, PEORIA, LASALLE, MACON: Anderson, Cameron, Fawcett, Frank, Jones, Kellar, Keller, Lane, O'Neal, Siscoe, Fowler
    Mrs. Betty J. Kellar, 6781 N. Oriole Ave., Pensacola, FL 32504
BUREAU: Metzinger
    J.W. (Bill) Schikora, 6117 Avon, Kalamazoo, MI 49002
SHELBY: Hart, Hish
    MaLinda Daniel, 860 Maple, Virginia, IL 62691
EDGAR: Morris, Hensley, Long, Drake, Spoonamore; CLAY: Morris, Hensley; FAYETTE: Morris; LEE: Hall, Fender, Taliaferro or Toliver, Duff, Black; OGLE: Fender; ADAMS: Fender; HANCOCK: Murphy, Lovell; MACON: Duff or Duft; WOODFORD: Stiteler, Mc Sparran; WHITESIDE: Brown, Lincoln; MACOUPIN: Redfern, Ruyle or Rule, Frouge or Frogge, Kaiser; SANGAMON: Redfern, Frouge or Frogge; UNION: Frouge or Frogge, Davidson; GREENE: Ruyle or Rule, Frouge or Frogge, Davidson, McVey, Emmens or Emmons; CARROLL: Emmens or Emmons, Fender; CUMBERLAND: Russell, McKinley
    Donna (Tice) Carnall, 606 East Ninth, Cherryvale, KS 67335
COUNTY NOT GIVEN: Adams, Black Hawk War
    Jean Adams Pyle, HCR Box 3385, Benson, AZ 85002
COOK: Hertel, Kuhlmanln, Proesch, Levering or Leverence
    Marilyn Scott, 400 Ellwood Beach No. 3, Goleta, CA 93117
MACOUPIN: Turner, Hart, White
    Susan Cross, P.O. Box 535, Jacksonville, IL 62651
KANE: Raymond
    Lois Raymond Mead, 2720 Alabama St., Bellingham, WA 98226
KANE, WILL, GRUNDY: Hale
    Tina Dunaway, P.O. Box 711, Jay, OK 74346
ALL COUNTIES: Ridlon or Ridlen or Redlon
    Nancy R. Welch, R 2, Box 389 A, Hollis Center, ME 04042
LOGAN: Shannon, Manley
    Marguarite Villarreal, R 2, Box 620, Bartlesville, OK 74006
MOULTRIE: Munson, McKenney
    Mrs. Jake D. Webb, 1220 Cedar Ridge Lane, Colorado Springs, CO 80919
RICHLAND, JASPER, CRAWFORD: Yates, Thompson
    Lodean Russell, Box 35, Farmersburg, IN 47850
BOND: Copple
    Oscar Copple, 195 Skyview, New Braunfels, TX 78130
BOONE: Frank, Postlewaithe
    Helen C. Aukerman, 5444 Overlook Drive NE, Albuquerque, NM 87111
MCLEAN: Hastings
    Mrs. Nan Heacock, High Noon Hollow, Bradyville, TN 37026
PEORIA: Breeding, Hale
    Sherry Chandler, P.O. Box 9110, South Lake Tahoe, Ca 95731
RANDOLPH: Surnames not given
    Lucille Wiechens, 69 St Edith Ct, St. Charles, MO 63301

PAID ADVERTISING

GEAR, GERE, GAER IN ILLINOIS
    Examples, Alarion/Almyron/Almerion Gear/Gaer/Geer born circa 1831 IL, county unknown, alive 1880 Iowa.
    Shelton Gear/Gaer born circa 1820, IL, county unknown, alive 1867 in Iowa.
    Carpender/Cavender/Carpenter Gear/Geer/Gaer, res. 1831 IL, county unknown.
    G. August, 32 Stetson, Princeton, NJ 08540
    ------------

NEED ANCESTORS of: Eliza J. Worley, born 3 Feb. 1819 in Johnson Co., Illinois. First wife of Captain William Jones, born 5 Feb. 1812 Adair Co., KY. and of: Eliza Noble, born 1828 in Illinois, wife of James W. Strickland Sr., born 1817-23 in Mo. and of: James Strickland, born circa 1790. He lived in Carbondale, IL.
Lewis Baker, P.O.B. 2805, Crossville, TN 38555
    ------------

**MENNONITE FAMILY HISTORY**

Periodical on Mennonite, Amish, and Brethren family history, published quarterly since 1982. ($15 annually)

P. O. Box 171, Elverson, PA 19520

SEARCHING ILLINOIS ANCESTORS
(ISSN 0886-7763)

ADVERTISING RATES
1 col. x 2" ....$5, one time
1/4 page........$10, one time
half page.......$17.50, once
full page.......$35, one time
    Deadlines: Feb. 21, April 21, June 20, Aug. 22 and Oct. 24
    Black on white only!
    8 x 11 1/2 format
FULL PAYMENT REQUIRED WITH COPY

## INDEX TO VOLUME III, NUMBER II

Abney, 42
Adams, 30,33,46,48
Allen, 38
Ament, 35
Ano, 31
Arnold, 46
Austin, 32,36
Baldwin, 46
Bare, 33
Barnett, 40,42,47
Barr, 46
Barringer, 45
Barth, 46
Bass, 46
Bean, 41
Beblehemer, 36
Beechum, 46
Belle, 46
Benseley, 33
Besley, 46
Black, 36,48
Bladget, 35
Blane, 40
Blount, 30
Bohannson, 36
Boon, 40
Borin, 32
Bousman, 32
Bradley, 33
Bragg, 31
Branger, 32
Breeding, 48
Breyley, 46
Brines, 46
Briton, 30
Bruner, 34
Buckley, 43
Bush, 30
Butterfield, 35
Cairns, 37
Callums, 35
Camerer, 35,36
Canady, 35,36
Canute, 35
Carlton, 47
Carr, 35
Caton, 33
Chaffin, 40
Charter, 41

Acheson, 47
Agnus, 46
Allison, 36
Anderson, 37,36,40,48
Archer, 41
Ashburn, 46
Bailey, 32,40,47
Bales, 39
Barker, 45
Barney, 36
Barrels, 41
Bart, 41
Bartlett, 31
Bateman, 40
Beard, 36
Bechel, 46
Beevers, 33
Bellus, 46
Berry, 35,36,42
Biggs, 37
Blackman, 42
Blake, 43,46
Blankenship, 30
Bluthardt, 32
Bohnhoff, 32
Boone, 36,37
Bost, 30
Bowerman, 41
Bradsby, 37
Bramlett, 42
Brazel, 40
Breese, 37
Bridges, 41
Brink, 38
Brooks, 40
Buchan, 40
Bullard, 39
Bussing, 37
Buyat, 40,41
Caldwell, 37
Calvin, 35,36
Cameron, 48
Canaday, 46
Carbaugh, 31
Carnes, 36
Carter, 33
Cauble, 45
Chamberlin, 31
Chatman, 35,36

Ackerman, 32
Alexander, 30,35,41
Altermont, 33
Andrews, 33
Arend, 32
Ashby, 34
Baker, 34,42,43
Barbeau, 40,41
Barlow, 34
Barns, 30
Barrickman, 43
Barter, 35
Bashford, 31
Baum, 46
Beattle, 41
Beck, 37
Behler, 32
Bennett, 35
Bertine, 34
Bilderback, 40,41
Blackwell, 32
Blanchard, 46
Blanton, 32
Boatman, 36
Bonneau, 47
Booth, 35
Bourland, 42
Bradford, 34
Brady, 46
Brandenberg, 34
Brazleton, 33
Brents, 31
Bright, 32
Brinkley, 46
Brown, 37,47,48
Buchannan, 46
Burkhardt, 32
Butler, 42
Cain, 42
Callaway, 35
Calvins, 36
Campbell, 31,33,41,46,47
Cankey, 35
Carbill, 30
Carney, 46
Cartwright, 33
Center, 35
Chapman, 30,34,35,36,41
Cheaney, 42

| | | |
|---|---|---|
| Cheek, 34,36 | Chenault, 42 | Chester, 45 |
| Childress, 35 | Chilton, 40 | Chism, 36 |
| Christopher, 32 | Chumley, 30 | Clark, 35,36,42,46 |
| Clarke, 34,41 | Clary, 42 | Claus, 32 |
| Clay, 33 | Clayton, 32,42 | Cloe, 36 |
| Club, 36 | Clyne, 41 | Coamer, 35 |
| Cochran, 40 | Coe, 37 | Coffin, 33 |
| Cola, 41 | Collins, 35 | Combs, 36 |
| Conery, 35 | Conger, 37 | Conner, 35,41 |
| Conover, 46 | Conrey, 36 | Cook, 31,35,46 |
| Coon, 37 | Coons, 34 | Coope, 34 |
| Cooper, 34,35 | Copple, 48 | Cornwell, 35 |
| Cossy, 41 | Cotteral, 36 | Couch, 46 |
| Coverdale, 32 | Cowgill, 31 | Cox, 34,35,40 |
| Cowan, 36 | Coy, 35 | Craig, 35,45 |
| Craine, 41 | Crandell, 34 | Crawford, 35 |
| Creath, 41 | Creek, 31 | Crogan, 45 |
| Crone, 46 | Cross, 36,38 | Culver, 35 |
| Cummings, 43 | Cummins, 35 | Cunningham, 46 |
| Curnett, 36 | Curry, 30 | Curtner, 42 |
| Cusick, 35 | Custer, 36 | Cyrus, 41 |
| Daly, 32 | Dameron, 41 | Daniels, 31 |
| Danforth, 46 | Darling, 34 | Darneal, 32 |
| David, 45 | Davidson, 30,48 | Davis, 34,36,37,38,40,41,42,43 |
| Deason, 40 | DeGoynle, 40 | Deitz, 37 |
| Demot, 31 | Dennison, 36 | Derby, 39 |
| Deriker, 32 | Devick, 33 | Dicken, 46 |
| Dickson, 31 | Diffenour, 32 | Dittoe, 43 |
| Dodds, 46,47 | Doing, 35 | Dolin, 40 |
| Dollarhide, 40 | Dory, 40 | Dove, 43 |
| Dover, 41 | Downing, 46 | Drake, 48 |
| Drew, 38 | Drury, 34,40 | Duff, 46,48 |
| Dumbeck, 32 | Dunlap, 36 | Dunsworth, 41 |
| Durham, 42 | Dwyer, 42 | Dyalie, 32 |
| Easington, 32 | East, 30 | Easton, 33 |
| Edmonston, 41 | Edwards, 30,40 | Elling, 33 |
| Ellis, 45 | Emmens, 48 | Empson, 42 |
| Engle, 32 | Engler, 33 | Epperly, 32 |
| Erwin, 33 | Eslinger, 36 | Evans, 35,42 |
| Ezell, 42 | Farmer, 45 | Farrington, 41 |
| Fawcett, 46 | Fear, 43 | Feese, 41 |
| Fender, 48 | Ferbroche, 33 | Ferguson, 40 |
| Field, 37 | Fields, 38 | Fink, 32 |
| Finley, 40 | Fisher, 41,45,46 | Fite, 38 |
| Fitzgerald, 31 | Fitzpatrick, 33 | Flanery, 40 |
| Fleming, 34 | Florin, 32 | Ford, 32 |
| Fortney, 47 | Foster, 35,36 | Fowler, 38,48 |
| Fox, 35,40,42 | Frame, 34 | Franciss, 34 |
| Frank, 48 | Frazier, 46 | Frear, 46 |
| French, 40,41 | Frey, 38 | Friend, 34 |
| Frost, 34 | Frouge, 48 | Fugate, 41 |

NOTE: CHECK ALL ALPHABETICAL ENTRIES FOR GIVEN LETTER

Furlong, 42
Gaddis, 32
Galbraith, 38
Galloway, 30
Garber, 32
Garner, 40,41,47
Garrard, 46
Gasaway, 42
Gaston, 40
Gatten, 41
Gault, 35
Gaultney, 38
Gavin, 45
Gear,Gere,Gaer, 49
Gebbiens, 35
Gendron, 41
Gibbs, 37
Gibson, 41
Giger, 40
Gilbert, 33
Gilham, 37
Gilliam, 36
Glasgow, 33
Glenn, 41
Goads, 47
Gadler, 41
Gibbs, 38
Gilmore, 33
Godier, 41
Godler, 40
Gold, 42
Golden, 46,47
Goodin, 45
Goodman, 35
Goodrich, 33,34
Goodwater, 47
Gordon, 36
Gore, 42
Gougar, 34
Grace, 42
Gragg, 40
Gramer, 45
Grayson, 47
Gredding, 33
Green, 40
Gregg, 42
Griffin, 33,40
Grob, 32
Grote, 33
Guill, 38
Habler, 32
Hacker, 32
Haddock, 34
Hahnn, 32
Haight, 34
Haines, 30,31
Halbrooks, 34
Hale, 48
Halford, 30
Hall, 30,42,48
Halley, 38
Hambleton, 37
Hamel, 31
Hamilton, 41,46
Hammon, 30
Hancock, 45
Hanna, 30
Hannford, 37
Hanon, 30
Hanson, 31
Harden, 30
Harper, 30
Harris, 30,31,40
Harrison, 35,38
Harrawood, 38
Harrel, 30
Harrington, 33
Harrod, 30
Hart, 33,48
Harter, 32
Hasting, 46
Hastings, 48
Hatchett, 30
Hatfield, 30,31
Hatmaker, 34
Hawkins, 30,34
Hawley, 35
Hays, 36
Hayward, 30
Head, 35
Heinmann, 42
Helmick, 30
Henderson, 34
Hendson, 30
Henshi, 30
Hensley, 48
Henson, 40
Hepner, 41
Herman, 31
Hertel, 48
Hesket, 31
Hesler, 46
Hesse, 32
Hide, 39
Higgins, 33
Hill, 30,31,41,45
Hillabrant, 30
Hilyard, 46
Hinton, 30
Hish, 48
Hobbert, 47
Hobson, 35
Hodges, 45
Hodson, 42
Hogan, 31,34,35
Hogue, 35
Holden, 31
Hollingsworth, 30
Holt, 40
Holston, 30
Honck, 41
Honnan, 41
Honsanan, 30
Hood, 47
Hoover, 30,31
Hopkins, 31
Hopper, 31
Hornaday, 43
Housley, 30
Howard, 30,40
Howell, 35
Hoyt, 47
Huddleston, 30,31
Hudson, 30,42
Huff, 38
Hufford, 30
Hughes, 41
Hulen, 30
Hulford, 30
Hull, 41,47
Hummer, 30
Humphreys, 30
Hunter, 30,31
Huntsucker, 45
Hurges, 30
Hurst, 30,36
Huss, 32

Hutchins, 30
Ingle, 33
Irwin, 32
Jester, 34
Joice, 46
Jordan, 38
Karnes, 42
Keen, 46,47
Kemmerer, 31
Keyes, 35
Kirby, 46
Kittlinger, 42
Knock, 33
LaChapelle, 40
LaFranbris, 40
Lamfear, 34
Land, 38
Langdon, 35
Lansdown, 41
Laughlin, 35
Lee, 40
Leigh, 31
Lethcoe, 31
Levering, 48
Lieven, 42
Lincoln, 48
Lively, 41,45
Lockhart, 40
Logan, 31
Lovell, 48
Lusk, 42
McCannaba, 33
McDaniel, 31
McElyea, 45
McGraw, 45
McIlrath, 42
McKamy, 41
McLain, 34
McMahon, 33
McNeese, 46
Maberry, 38
Macklin, 42
Maggard, 34
Mallen, 34
Manley, 48
Marsh, 42
Matteson, 47
Maxwell, 31
Mayes, 33
Merritt, 33,34
Middlesworth, 43

Hutton, 40
Ireland, 32
Jackson, 32,41,46
Jobe, 41
Jone, 40
Joy, 31
Kean, 46
Keller, 48
Kennerly, 47
Kimball, 39
Kirkham, 32
Klauberg, 41
Koone, 32
Lacy, 40
Lake, 33
Lampseed, 34
Lander, 33
Langham, 37
Larkin, 34
Lazadder, 41
Leech, 37
Lemsis, 34
Levellett, 47
Lewis, 36,42,46
Lillard, 41
Lindley, 40
Livingston, 46
Lockwall, 37
Long, 38,48
Low, 37
Lyon, 46
McCord, 36
McDonald, 32
McFarlin, 32
McGregor, 37
McImoy, 33
McKenney, 31,48
McLean, 37,45
McMillen, 47
McSparran, 48
Mace, 32,33,42
Macy, 46
Malehorn, 32
Mallicoat, 34
Manning, 35,37,46
Martin, 46
Maulding, 37
May, 41
Mayo, 36,46
Metzinger, 48
Middleton, 36

Hyde, 39
Irvine, 45
James, 35
Johnson, 32,34,37,38,39
Jones, 37,38,42,48,49
Judd, 46
Kearne, 35
Kelly, 42
Keran, 36
King, 35
Kirkpatrick, 37
Knight, 39
Kuhlmanln, 48
Lafham, 37
Lamb, 30,33
Lance, 45
Lane, 41,48
Langley, 30,45
Lathatt, 37
Leatherland, 46
Lefton, 37
Leone, 41
Leverence, 48
Leyland, 39
Limerick, 42
Lingle, 45
Lockard, 30
Lockwood, 33,42,47
Lough, 37
Ludwick, 47
McCall, 45
McCorkle, 37
McDonough, 40
McGee, 41
McGrew, 31
McIntosh, 45
McKinley, 48
McLure, 37
McNamer, 46
McVey, 48
Machen, 41
Maddux, 32
Malfaffy, 46
Malone, 33,37
Mapes, 35
Matthews, 30,34,41,42
Maxey, 46
Mayberry, 38
Melk, 33
Mick, 42
Milholland, 46

| | | |
|---|---|---|
| Miliner, 46 | Miller, 41,45,47 | Milligan, 43 |
| Millink, 32 | Milner, 46 | Minnis, 30,46 |
| Mitchell, 42,44,46 | M'Leof, 36 | Moberley, 44 |
| Moffatt, 44 | Moland, 45 | Moll, 44 |
| Moore, 30,31,33,44,46 | Moran, 44 | More, 34 |
| Morgan, 44,45 | Morisette, 47 | Morris, 33,44,45,4 |
| Morrison, 44 | Morrow, 36 | Morse, 44 |
| Mort, 44 | Mortimer, 44 | Mortin, 31 |
| Moseley, 31 | Moutroy, 41 | Mowell, 34 |
| Munson, 46 | Murphy, 36,45,48 | Murray, 32,35 |
| Myers, 33,34 | Nabeck, 34 | Napier, 35 |
| Neel, 38 | Neely, 40 | Nelson, 31,34 |
| Newcomb, 36 | Newlon, 46 | Newton, 45 |
| Nicholson, 31 | Niernan, 32 | Nipper, 38 |
| Niserwaner, 31 | Noble, 49 | Nolen, 42 |
| Norman, 34 | Norton, 40 | Nowland, 41 |
| Nunsmaker, 46 | Ochletree, 47 | Oliver, 37 |
| Onslott, 31 | Opdycke, 46 | Orsborn, 41 |
| Osborn, 46 | Osburn, 30 | Otey, 42 |
| Owen, 37 | Pace, 37 | Padfield, 37 |
| Paine, 35 | Painter, 41,47 | Palmer, 41 |
| Pankey, 42 | Parker, 32,36,46,47 | Parks, 32 |
| Parmer, 45 | Parmeter, 47 | Parr, 47 |
| Parsons, 35 | Partridge, 46 | Paskal, 34 |
| Patrick, 36 | Patterson, 31 | Patty, 46 |
| Payne, 46 | Payten, 46 | Peck, 35 |
| Pennington, 41 | Penrad, 45 | Perkins, 41 |
| Perry, 32,36 | Peslo, 41 | Pettijohn, 34 |
| Phelps, 36 | Philhart, 41 | Phillips, 37,42 |
| Pickering, 32 | Pickett, 42 | Pierce, 39,46,47 |
| Pillet, 41 | Pixley, 47 | Poor, 34,35 |
| Porter, 42 | Poscal, 41 | Postlewaithe, 48 |
| Powell, 37 | Prather, 34 | Pratt, 39 |
| Preashel, 32 | Prevo, 36 | Price, 37 |
| Proesch, 48 | Provost, 37 | Pruitt, 40 |
| Pyle, 41 | Quest, 34 | Quick, 34,35 |
| Quillman, 45 | Rader, 32 | Ramsey, 36 |
| Ratcliff, 37 | Ratroff, 46 | Rawlings, 36,42 |
| Rawlison, 40 | Raymond, 48 | Reading, 31 |
| Ream, 47 | Reavis, 40 | Redfern, 48 |
| Reeder, 32 | Reel, 47 | Reese, 30 |
| Rendlemen, 45 | Rentfro, 42 | Reynolds, 42 |
| Rice, 35 | Richards, 39,40 | Richardson, 30 |
| Rickets, 33,34 | Ricks, 30 | Ridgely, 47 |
| Ridlon, 48 | Riggs, 34 | Robb, 35 |
| Robbason, 32 | Robert, 40 | Roberts, 38,40,41 |
| Robertson, 37 | Robinson, 33,32,37,38,41 | Rockwell, 47 |
| Rodgers, 35,46 | Rogers, 31,38 | Rolfe, 39 |
| Roper, 32,33 | Rose, 42 | Rowley, 35 |
| Roy, 40 | Rumsey, 45 | Russell, 30,42,46 |
| Ruyle, 48 | Runyan, 34 | Ryan, 46 |

| | | |
|---|---|---|
| Sager, 32 | St. John, 40 | Salisbury, 35 |
| Sallie, 33 | Salmons, 34,45 | Sanders, 46 |
| Sanford, 47 | Sargent, 30 | Sayres, 34 |
| Scenn, 32 | Scharlier, 32 | Schepfur, 32 |
| Schlenker, 32 | Schram, 32 | Scott, 34,35,37,41,42,46 |
| Seabon, 30 | Seission, 34 | Seward, 42 |
| Sexson, 42 | Seybold, 41 | Shaffer, 34,46 |
| Shall, 36 | Shannon, 48 | Sharp, 32 |
| Shaw, 35,42 | Shelby, 42 | Shelton, 42,43 |
| Shepard, 43 | Shepherd, 45 | Sherburn, 43 |
| Shoemaker, 32 | Shook, 42 | Showell, 35 |
| Shultz, 34 | Simmons, 38 | Sims, 43 |
| Sincoe, 31 | Siscoe, 48 | Sisk, 42 |
| Sittler, 43 | Skeggs, 42 | Skief, 31 |
| Slatter, 42 | Sloan, 42 | Smalley, 32,33 |
| Smeiser, 40 | Smelson, 40 | Smiley, 32 |
| Smith, 32,34,35,36,38,39,41,47 | Songer, 31 | Snodgrass, 40 |
| Solomon, 46 | Songer, 31 | Speaker, 31 |
| Spence, 33 | Spoonamore, 48 | Springer, 40 |
| Staats, 46 | Stallings, 31 | Stansberry, 43 |
| Starkey, 46 | Staten, 45 | Steel, 35 |
| Steele, 41 | Stephens, 34,35 | Stephenson, 38 |
| Steptoe, 47 | Stevens, 35 | Stevenson, 38 |
| Stiteler, 48 | Stites, 46 | Stowell, 35 |
| Stratton, 46 | Street, 37 | Strickland, 34,49 |
| Stubblefield, 40 | Sturman, 38 | Suber, 32 |
| Summer, 47 | Sutton, 31 | Swartz, 32 |
| Swett, 35 | Tackett, 35 | Taggert, 33 |
| Taliaferro, 48 | Tamaraoa, 41 | Tarter, 31 |
| Tayes, 40 | Taylor, 39 | Teabeau, 40 |
| Temple, 34 | Tetricks, 40 | Thomas, 37 |
| Thompson, 40,46,48 | Thornberry, 42 | Tieling, 32 |
| Tilford, 37,40 | Titus, 34 | Tompkins, 31 |
| Towle, 42 | Townsend, 37 | Travelstead, 42 |
| Turnerr, 35,47,48 | Turney, 37 | Tweedy, 46 |
| Umbarger, 32 | Umphries, 34 | Ury, 45 |
| Utter, 47 | Vance, 41 | VanCleave, 31 |
| Vanderhoof, 47 | VanHoozer, 40 | Vanhorn, 34 |
| VanHorne, 35 | Varley, 35 | Venters, 43 |
| Vermillion, 30 | Vincent, 45 | Vires, 38 |
| Vita, 33 | Von, 34 | Waddle, 30 |
| Wadley, 41 | Waistcoat, 35 | Walchaber, 33 |
| Waldrop, 34 | Walker, 31,33,34,37,40,41 | Wallace, 34,41 |
| Waller, 35 | Wallis, 30 | Walters, 38 |
| Waltrip, 34 | Wangaman, 46 | Warden, 36 |
| Wares, 35 | Warfield, 42 | Warnock, 37 |
| Waters, 30 | Watts, 46 | Wear, 47 |
| Weatherspoon, 37 | Weber, 33 | Weller, 30 |
| Wentworth, 34 | Weselfall, 38 | West, 33,34,46 |
| Westbrook, 30,42 | Westley, 34 | Weston, 46 |

White, 33,34,38,40,46,48   Whiteley, 31   Whitley, 40
Wickersham, 31            Wicoffe, 35     Widen, 37
Wilcox, 30,46             Wilkinson, 37   Willard, 46
Williams, 34,38,42,46     Williamson, 38  Williford, 42
Wills, 42                 Wilmarth, 46    Wilson, 30,34,35,37,38,
                                              42,46,47
Wilton, 33                Winders, 47     Winghart, 40
Wiseman, 32,33            Witters, 38     Wolrick, 40
Wolverton, 42             Woodruff, 39    Woods, 33,46,47
Woodside, 41              Woodsides, 31   Woodward, 33
Wooten, 41                Worley, 49      Wray, 46
Wren, 47                  Wright, 31,45   Wrightmire, 46
Yates, 48                 Yeomans, 47     York, 38
Young, 31,39,40

SEARCHING ILLLINOIS ANCESTORS

VOLUME III NO. III

March April 1987

INDEXED IN GENEALOGICAL PERIODICAL INDEX

Issued bi-monthly by Helen Cox Tregillis. Publication and advertising offices: Box 392, Shelbyville, IL 62565. Current single copy price, $2 plus 69 cents postage. Yearly subscription, $12. Send check or money order payable to: Helen Cox Tregillis, Box 392, Shelbyville, IL 62565. Surnames, articles appearing in publication are indexed in GENEALOGICAL PERIODICAL INDEX. Postage paid at Shelbyville, IL. Send address changes, queries, advertising to above address.
ISSN 0886 - 7763
PAYMENT MUST ACCOMPANY SUBSCRIPTION, QUERY AND ADVERTISING

NO BACK ISSUES AVAILABLE

# SEARCHING ILLINOIS ANCESTORS
## TABLE OF CONTENTS
### MARCH APRIL 1987

| | |
|---|---|
| Christian County, Illinois | |
|     Marriages 1839-1866 | 57 |
| Crawford County, Illinois | |
|     Genealogical Sources, Help | 58 |
|     Capt. Highsmith's Co., Black Hawk War | 58 |
| Cumberland County, Illinois | |
|     Genealogical Sources, Help | 59 |
|     21st Ill. Infantry, Civil War | 59 |
| DeKalb County, Illinois | |
|     Genealogical Sources, Help | 60 |
|     13th Ill. Infantry, Civil War | 61 |
| DeWitt County, Illinois | |
|     Genealogical Sources, Help | 62 |
|     20th Ill. Infantry, Civil War | 62 |
| Edgar County, Illinois | |
|     Early Marriage Records | 63 |
| Fayette County, Illinois | |
|     1821 Tax List for Vandalia | 64 |
|     1822 Post Office List, Vandalia | 65 |
| Franklin County, Illinois | |
|     Biographies in 1887 History | 65 |
| Hamilton County, Illinois | |
|     Newspaper Abstracts, 1890 | 66 |
| Illinois: War of 1812 | |
|     Capt. Moore's/Capt. Chambers' Co. | 68 |
| Illinois: Early Settlers | |
|     Abstract from Illinois Libraries | 68 |
| Shelby County, Illinois | |
|     Newspaper Abstracts | 69 |
| Stark County, Illinois | |
|     Genealogical Sources, Help | 71 |
|     33 Ill.Inf., Civil War (Not indexed) | 72 |
| St. Clair County, Illinois | |
|     Capt. Thomas' Co., Black Hawk War | 73 |
| Stephenson County, Illinois | |
|     Genealogical Sources, Help | 73 |
|     Known Cemeteries with Military Burials | 74 |
| Tazewell County, Illinois | |
|     Genealogical Sources, Help | 74 |
|     Capt. Adams' Co., Black Hawk War | 74 |
| SEARCHING ILLINOIS ANCESTORS | 75 |
|     Paid Advertising | 77 |
| Index | 78 |

Christian Co., Ill. Marriages
Book I 1839-1866, County Clerk

Elisha JOHNSON and Sarah A. MATHEWS, page 7
Samuel JACOBS and Martha KANFIELD, page 11
William JOY and Maloma HAFORD, page 53
Samuel JOHNSON and Margaret A. CONLON?, page 75
Z.M. JOHNSON and Mazilla ROWMANS, page 82
Henry C. JOHNSON and Cyrena A. CLARK, page 85
William B. JACKSON and Margaret E. DUNKERSON, page 92
Samuel JOHNSON and Louisa TAFT, page 93
George W. JACOBS and Malinda HAYS, page 102
Churchwell JOHNSON and Ruth Ann DENTON, page 108
William J. JORDAN and Ersella M. BROCKMAN, page 109
Almeron JENKINS and Mary Ann ABBOT, page 111
Jesse JACOBS and Elizabeth GARREN, page 111
Sylvester JAINLEE, Jr. and Ellenor MURPHY, page 114
George JUNKIN and Maria HURST, page 114
Austin JONES and Eliza J. HARRIS, page 116
Daniel JACOBS and Sarah E. ANTERBURY, page 117
Adam JACOBS and Clarinda WALCOTT, page 118
Henry JEFFERY and Mary I. ROSENBAUGER, page 125
John W. JOHNSTON and Sarah A. PULLEN, page 127
Peter JACKSON and Elizabeth P. WEEKS, page 128
James D. JOHNSON and Nancy J HAYWARD, page 133
Andrew JOHNSON and Mary e. SKIFFY, page 135
Gabriel JONES and Malinda RUSSEL, page 141
Joseph M. JOHNSON and Rebecca M. HARRISON, page 141
Richard JOHNSON and Matilda BAKER, page 143
Gustavus A. JACKSON and Melissa J. SMITH, page 145
Robert A. JONES and Rachael A. SPEER, page 155
Dennis O. JOHNSON and Mary a. BRENTS, page 160
Ralph JOHNSON and Ellenor CARPENTER, page 160
Philip V. JOHNSON and Martha L. SANDERS, page 166
Henry W. JACOBS and Mary E. CROSS, page 173
John O. JONES and Louisa AMBURN, page 196
Next row of names difficult to make out.
James W. JAMES and Mahala MILLER, page 197
Lewis H. JARNIGAN and Amanda BLOUNT (?), page 224
Allen JONES and Susan DURBIN, page 233
Alexander JONES and Caroline MAUZY, page 236
Thompson KIPPER and Rebecca ELLIOTT, page 7
James KETCHAM and Mary Ellen RAY, page 12
Robert KITTS and Julia Ann FRENCH, page 23
David KIZE and Sarah DAVIS, pyae 25
Christopher KETCHAM and Mary Ann TRAUBER, page 29
Christopher KETCHAM and Polly Ann BROWN, page 38
Dearman W. KING and Mary RUSK, page 62
Cornelius KLINEFELTER and Agnes P. MILLER, page 69
Jacob B. KLINEFELTER and Amanda C. PIERCE, page 72
Culbert H. KELLEY and Nancy W. SCALES, page 74

John KETCHUM and Sarah E. McDONALD, page 82
John M. KING and Susan NUCKOLLS, page 87
James KELSO and Sarah HENSLEY, page 98
Sollomon KNEE and Nancy S. BOST, page 100
Eli KING and Mary E. LANTZ, page 105
Edward KELLER and Mary E. DICKSON, page 107
G.M. KEIZER and Mary E. MIDDLEHOFF, page 110
Henry T. KELLY and Margaret COPPLE, page 129
Josephus KETCHUM and Amanda E. McDONALD, pgae 137
Wilford B. KING and Optha J. DICKERSON, page 141
J.P. KEITH and Sarah L. TABLE, page 143
Francis M. KELLEY and Louisa D. SELBY, page 144
Mitchel KING and Samantha A. FLEMING, page 146
James B. KENEDY and Mary J. BOZARTH, page 150
Henry KIRKPATRICK and J.C. McCAFFEE, paeg 159
James KELSO and Louisa NATION, paeg 168
Otha W. KELLAMS and Effa MATHEWS, page 172
Samuel P. KEMMERERK and Sarah E. HERDMAN, page 173
John B. KELLER and Mary PULLIN, page 182
William S. KNOTT and Elizabeth ALLEN, page 183
William O. KELLEY and Mary HAYWARD, page 197
Christian HOERNER and Caroline GRUP (?), page 208
Dial W. KISER and Mary A. TABLER, page 213
Edwin W. KEMP and Nancy S. WERMAN, paeg 216
P.B. KNIGHT and Lucinda SKINNER, page 52

---

## Crawford County, Illinois
### Genealogical Sources, Help

County created 31 Dec. 1816 from parent county of Edwards. Named for William H. Crawford. County seat at Robinson, IL 62454 has vital, land records (county clerk, 618-546-1212) and court records (circuit clerk, 618-544-3512). Courthouse hours, M-F, 8 - 4 p.m. Illinois genealogical society that covers this county is Crawford Co. Genealogical Society, P.O. Box 110, Robinson, IL 62454.

### Sources

1860 Census of Crawford County, Ill. Deanne McNeely Bennett. 1981.
1850 Federal Census of Crawford Co., Ill. Decatur Genealogical Society, 1970; reptd. 1976.
Our Crawford County, Ill. Donna Gowin Johnston, 1983.
Quaker Lane and Other Upper Crawfordd Co., Ill. Placenames. William F. Medlin, 1984.
History of Crawford and Clark Counties, Ill. W. H. Perrin, 1883.
Check with the society for other sources, help.

---

## Captain Highsmith's Detachment
### Black Hawk War, May 15, 1832 to 2 Aug. 1832
### Crawford County, Illinois
### Illinois Adjudant General

Capt. William Highsmith
First Lt. Samuel V. Allison
Second Lt. John H. McMickle

Sgts. Thomas Fuller, 2nd.; William McCoy, 3d.
Corps. Nathan Highsmith I; Maratin Fuller, 2d; John Lagon 4th.
Pvts. John Allison, Samuel H. Allison, John Brimbery, Benjamin
    Carter, Thomas Easton, Peter Garrison, John Johnston, George W.
    Kinney, James Lewis, And'w Montgomery, Isaac Martin, John
    Parker Jr., Thomas N. Parker, Amos Phelps, Thomas Stockwell,
    William Rece, James Weger.

Capt. A.M. Houston's Co. 2d Regiment, 2d Brigade

Corps. Cornelius Doherty, Joseph Jones.
Pvts. George Baugher, George R. Donden, Joseph Hacket, William
    Hawkins, John McCoy, Joseph Pearson, Edward Pearson, William
    Pearson, Zilman Phelps, John Vanderinder.

---

## CUMBERLAND COUNTY, ILLINOIS
## GENEALOGICAL SOURCES, HELP

County created 2 March 1843 from parent county of Coles. Named for Cumberland Road. County seat at Toledo, IL 62468 has vital, land records (county clerk, 217-849-2631) and court records (circuit clerk, 217-849-3601). Courthouse hours, Monday through Friday, 8-4. Illinois genealogical society that covers this county is Cumberland Historical Society, Greenup, IL 62428.

NOTE: THE COURTHOUSE BURNED CIRCA 1885 THEREBY DESTROYING ALL RECORDS BEFORE THAT DATE. ONLY A FEW DELAYED BIRTHS BEFORE THAT DATE EXIST.

### Sources

1850 Federal Census, Decatur Genealogical Society, 1969.
1860 Federal Census, Decatur Genealogical Society, 1983.
Johnstown Lives in Memory by Freda L. Misenheimer, 1980-81, oral
    family histories.
The Johnstown Story, 1776-1976. 1976 by Freda L. Misenheimer. Oral
    family histories.

---

### 21st Illinois Infantry, Civil War
### Cumberland County, Illinois
### Adjutant General's Report
### Company B

Capts. Jesse P.H. Stevenson, Philip Wolshimer, Austin Blake.
First Lts. Philip Wolshimer, Charles L. Smeldell, Austin Blake,
    Hezekiah A. Ashmore.
Sec. Lts. Charles L. Smidell, Austin Blake, Ambrose T. Hart, Orville
    Goodin.
First Sgt. Austin Blake.
Sgts. Ambrose T. Hart, Allen Gordon, Armond S. McComas, Samuel F.
    Wilson.
Corps. John W. Lewis, AllenH. Sacrider, James Martin, William
    Ziegler, James Sell, Ephraim Kensell, William Pitt, Edwin
    Rhodes.
Musicians: Edward Kise, Henry C. Kurts.
Wagoner: Wiley Jones.
Pvts. Lewis F. Allison, Joseph H. Allsback, George Agers, Thomas J.
    Ashmore, John H. Ashmore, Hezekiah A. Ashmore, Albertis Akers,
    Lewis F. Benge, George Bennette, William N. Berry, William W.
    Buchanan, Christopher Brannon, William H. Bigelow, Edwin

Curtis, William H. Compton, William J. Clark, Thomas H. Curtis, John G. Cain, Jacob H. Condit, John G. Collins, William J. Dunn, Thomas Dodds, Eli Davis, George W. Devere, Aaron Elliott, Milton A. Ewing, John E. Forcum, William Furgason, James Filson, James Furgason, Robert S. Gordon, Leander Gilleland, Orville Goodin, Francis Hildearbrant, Wesley Hoge, Charles B. Hackett, Columbus Halbrooke, Chesterfield Heart, Samuel Howard, Oliver C.W. Kenny, Alfred W. Kimery, William Kennett, George W. Kiger, John Lake, Andrew J. Lake, William Lake, Marion Lansdown, James E. Lansdown, Hugh L. McCormack, Hiram C. Miller, John Maynard, Robert Mundell, James M. Moffett, Henry M. Newbanks, William Pool, Noah Poorman, Thomas J. Phipps, Francis M. Potter, James B. Pemberton, Samuel D. Russell, John H. Redfern, Thomas Robinson, John C. Ramsey, William Rice, Henry Ross, Jacob E. Rhodes, John Stone, Thomas P. Sayre, Jerome Tefft, Franklin Waller, John T. Waller, Daniel Williams, Thomas J. Wilson, Horace M. Woolley, Joseph Wolf, Henry Wharton, David West, Richard W. Wright.

Veterans: Hezekiah A. Ashmore, William W. Buchanan, Louis F. Bange, Jacob H. Condit, Eli Davis. Aaron Elliott, George Eggers, James Filson, Allen Gordon, Robert S. Gordon, Orville S. Goodin, James E. Lansdown, William Rice.

Recruits: John Able, Thomas H. Brannon, William W. Benge, George Bingham, Robert Bryson, Elisha r. Bennett, Frederick L. Clark, William H. Collins, James Delaney, Henry A. Davis, Charles Ebby, William Gayetty, Samuel Hendrix, Samuel N. Hoover, Balaam Hull, Arthur T. Higley, William Hilderbrand, John Hefty, Christian Kuntz, Robert Maller, Leonard Metcalf, Christopher Metcalf, John Metcalf, James Metcalf, John McCoy, James H. McAlister, Christopher Mencimer, John Martin, James Nicholas, William Oliver, Franklin Rhodes, Herman Radeke, Joseph Rubado, Henry Rosenthal, David Reed, John Samson, Charles Skemp, Chapman Thistlewait, William H. Tippett, Robert Virtue, John Winkler, Frederick Wohlfurt, Henry Wayman, Robert B. Wilson, Frederick Weamers, Henry Willey, Gregory Weltzenaker, George Woodard, Thomas Winters.

---

DeKalb County, Illinois
Genealogical Sources, Help

County created 4 March 1837 from parent county of Kane. County named for Baron DeKalb. County seat at Sycamore, IL 60178 has vital, land records (county clerk, 815-895-9161) and court records (circuit clerk, 815-895-9161). Courthouse hours, Monday through Friday, 8:30-4:30. Illinois genealogical society that covers this county is Genealogiical Society of DeKalb Co., Ill., P.O. 295, Sycamore, IL 60178.

Sources

1885 Portrait and Biographical Album of DeKalb Co. by Chapman Brothers.
1898 Biographical Record of DeKalb County, Ill. by S.J. Clarke Pub. Co.

DeKalb Chronicle Souvenir, 1899. JF. Glidden Publ. Co.
1967, Past and Present of DeKalb Co., Ill. Lewis M. Gross.
Tombstone Inscriptions and Recorded Burials, St. John the Baptist Catholic Cemetery. Virginia Hann.
Fairview Cemetery Records, 1903-1982. Florence Houghton Marshall.
1928, History of Somonauk United Presbyterian Church. Patten and Graham.
1850 DeKalb Co., Ill. Census. Bernice C. Richard.
1860 DeKalb Co., Ill. Census. Marilyn Robinson.
DeKalb Co. 1855 Census Index. Mrs. Harlin Taylor, 1972.
Check with the society for other genealogical aids, help.

---

13th Illinois Infantry, Company E
Civil War, DeKalb County
Illinois Adjutant General Records

Capt. Fred'k W. Partridge, A.J. Brinkerhoff, George H. Carpenter.
First Lts. A.J. Brinkerhoff, George B. Devoll, George H. Carpenter, William Wallace.
Second Lts. George B. Devoll, Henry T. Porter, George H. Carpenter, William Wallace, Benjamin J. Gifford.
First Sgt. E.W. Dewey.
Sgts. E.J. Gifford, Zenas S. Harrison, William Wallace.
Corps. James M. Dobbin, James R. Neer, Robert Skinner, Wm. E. Underwood.
Musicians: Effingham T. Bowers, Sanford W. West.
PVts. George W. Atwood, Henry Ankle, Total Antol, Jacob Bagley, Lewis Bish, Philip Boyles, Joseph M. Bashaw, James Brookins, Thomas Blake, John Burbank, Jacob Brainard, Frank Colgrove, Thomas Cooper, Enoch Darnell, Marcus B. Doolittle, Jefferson J. Eastman, Horace M. Ellsworth, Erick Erickson, Jacob Fifer, Francis M. Fox, Charles O. Fuller, William Fullerton, Albert C. Fitch, Judson Grammon, Joshua Hough, Robert Holley, Lewis Hermis, John F. Itiff, William Joles, John H. Jordan, Michael Judge, James Kelly, Michael Kouth, Nicholas Liter, John Leitch, Nicholas Miller, Andrew Mullin, George Middlemas, Martin McNett, Paul D. McGilvery, James Dana Mattison, John W. Neer, Thomas Nicholas, Aquillian W. Noe, Alfred B. Orr, William B. Patch, Thomas B. Potter, Camilus L. Palmer, Alfred Benj. Peirce, Rizziner Root, Abraham B. Serene, Martin V.B. Stearns, Othello Smith, Henry J. Seaman, Daniel Stewart, Aaron A. Sheridan, John Seeley, Perry G. Tripp, Daniel Trombla, Sam H. Trowbridge, John Trowbridge, Lucien L. VanValzer, Ole H. Valder, Speed VanOrder, Irwin J. Walker, Henry Wright, Otis Wilcox.
Recruits: William H. Alger, Benj. B. Courtright, Oscar J. Cone, Louis Clemens, William J. Chittenden, Thomas Darnell, Charles F. Fairbanks, Edward C. Hinkley, Wallace Henry, William B. Howe, Jared M. Hinkley, William Laing, John W. Livingston, Stephen H. Marcy, John Mullin, James McGuire, William A. Mitten, George Morgan, Patrick H. Quinlisk, Francis E. Reed, Silliman H. Sherman, Joseph Simpson, John R. Swarthout, Frederick Trapp, John VanSickle.

DeWitt County, Illinois
Genealogical Sources, Help

County created 1 March 1839 from parent counties of Macon and McLean. Named for DeWitt Clinton. County seat at Clinton, IL 61727 has vital, land records (county clerk, 217-935-2119) and court records (circuit clerk, 217-935-2195). Courthouse hours: Monday through Friday, 8:30 - 4:30. Illinois genealogical society that covers this county is DeWitt Co. Genealogical Society, Box 329, Clinton, IL 61727.

### Sources

1882, History of DeWitt County. W.R. Brink & Co.
1891, Portrait and Biographical Record of DeWitt and Piatt Counties. Chapman Brothers.
1901, Biographical Record of DeWitt County. S.J. Clarke Pub. Co.
Cemetery Inscriptions, 5 volumes by Decatur Genealogical Society.
1840 and 1850 Census of DeWitt County by Decatur Genealogical Society.
1910, History of DeWitt County. Pioneer Publishing Co.
1875 Patron Index to Atlas by Decatur Genealogical Society.
1894 Patron Index to Atlas by Decatur Genealogical Society.

---

Co. E 20th Illinois Infantry, Civil War
DeWitt County, Illinois
Illinois Adjutant General

Capts: Evan Richards, James M. North, John A. Edmiston.
First Lts.: Henry C. Pharres, John A. Edmiston, Samuel Denton.
Second Lts.: James M. North, Vespasian Warner, John M. Porter.
First Sgt.: John R. Conklin.
Sgts: Edwin W. Gideon, Ephraim D. Carruthers, John M. Porter, Vespasian Warner.
Corps.: James M. Lemon, James McAlhaney, Samuel B. McMurray, William H. Brewster, John N. Derby, Thomas N. Byerley, Lafayette Lucas, Martin Moreley.
Musicians: Chas. Aughenbaugh, William H. Bayles.
Wagoner: Martin L. Harrison.
Pvts: Riley Aler, William A. Allen, John G. Bolton, Gustavus Bavha, John W. Batty, Benjamin S. Brown, Francis M. Bates, Thomas Butler, James R. Brewster, George Bayler, Asa W. Cain, John W. Cain, John C. Cain, Gideon Chenoweth, William D. Cole, William J. Comstock, Thomas Clark, William Carty, John Drury, Samuel Denton, Dr. Benj. Franklin, Reuben B. Gibbs, John M. Griffin, James M. Hall, Oliver Harrold, Joshua C. Hull, Lucian A.B. Harnell, George A. Hull, Ephraim A. Hubbell, Joseph M. Jones, Milton Y. Judd, Abner C. Kneadler, John A. Kelly, John J. Kinney, Sylvester M. King, John W. McDonald, John McFarland, Joseph Morrison, Theodore McGee, Reuben B. Moody, Robert H. Mecumb, Patrick Malony, Alexander Martin, William H. Miller, Samuel P. Martin, William H. Marrs, James McGough, Thomas Nicholson, John M. Osborn, Reuben E. Ogborn, Daniel O'Larry, John A. Porter, Thomas Patterson, Samuel Proud, John Ross,

Stephen D. Robb, Joshua C. Robb, Eli Ratcliff, Orestes S. Sampson, John F. Street, David Schmidt, James W. Scate, John Solomon, John Short, Charles A. Stewart, James A. Statton, William H. Thomas, David West, Charles A. Winston, Reuben J.W. Winn, Asa Wilson, James P. Yeaman.

Veterans: James H. Bean, William R. Bayless, Samuel Denton, Doctor B. Franklin, Oliver Harrold, Joseph M. Jones, Lewis Long, Martin Morely, John McFarland, Joseph Morrison, Alexander Martin, Samuel P. Martin, George F. Marsh, Robert H. Mecumb, John M. Porter, Samuel Proud, Orestes S. Sampson, John F. Street, George M. West.

Recruits: Reuben E. Augburn, Jaames H. Bean, Alexander G. Dettis, Stephen R. Carter, Isaac F. Dawson, Jacob Hogle (Listed twice), James H. Hutchinson, J. Howard Hudson, William R. Kelley, Joel E. King, Lewis Long, Fred'k Moldenhaur, George F. Marsh, James A. Morrison, John F. Miller, George W. Morgan Thomas McCaragan, Thomas B. Phillips, Isaac R. Porter, Charles E. Pearce, Samuel Richards, William R. Smith.

Under cook: Henry B. Rounds.

Drafted & substitute recruits: Henry Anderson, William Adock, George Dealing, John Berlein, Thomas Burnfield, Allen Baker, James Cook, Simon Cooper, John Davidson, John Derst, Charles Derillo, James DeWitt, Frederick Daub, Henry Dorman, Jonathon Elkins, James Farrell, Charles Fuller, John A. Floyd, Aaron L. Gelvin, Philip Graves, Joseph C. Hoffman, James H. Hickman, Emanuel Jackson, Henry Jackson, William D. Lawerence, Thomas Lynch, William H. Lott, Solomon W. Miller, Michael McMahon, Scott McNown, Eucebia Maitlett, Finley C. McClerrin, William F. Peppard, Edward Quirk, James Riley, Gustavus Reidkey, Samuel Rampff, Frederick Schrader, William W. Stabler, Herman Shrader, Christian Shuman, Thomas A. Smith, John Williams, William Wood, William Washington, Azirus Walgrove, Peter Weiss.

---

Edgar County, Illinois
Early Marriage Records
County Clerk

Jan. 25, 1843 William CHAPMAN and Jamima CURNUTE
March 4, 1843 Elisha CLARK and Mary MATHEWS
March 7, 1843 William CURRY and Rebecca COX
June 16, 1843 John CHRONICK and Elizabeth WYNN
August 2, 1843 Major D. CASSADAY and Catherine WELLS
Sept. 6, 1843 Abram L. COWREY and Nancy HANNAH
Sept. 14, 1843 Oliver J. CHESNUT and Mary E. ALEXANDER
Oct. 6, 1843 Alexander CLARK and Nancy NEWCOMB
Nov. 18, 1843 William A. CONKEY and Elizabeth WILSON
Dec. 18, 1843 William M. CLINE and Abigail MURPHY
July 5, 1844 Obadiah CARTER and Lucy BRITMAN
July 13, 1844 Joseph COOPER and Ellen GAITHER
Aug. 19, 1844 Gilbert CURTIS and Louisa H. DUDLEY
Sept. 27, 1844 Esquire CALLOWAY and Martha I. FERGUSON

Oct. 3, 1844 Reson CLAPP and Sumillia BOILS
Nov. 6, 1844 Thomas B. CLINTON and Sarah McCLELLAND
Dec. 20, 1844 William A. CALE and Judith Ann GREAVER
Feb. 18, 1845 Samuel CHRONIC and Elizabeth Ann ASHLEY
March 13, 1845 John CRANDALL and Louisa CASSADY
April 18, 1845 Andrew J. CANADY and Nancy INGRAM
June 4, 1845 Caleb COX and Sarah LONGFELLOW
Aug. 28, 1845 William G. CRAIG and Paulina BAILEY
Nov. 27, 1845 Benjamin CARROLL and Elizabeth FARIS
Feb. 7, 1846 John C. COLVIN and Elizabeth Ann LEWIS
March 23, 1846 Virgil COLLINS and Amanda E. WHEELER
April 7, 1846 Leonard CRAWFORD and Susan REED
Nov. 4, 1846 Samuel COOPER and Nancy Jane FRANCIS
Dec. 5, 1846 James COCKCROFT and Sarah HOLLEY
Dec. 26, 1846 Marques CAMERON and Dicy Jane ADAMS
Dec. 31, 1846 Abram L. CONREY and Elizabeth CHASTAIN
April 22, 1847 Uriah CLARK and Ann E. DAVIS
June 29, 1847 James D. CRANE and Elizabeth MAYO
Sept. 24, 1847 Daniel CAMERER and Mary HOWREY
Sept. 27, 1847 George W. CRAIG and Louisa BAILEY
Oct. 7, 1847 John F. CAMPBELL and Elizabeth DAVID
Oct. 23, 1847 William COVINGTON and Martha COVINGTON
Dec. 1, 1847 James CURNUTT and Malissia STUMP
Jan. 1, 1848 John CALDWELL and Sarah CUSTER
Jan. 10, 1848 James H. CUNNINGHAM and Abigail JAMES
Jan. 22, 1848 John COVINGTON and Addona ESTES
Feb. 9, 1848 Crawford H. COLEMAN and Henrietta E. REDMON
March 6, 1848 Levi COMSTOCK and Lucy REDMON
March 8, 1848 James COSLET and Margaret PHARIS
June 28, 1848 William CRAIG and Margaret ELLEDGE
July 3, 1848 Clarkson CANNON and Sarah CUNNINGHAM
July 20, 1848 Robert CLARK and Sarah Elizabeth SHRADER
July 25, 1848 David S. CURTIS and Frances R. DICKENSON
Aug. 4, 1848 Elijah CAMPBELL and Dulcenia BLAIR
Aug. 15, 1848 Obadiah CARTER and Elizabeth REDMON
Aug. 10, 1848 Alexander CROCKET and Mary McFARREN
Nov. 8, 1848 Edward COVINGTON and Elizabeth C. HUMPHREY
Dec. 2, 1848 David W. CLARK and Ann THOMPSON
Dec. 19, 1848 Lot COX and Sarah FARNHAM
Dec. 20, 1848 Joseph CHASTAIN and Frances KING

---

Newspaper Abstracts
The Illinois Intelligencer, Vandalia, Ill.
Microfilm

Tuesday, Nov. 6, 1821
    Lists of lots for taxation in town of Vandalia, with the taxes annexed, belonging to non-residents, which, if not paid in one month, will be sold to satisfy the same. Isaac Dubois, collector.
    William Otwell, Job Budgley, Thornton Peeples, John Dew, James Cowan, Wm. B. Whiteside, John B. Stovall, Tarlton Gaines, John L.

Bogardus, Wm. Gruen, Samuel Stubbens, Josiah Craft, Wm. M. Brewst, Daniel Field, Burwood Miller, Labah Payne, Elias K. Kane, James B. Moore, Patrick Kavanaugh, John Forster, John Rankin, Cyrus Birge, George Webb, Seymour Kellogg, Wm. H. Thompson, John H. Spencer, John P. McCollum, James Whiteside, Thomas Kirkpatrick, Saml. McClintock, Thomas N. Durvin, Wm. Bennett, Saml. Morrison, Abram Prickett, M.S. Davenport, Joseph Cann or Cain, John Reynolds, Saml. Hays, Wyatt Stubblefield, Saml. Davidson, Ben Johnson, Evan Burns, John Boling, Jake Steel, James E. Wills, Theophilis W. Smith, Chas. R. Matheny, Thomas Jordan, Henry Collins, Robert Lemen, Benj. Johnson, Francis Kirkpatrick, Shadrach Bond, Wm. L. Dickerson, Henry Eddy, A.P. Hubbard, Nelson M'L Johnson & Brown, Jesse Philips.

Tuesday, Jan. 3, 1822, page 3

List of letters remaining at post office at Vandalia, on the first day of Jan. 1822, which, if not taken out in three months, will be forwarded to the general post office, as dead letters.

John Beck, Danl. Bohers, Paten Bankson, Paul Beck, L. Burbanks, D.J. Baker, G. Beck, Filow Beaumont, Newton Coffey, Henry Connar, John S. Duncan, Jas. M. Duncan, Ferdinand Ernst, John Foley, Walter Goff, Richard R. Howard, Thos. Hopkins, Benjamin Jones, John Jones, W. Jernold, Harvey Lee, Harris McGregor, R. K. M'Laughlin, B.L. Morrison, William Marshall, John P. Ross, William Sprigg, John Shields, Ab. Starnes, Adam Smith, Robert Thompson, Levi Thornton, Henry Walker, John Ward, Peter Winters. John Warnock, p.m.

---

Biographies Contained In
History of Gallatin, Saline, Hamilton, Franklin
& Williamson Co., Ill.
Chicago: Goodspeed Pub. Co., 1887

Franklin County

James M. Akin, L.R. Auten, Daniel Bain, James S. Barr, C.C. Biggs, Wm. H. Boyer, William G. Brown, Levi Browning, Daniel M. Browning, A.M. Brownlee, James Burkill, T.B. Cantrell, William S. Cantrell, Dr. L.C. Carter, E.H. Casaey, A.C. Clark, F.E. Clinton, Braxton Cook, Elder W.L. Crim, A.J. Crisp, Thomas Croslin, Nehemiah Davis, M.B. Dimmick,; S.H. Dorris, Dr. James A. Durham, N. A. Durham, W.L. Eskew, R. H. Flannigan, D. W. Frailey, Dr. S. Hamilton, F.O. Harrison, T.P. Harrison, Dr. James T. Harris, Zachariah Hickman, John P. Hill, James B. Hill, John W. Hill, W.H. Hill, J.J. Hudson, Ulysses Hutson. Dr. E.G. Hutson, H.K. Jones, W.R. Jones, Allen Jones, C.O. Kelley, W.A. King, Willis B. King, Thos. J. Layman, J.B. Link, Rr.R. Link, T.J. Link, Dr. A.J. McIntyre, Prof. J.W. Maddux, Overton R. Mallory, Col. G.R. Marvel, James F. Mason, J. G. Mitchell, Hon. F.M. Mooneyham, Daniel Mooneyham, John B. Moore, Capt. Carroll Moore, W.J. N. Moyers, W.H. Mulkey, Thomas Neal, Addison Odum, A.G. Orr, W.C. Pearce, Hon. Peter Philips, Dr. B. Poindexter, C.D. Rea, S.M. Robinson, M.D., George C. Ross, Dr. E.M. Rotramel, Dr. R. H. Rotramel, James W. Royall, John J. St. Clair, George W. Sims, W.F. Spiller, John Sullivan, Ambrose Summers, Prof. R.D. Swain, Z.M.

Swisher, R.J. Taylor, R. Thompson, Dr. C.M. Thornton, C.D. Threkeld, W.H. Thurmond, James R. Turner, Rev. Hosea V?se, W.R. Ward, John Washburn, D.D., L.M. Webb, A.U. Whiden, W.H. Williams, John Willis, F.M. Youngblood.

---

Abstracts from McLeansboro, Ill. The Leader
Newspaper Microfilm/Hamilton County
Illinois State Historical Library

Date of newspaper
- Dec. 4, 1890/Marriage licenses
    - William Huffstatler, 22, and Rosa F. Betts, 16
    - Henry Betts, 45, and Alice Smith, 23
    - Charles Griswold, 20, and Francis Barker, 16
    - Emery M. Webb, 21, and Indiana Cox, 16
    - Larkin Gwaltney, 35, and Mary J. Wilson, 30
    - Thomas I. Todd, 22, and Hester A. Barbee, 17
    - Robert Spain, 21, and Nancy Laskins, 19
    - John W. Jameson, 27, and Mary A. Loyd, 29
    - James T. Fields, 38, and Mary J. Johnson, 29
- Dec. 11, 1890

Terrible accident/ accidental killing of Charles L. Anderson, son of Capt. and Mrs. John T. Anderson; interred in Odd Fellow's Cemetery; aged 24.

- Dec. 25, 1890/Marriage licenses
    - B.R. Hicks, 22, and Fannie E. Pittman, 21
    - Jas. Hamontree, 34, and Sarah Bond, 20
    - William Moore, 22, and Rosa Todd, 21
    - Jas. K. Mezo, 24, and Ollie Coin, 18
    - W.W. Crawford, 36, and Mary Myers, 27
    - O.P. Holland, 23, and Mary A. Sullivan, 16
    - J.D. Latham, 21, and Sarah Upchurch, 19
    - C.L. Driskell, 21, and Rosia Coblson, 16

Obituary: Carmi Courier: Rev. John W. Lowe, who was pastor of the M.E. Church in Grayville sixteen years ago, died, last month, in Preston, Kansas. He had been a minister of the gospel for 32 years. His wife survives him.

- Jan. 1, 1891/Marriage licenses
    - David F. Kennedy, 29, and Martha M. Wilcox, 34
    - Samuel L. Porter, 19, and Julia A. Barlow, 17

Obituary: Frank Burnett, 30, killed at Walpole by John Smith; left young widow, daughter of W.R. Jennings, late p.m. at Walpole

- Jan. 8, 1891/Marriage licenses
    - Carrol Duckworth, 21, and Mary Lampkin, 17
    - Leonard D. Durbin, 30, and Laura A. Durbin, 17
    - Ulysses S. Collins, 22, and Matilda M. Esary, 19
- Jan. 15, 1891/Marriage licenses
    - J.L. Sinks, 25, and Nancy V.E. Burton, 19
    - William G. Johnson, 19, and Lydia Penell, 20
    - Frances Cotter, 23, and Con. Smith, 19
    - Francis J. Daily, 43, and Malissa C. Damon, 39

Samuel E. Wouldridge, 20, and Alice Johnson, 20

Jan. 22, 1891/Marriage licenses

Luther F. Jones, 30, and Eline Gregory, 24
William L. White, 44, and Perlia e. McLanield, 34
Charles Duckworth, 18, and Dora F. Craddock, 18

Jan. 29, 1891/Obituary

The mother of Samuel Drake, mail carrier between this place and Macedonia, died on Wednesday night of last week of paralysis at her home near Macedonia.

Feb. 12, 1891/Marriage licenses

Henry Shuster, 32, and Mrs. Anna Karcher, 34
Howard H. Smith, 22, and Cordelia Stocker, 16
William Mezo, 20, and Ida E. Johnson, 16
James Lane, Jr., 20, and Martha L. Crisel, 18
Elbert L. Haster, 26, and Francis L. Crisel, 22
Orlando Poindexter, 31, and Dora Sothard, 22
C.H. Karns, 17, and Amy J. Sloan, 18
David E. Sharp, 27, and Martha L. Shields, 19
M.C. Harrawood, 20, and Hattie E. Robinson, 17
Hiram Williams, 21, and Carie Clark, 19
John Rhodes, 22, and Letha Call, 19
John E. Lyons, 19, and Mary Aldridge, 19

March 5, 1891

Joseph Ingram, 21, and Cora E. Cullins, 15
Isaac A. Oglesby, 19, and Sarah H. Tatem, 17
McClintock Hardesty, 19, and Maud McKinzie, 18
Silas Cross, 25, and Elsie Allen, 24
John Bruner, 23, and Ida A. Richardson, 23
Larden J. Biggerstaff, 18, and Daisy A. Bigerstaff, 14
Aaron Austin, 29, and Martha Chapman, 28
Jas. P. Barlow, 25, and Gustavia Collard, 24
Marion T. Severs, 23, and Elzora Moore, 22
Robert E. Call, 22, and Mary L. Burton, 22
James W. Allen, 26, and Lillie Groves, 19
Chas. K. Hungate, 20, and Dollie Reed, 17
John P. Moore, 24, and Cazza Mayberry, 19
Chas. I. Cuin, 21, and Jennie J. Simons, 21

Obituary/Marion Cross, of Dahlgren Twp. died yesterday morning of pneumonia, aged 58 years. Mr. Cross caught a severe cold while attending court here last week, which developed into pneumonia with the result stated. Mr. Cross was a good citizen and one of our best farmers.

Obituary/Thos. Shepard, an aged citizen of Cryville, died in that city last week. He was one of the last of the early settlers of Edwards County.

March 19, 1891

Obituary/Miss May Handley of Hawthorne died last Monday night and was buried on Wednesday p.m. She was a most estimable young lady of an amiable and lovable disposition, and her death is mourned by a host of friends. Grayville Mercury.

March 26, 1891/Marriage licenses

Silas Yates, 22, and Cora Roach, 15

Jarrett Riddle, 22, and Minnie M. Floyd, 23
Jarrett Plasters, 34, and Viola Hungate, 25
Elisha Lawson, 23, and Mrs. Hannah Fisher, 28
H.M. Barker, 25, and Ida J. Madison, 17
Jacob Clark, 22, and Mrs. Charlotte Shields, 24
Willie Moore, 20, and Eliza Johnson, 18
John Leathers, 29, and Amy Moorman, 25
Columbus Bullock, 21, and Annie Shelton, 19
Chester C. Head, 28, and Ellar Hale, 18

---

War of 1812, Illinois Regiments
Adjutant General's Records
Illinois State Archives
Springfield, Illinois

Lt. Daniel G. Moore's Company: Service from May 9, 1813, to June 9, 1813

Lt. Daniel G. Moore

Sgts.: Martin Jones, William P. Rowdon, Benjamin Stidman, Zadock Newman

Corps.: George Moore, James Beaman, John Russell, Eli Savadge

Pvts.: John Bows, John Beck, John Kirkpatrick, Thomas Kirkpatrick, Harrison Kirkpatrick, Henry B. Riggor, Joseph Newman, William Jones, John Newman, Jesse Starkey, Abel Moore, Jesse Ennis, William Ennis, James Beck, John Braman, John Fullmore, Hezekiah Cosby, William Bartlett, Burrill Hill, James Hill, John Lorton.

Captain Nathan Chamber's Company: Service from 12 April to 12 May 1813

Capt. Nathan Chambers

Ensign: John Savage

Sgts.: Henry Carr, John Nichols, James Bankson, Joseph Duncan

Corps.: William Scott, James Crocker, Charles Cox, Henry White

Pvts.: George Nichols, Pleasnt Nichols, Abraham Baker, Abram Minson, Francis Swann, Malcom Johnson, William Dunkin, John Broom, Robert Farrar, Thomas Nichols, Leven Maddox, William Armstrong, James Chambers, Samuel Scott, Abraham Pike, Nathan Langston, Joseph Holcomb, John Robertson, Daniel Peck, Bond Bernett, Benjamin Hagerman, Robert Middleton, Reuben Middleton, Robert Abernathy, Miles Abernathy, Robert Moore, Arthur Crocker, William Crocker, Job Vanwinkle, Simeon Wakefield, Henry Hutton, Jonathon Hill, Patton Bankson, John Pea, John Journey Sr., Robert Dunkin Sr., James McCracken, Barnet Bone, Robert Dunkin Jr., James Petty, Bryant Mooney, John Crocker, Hugh Gilbreath, Paul Gasgill, Jonathon Gasgill, William Wakefield.

---

Interesting Abstracts from
ILLINOIS LIBRARIES, Vol. 59 Number 5
Springfield, Ill. May, 1977

This issue contains the Illinois militiamen for Aug. 1, 1790; squatters in territorial Illinois; squatters report of 1807, and squatters report of 1813. All of the information was from original documents preserved in the Illinois Archives.

"An estimate of the number of settlers on lands belonging to the United States within the District of Kaskaskia before the 3d of March 1807, and who have not applied for permission to remain thereon--

30 families on the Mississippi and the waters emptying into it, above the mouth of the Ohio and South of the base line

32 families on the waters of the Ohio -- Grand Pierre, Big Bay & Big creek South of the base line

59 families in the neighbourhood of the Shawano Town on the Ohio & the waters of the Saline Creek -- South of the base line

23 families on the waters of Kaskaskia River, in Randolph County -- North of the base line--

38 families in Goshin, St. Clair County, north of the base line

182 Total"

---

Newspaper Abstracts, Microfilm
Shelby County, Illinois
Date, issue of newspaper following

Sittler, Jacob        Died 6 December 1897

Born 27 Dec. 1813 Westmoreland Co., Pa.; married 1839 Sidney Cummings: 12 children, 6 deceased; came to Shelby Co., Ill. 1841; surviving, widow; children: Thomas J., Henry C., Mrs. Emma Dove, Mrs. Mary Fear, Mrs. F.A. Hornada of Ft. Scott, Ks., Mrs. Sallie A. Stansbery of Pana, Ill.

Shelbyville Democrat, 16 December 1897

Sleeth, Mary Ann        Died 6 April 1889

Mother of Mrs. James Skaggs; born 15 Oct. 1834 Jefferson Co., Kentucky; burial, city cemetery

Our Best Words, Shelbyville, 20 April 1889

Smith, Amos        Died 31 May 1878

Born 1821 Fenton Co., Tennessee; lived Kentucky, Hamilton Co., Ill.

Shelbyville Democrat, 6 June 1878

Smith, Annes P.        Died 15 Jan. 1908

Born 10 July 1826 Lexington, Ky.; maiden name Tanby; married 1846 Elias Smith in Tennessee; came to Shelby County 1856; surviving, two sons, Frank of Shelbyville and Edward of Florida; 3 brothers, G.W. Tanby of Jacksonville, Walter of Lincoln, H.C. of California; burial, Glenwood Cemetery, Shelbyville.

Shelbyville Democrat, 16 Jan. 1908

Smith, John B.        Died 13 Aug. 1890

Born 3 Dec. 1823 Butler County, Ohio, near Hamilton; lived in Brookville, Franklin Co., Ind.; married Sarah E. Munson, Brookville; 7 children, 2 deceased, Emma Middlesworth and C.N. Smith.

Shelbyville Democrat, 28 Aug. 1890

Smith, Louisa Churchill        Died 2 March 1894 Mansville, Florida

Born 25 April 1838 Sangamon County, Illinois; married 10 April 1860 Reuben Smith: 9 children, 5 died in infancy; surviving, husband; children: George C. Smith, Ada Smith and Gertrude Smith of Windsor

and Herbert Smith of Decatur, Ill.; burial, Windsor Cemetery
      Shelbyville Democrat, 15 March 1894

Smith, Mary Killam                 Funeral 1 Feb. 1880
    Born 2 Dec. 1799 Nicholas County, Ky.; parents originally of Maryland; married 22 April 1819 Nathan Smith who died 15 Aug. 1830; came to county 1831 with children and relatives; surviving, 5 sons, and one dau. Mrs. Chatten Kelley.
      Shelbyville Democrat, 4 Feb. 1880

Smith, Sarah J. Trusler            Died 14 Nov. 1899
    Born 4 May 1833 Franklin Co., Ind.; maiden name, Trusler; married 29 Jan. 1850 Elijah Smith who died 2 Sept. 1885; 9 children, one dau. Kate deceased; surviving, children: Charles Edward, Mrs. Lida J. Thomas, John Freemont, William Nelson, Noble Ellsworth, Effie Hall, George Sydney, Emma May Proctor; burial, Henton Cemetery.
      Shelbyville Democrat, 23 Nov. 1899

Smith, William                     65th birthday
    Born Nicholas County, Kentucky; married 2 March 1843 Lucinda Virden, daughter of James and Nancy Virden.
      Shelbyville Democrat, 5 Feb. 1885

Smith, William                     Died 14 Jan. 1898
    Born 1820 Nicholas County, Kentucky, son of Nathan and Mary Killam Smith; came to Shelby County, Ill. 1831 with mother; father had died in 1830; surviving, children: Joseph, Mrs. Henry Bullington, Lizzie; brothers, Samuel, Daniel; burial, Craig Cemetery, Henton.
      Shelbyville Democrat, 20 Jan. 1898

Smock, Delilah Casey               Died 3 May 1898
    Born 28 June 1838 Shelby County, Ill., daughter of John Casey; married 30 Oct. 1862 Barnett Smock; surviving, husband; children: Albert B., Lydia A. Longenbaugh, John C.; sisters, Mrs. James Thomas of Obed, and Mrs. J. J. Smock of Iowa; brother, Levi Casey of Iowa.
      Shelbyville Democrat, 23 June 1898

Smyser, Capt. A.N.                 Died 20 Jan. 1880 Sullivan, Ill.
    Born 27 Nov. 1828 Harrison County, Kentucky, son of Samuel M. and Rebecca Smyser; family moved to Moultrie County, Ill. 1831; married April 1847 Isyphena Edwards; surviving, widow; children: Henry, Kittie, Ollie, Josie, Sammy.
      Shelbyville Democrat, 29 Jan. 1880

Snow, John Caswell                 Died 3 Feb. 1890
    Born 7 Nov. 1828 Amherst County, Va.; 1844 with father moved to Green County, Ky.; then 1858 Green County, Ill.; married first, 6 Sept. 1857 Asenath Evans who died 27 Sept. 1858, twins died in infancy; married second, 2 March 1859 Sarah E. Young; 3 children, all dead - one daughter died 1877.
      Moweaqua Mail Call, Moweaqua, Ill. 6 Feb. 1890

Souther, Hester Davis              Died 15 Oct. 1895
    Born 20 Jan. 1824 Union Co., Pa.; moved with parents to Ross County, Ohio 1826; 1846 moved to Coles county, Ill.; married 1850 Jeremiah Souther and settled Moultrie Co., Ill.; 5 children, two sons and 3 daughters, one deceased; she moved to Shelbyville, 1893.
      Shelbyville Democrat, 7 Nov. 1895

Souther, Jeremiah                  Died 11 March 1891
    Born 6 March 1803 Virginia; moved to Kentucky till 1834 and

then to Moultrie Co. then Shelby County 1868; married first, July 1825 Barbara Ann Smith, 11 children; married second, Hester Davis 11 April 1850, 5 children.

Shelbyville Democrat, 19 March 1891

Spraker, Mrs. S.E.                    Died 10 April 1898

Born 9 Nov. 1851 Shelby County, Ill.; maiden name Sarah Ellen Wallace, daughter of Samuel Wallace; married 19 April 1876 Simon E. Spraker; one daughter Ada; surviving, daughter and husband; burial, Windsor Cemetery.

Findlay Enterprise, 21 April 1898
Shelbyville Democrat, 21 April 1898

Spain, Mitch                    Died Nov. 1877 Stewardson

"Aged about 50 years, died recently. His remains were interred at Big Spring Cemetery. He leaves a large family and many friends to mourn his departure into the silent land."

Shelbyville Democrat, 22 Nov. 1877

Stables, Mrs. William            Died 10 March 1877 Prairie Home

Died from parturtion? Deceased left husband, 3 small children; funeral preached by Rev. Mr. Spencer.

Shelbyville Democrat, 15 March 1877

Stamps, Capt. Lewis            Died 1 May 1893 Decatur, Ill.

Born 1 Nov. 1800 Georgia; moved to Rutherford Co., TN 1810 then to Franklin Co., TN 1812; married first, 1824 Sarah Blackman who died 1825; moved to Morgan County, Alabama; married 1827 Tena Cauthin in Bedford County, TN; moved to Vandalia, Ill. 1832, helped build Fayette County Courthouse; came to Shelbyville, Ill. 1849; he and Peter Kern helped with cholera epidemic; city paid each $50 for seven weeks work with the dead; surviving, 5 children in Tennessee, and stepson J. B. Tucker in Decatur, Ill.; burial, Glenwood Cemetery, Shelbyville, Ill.

Shelbyville Democrat, 4 May 1893

---

Stark County, Illinois
Genealogical Sources, Help

County created 2 March 1839 from parent counties of Knox and Putnam. Named for Gen. John Stark. County seat at Toulon, IL 61483 has vital, land records (county clerk, 309-286-5911) and court records (circuit clerk, 309-286-5941). Courthouse hours, Monday through Friday, 8:30 - 5. Irene R. Williams Berg, East 15407 Springfield, Versdale, WA 99037 has census.

Sources

1860, 1870, 1880 Stark County, Ill. Census. by Irene R. Williams Berg. Published 1982, 1983.

1860, History of Putnam and Marshall Counties with early progress of Bureau and Stark Counties. By Henry A. Ford.

1887, Documents and Biography Pertaining to the Settlement of and Progress of Stark County. W.A. Leeson.

1876, Stark County and Its Pioneers. By Mrs. E.H. Shallenberger.

Index to Persons in Shallenberger's 1876 History. By Winnetka Genealogical Project Committee. 1973.

COMPANY B, 33 ILLINOIS INFANTRY
STARK COUNTY, ILLINOIS
ILLINOIS ADJUTANT GENERAL'S REPORT
ILLINOIS STATE ARCHIVES, SPRINGFIELD, ILL.

Surnames listed in the regiment

Captain: Moses I. Morgan

Gill, Durant, Gove, Brown, Moray, Cambridge, Lyon, Martin, Barr, Hall, Capron, Graves, Cotter, Green, Ingraham, Wakeman, Packer, Austin, Aiken, Armstrong, Andrews, Allison, Ballow, Block, Bailey, Biggs, Blodgett, Clarke, Cross, Coffey, Chatfield, Cry, Clifford, Durant, Donovan, Dewey, Day, Ellis, Fisher, Fezler, Fetterman, Grothman, Hess, Heartt, Hebbard, Harberger, Hotchkiss, Holchamp, Hummer, Johnson, Jacobson, Koshner, Keyes, Kalb, Lomon, Leistecon, Mayo, McClintock, McCampbell, McQuaid, McKee, Morgan, Marvin, Muir, Moore, Owen, Porter, Radke, Robinson, Rodgers, Ridge, Smart, Starks, Schmidt, Schwartz, Skinner, Shinn, Sipe, Sharpe, Smile, Thomas, Turtelot, Upperman, Utting, Vanvranken, Wolf, Wadleigh, Whitley, Wheatley, Forrestor, Rew, Cry, Degeare, Wright, Ankel, Albee, Adams, Butler, Beatty, Curson, Chase, Church, Carroway, Dyer, Ellis, Fell, Foxtox, Graunke, Godfrey, Galley, Gibbs, Grothman, Jonderweine, Jones, Kobel, Kempin, McClelland, Manning, Nehring, Palmer, Ray, Richardson, Rule, Renker, Stewart, Strowbridge, Stickney, Shipley, Sacrider, Turnball, Way, Weed, Wilson, Wonders, Wilkins, Zumbrun, Zang, Ayers, Allen, Byrne, Carrington, Coats, Eastwood, Frost, Fornberitt, Gros, Holmes, Hamilton, Harriot, Loud, Lauberg, McQueen, Merriam, Pincott, Parkinson, Potman, Quinn, Renshawsen, Shea, Swanson, Trevitt, Whitman.

---

St. Clair County, Illinois
Genealogical Sources, Help

County created 27 April 1790 from Northwest Territory. Named for Governor Arthur St. Clair. County seat at Belleville, IL 62220 has vital, land records (county clerk, 618-277-6600) and court records (circuit clerk, 618-277-6600). Courthouse hours, Monday through Friday, 8:30 - 5. Illinois genealogical society that covers this county is St. Clair Genealogical Society, P.O. Box 431, Belleville, IL 62222.

Sources

1881, History of St. Clair County. Brink, McDonough and Co.

1806-1965, County Naturalizations. By Robert Buechner. 1976.

1820 Federal Census of St. Clair County, Ill. St. Clair County Genealogical Society Quarterly, Vol. 3, No. 1, 1980.

1840 Census Transcriptions. St. Clair County Genealogical Society, 1973.

1806-1812 Indentured Servants of St. Clair County, Ill. St. Clair Genealogical Society Quarterly, Vol. 6, No. 1, 1983.

There are many other sources. Check with the society for other help.

St. Clair County, Illinois
Enrolled April 18, 1832 Black Hawk War
Illinois Adjutant Generals Records
Illinois State Archives, Springfield, IL

### Capt. John Thomas Company

First Lt. Gideon Simpson
Second Lts. George Kinney, Wm. S. Thomas
Sgts. John W. Woods, Parker Adams, Prettyman Boyce, James Nearen, Enoch Bridges
Corps: John McDonald, Andrew Terry, James H. Ashby, George West
Pvts.: Isaac Abbott, John Bird, Joseph O. Casterline, Abner Crocker, James Davis, Saml. D. Enochs, Robt Furgerson, Daniel McHenry, Benjamin Ogle, Richard Roman, Solomon Spann, Benjamin Scott, Chas. Scott, Wm. Twiss, Jos. Welker.

### Captain John Tate's Company

First Lt. Joshua Hughes
Second Lt. Abram B. Vandigrif
Sgts. Jacob Miller, Joseph Ogle, William Tate, George W. Hook
Corps.: James Phillips, Jacob Phillips, William Woods, Mathew Cox
Pvts.: Robert Ashlock, Charles Aspens, Peter B. Bear, Bonham Bear, James Blair, James N. Charles, John Dunlap, Atason Dingle, Peter Dun, I.C. Edwards, George Glass, Robert Higgins, Ichabod Higgins, Christopher Holt, Samuel Hootes, Anthony Hootes, Robert Leach, A.H. Leach, Jefferson Lyndon, Joseph Lindon, James McClintock, Absalom Miller, John Million, Hopson Owens, Charles Owens, Elit Owens, William Phillips, Horland Patason.

---

Stephenson County, Illinois
Genealogical Sources, Help

County created 4 March 1837 from parent counties of JoDaviess and Winnebago. Named for Col. Benjamin Stephenson. County seat at Freeport, IL 61032 has vital, land records (county clerk, 815-235-8289) and court records (circuit clerk, 815-235-8266). Courthouse hours, Monday through Friday, 8:30 - 4:30. Illinois genealogical society that covers this county is Stephenson County Historical Society, 1440 So. Carroll Ave., Freeport, IL 61032.

### Sources

1888, Portrait and Biographical Album of Stephenson County. Chapman Brothers.
1910, History of Stephenson County, biographical sketches. Addison L. Fulwider. 2 volumes.
Churches of Stephenson County, Sketches by Roger Hill.
1900, The Footprints of the Pioneers. Pioneer Publishing Co.
Cemetery Inscriptions. Stephenson County Historical Society.
1880, History of Stephenson County, Ill. Western Historical Company.
    Check with the society for other genealogical help.

---

Stephenson County, Illinois
Known Cemeteries with Military Burials
Roll of Honor: Record of Burial Places
Springfield, Ill. 1929

Adeline -- Apolkey at Freeport -- Babb's Grove at Elroy -- Beim Chapel at Rock Grove -- Beuna Vista -- Catholic at Elroy -- Cedarville at Cedarville -- Christian Hollow at Winslow -- City Cemetery at Freeport -- Cross Road's Church at Winslow -- Dakota at Freeport -- Davis at Freeport -- Dublin at Kent -- Eldorado at Oneco -- Florence at Florence -- German at Freeport -- German Catholic at Freeport -- Greenwood at Greenwood -- Harts at Elroy -- Irishe at Freeport -- Kent at Kent -- Lancaster at Elroy -- Lena at Lena -- Lutheran at Kent -- Manny at Waddams -- McConnell at Waddams Twp. -- Mennonite at Freeport -- Mt. Pleasant at Orangeville -- Oakland at Freeport -- Oneco at Orangeville -- Orangeville at Orangeville -- Quincy -- Ridott at Ridott -- Rock City at Freeport -- St. James at Waddams Twp. -- St. Mary's at Freeport -- Salem at Waddams Twp. -- Scott near Baileyville -- Silent Hill at Waddams Twp. -- Silver Creek at Freeport -- Silver Springs at Freeport -- Stone Church at Elroy -- Winneshiek at Dakota -- Winslow at Winslow -- Winslow Village -- Yellow Creek Union at Kent -- Young at Freeport

------------

Tazewell County, Illinois
Genealogical Sources, Help

County created 21 Jan. 1827 from parent county of Sangamon. Named for Gov. Lyttleton W. Tazewell. County seat at Pekin, IL 61554 has vital, land records (county clerk, 309-347-4148) and court records (circuit clerk, 309-347-4177). Courthouse hours, Monday through Friday, 9 - 5. Illinois genealogical society that covers this county is Tazewell County Genealogical Society, Box 312, Pekin, IL 61554.

Sources

1894, Portrait and Biographical Record of Tazewell and Mason Counties. Biographical Publishing Co.
1850 Census, 2 vols. Bloomington Normal Genealogical Society, 1979.
1879, History of Tazewell County, Ill. Chapman.
Tazewell County, Illinois Cemeteries. by Betty Weghorst Murphy. 7 vols.
1860 Census by Tazewell County Genealogical Society.
Tazewell County Marriage Records. 3 volumes. Tazewell County Genealogical Society, 1982,1983,1984.
Check with the society for other help.

------------

Capt. John G. Adams' Company
Pekin, Illinois Regiment
Black Hawk War, Enrolled April 27, 1832
Illinois Adjutant General's Records, Springfield, Ill.
Illinois State Archives

Capt. John G. Adams

First Lt. Benj. Briggs
Second Lt. Jno. O. Hyde
Sgts.: Michell Reeder, James Wright, Seth Wilson, John Ford
Corps.: Henry Cline, Conaway Rhodes, Hartside Hittle, D. Hanger
Pvts: David Alexander, Phenis Be;rry, Jacob Ballard, Thomas Briggs, Eli Bemis, Samuel Baxter, Jno. M. Barlow, Redick Council, Green Cullum, William Cline, John Coffey, Orison Craig, James conner, David Carter, Jas. W. Crain, Pinkney Dunbough, Abner Drum, Jesse Date, D.S. Evans, Geo. Gordon, Geo. W. Hughes, Jonathon Haynes, Wm. A. Hendricks, Samuel Henson, William Harper, Jonathon Helme, Jas. Judy, David Kreeps, Bazwell Lewis, Joseph Laudes, Reese Morgan, Hugh McJenkins, Ferdinand Maxwell, Stephen T. McCann, Zadock Mendinall, Alex McKnight, Benj. Orendorff, Robt. Paisley, John Paul, Isaac Perkins, Will Ryon, Joseph Reeder, Samuel Rickey, William Ramsey, Jas. Sumner, Elmore Shoemaker, Samuel Stout, Chapan Williamson.

---

## Searching Illinois Ancestors
### County, Surname and Person Searching

County Unknown: Sparika, Copas
    Betty Heide, 51537 Myrtle Ave., South Bend, IN 46637
ALL COUNTIES: Frad, Fred, Fread; SHELBY, LIVINGSTON: Beal
    Anna Logan, 482 Linden Lane, Oakville, Ont. L6H 3K1 Canada
BOND, EDWARDSVILLE, FAYETTE, SANGAMON, SHELBY, MONTGOMERY: Maryman, Merriman, Merryman, Armstrong, Renfro, Petty
    Dorothy Dodd, R. 4, Box 672, Carthage, MO 64836
BOND: Carson, Etheridge
    Harriett Mead, 1937 Manchester Rd., Sacramento, CA 95815
BRISTOL, ILL.: Kenny
    LaVerne Van Cleave, 718 N. Lincoln St., West Point, NE 68788
CARROLL: Winston, Shipley
    Frances S. Prestridge, 1402 Minter Lane, Abilene, TX 79603
CASS, MORGAN, HANCOCK: Surname not given
    Marjorie Hughett Gapinski, 1440 LaFayette St., LaSalle, IL 61301
CHRISTIAN: Purcell, Ralph
    H. Byron Landholt, 607 North Liberty, Plymouth, IN 46563
CHRISTIAN: Laymon
    Georgianna Gibson, 30 Circle Drive, Richmond, IN 47374
CLARK, CUMBERLAND, EDGAR: Surname not given
    Eva J. Chism, 1253 Henke Road, Lake St. Louis, MO 63367
CLAY, EFFINGHAM: Stevens, Stephens
    Alice L. Friend, Rt 1, Box 39, Colcord, OK 74338
COLES, SHELBY: Martin, Hanley
    Doris D. Martin, 314 Earle, WaKeeney, KS 67672
COLES: Johnson, Johnston
    Mrs. Earl Ball, 5260 Griggs Rd., Logan, OH 43138
COLES: Muns; PEORIA: Kennington; SHELBY: Anderson, Boston, Piper
    Virginia Kelley, 1441 Madison Ave., San Diego, CA 92116
COOK, VERMILLION: Lucas, Stettnisch, Gurgle
    Mrs. Barbara Ferguson, 286 Hibbing Circle, Marina, CA 93933

COOK: Budlong, Newton
    Margaret B. Wootton, Box 1605, Idyllwild, CA 92349

COOK, FAYETTE, LOGAN, MACON, MORGAN, SHELBY: Richhart, Ritchart, Tolly, Vermillion, Plyler, Booth, Schaniel, Nichols, Stine, Stump, Cox, Rubart, Jacobs, Nordyke, Zobel, Brainer, Johnson, Patten, Taylor
    Bettye Richhart, 7300 Ellis Rd., Fort Worth, TX 76112

CRAWFORD: Moore, Crownover
    Dorothy M. Parker, 307 Woodlawn Road, Lincoln, IL 62656

DEERPARK, ILL: Allen, Peck
    J.L. Cummings, 2010 W. Olive, Burbank, CA 91506

EDGAR, KANAKEE, VERMILLION: Jones, Mattocks, Reagan, Downs, Goodwin
    Maxine Hobble, 902 Wayne, Topeka, KS 66606

FULTON: Essex; JEFFERSON: Young; MACOUPIN: Davis, Fisher, Young; KNOX: Essex; MCHENRY: Wenkel; ROCK ISLAND: Essex; STARK: Tapp, Biggs, Ware; UNION: Essex
    J'Anette Vidunas Scott, 18303 NW 41 Ave., Ridgefield, WA 98642

HENRY: Hitchcock, Rivenburg; PEORIA: Hitchcock, Hume; SHELBY: Gregg, Allen; STARK: Newton, Hitchcock, Shaver
    Ruth E. Harrison, 1526 Grand Ave., Ojai, CA 93023

KNOX: Bixby, Butterfield
    Bob Bixby, 2709-57th, Des Moines, IA 50310

LEE, BUREAU, KANE: Derr
    E. Mitchell App, 217 Giotto Dr. Sorrento East, Nokomis, FL 33555

LIVINGSTON: Smith, McFann, Rickey
    Esther Jeffries, R. 1, Box 68, Rockville, IN 47872

LOGAN, McLean: Coons, Irvin, McCarrel; WAYNE: Bell
    Maryln Tetzloff, 3335 Pursell Lane, Pensacola, FL 32506

MORGAN: Keohoe, Ferry
    Mrs. Basil T. Kehoe, P.O. Box 195, Tahoe City, CA 95730

MOULTRIE, SHELBY: Montonye
    M. Tracy Carpenter, 315 E. Sale St., Tuscola, IL 61953

PERRY: Jones; UNION: Jones
    Edith L. Lowen, 26 South Drive, Decatur, IL 62526

PERRY, MORGAN: Gilliam, Gillam
    Jackson E. Gilliam, Shoreline Route, Polson, MT 59860

ROCK ISLAND: DeNolf, Van Echantle
    Virginia Bosford, 2915 Seneca St., Ft. Pierce, FL 33450

ST. CLAIR, WASHINGTON: Hardebeck, Hendricks, Haentschel, Spitsnas, Land
    John W. Hardebeck, MD., 7430 Jackson Dr., San Diego, CA 92119

SHELBY: McNear
    George C. McNear, Box 704, Brighton, IL 62012

SHELBY: Vaughn, Farrar
    Alton Orr, 4619 Holt, Bellaire, TX 77401

SHELBY: Masters
    Dorothy e. Hoglund, 109 E. Line Oak, San Gabriel, CA 91776

SHELBY, ETAL: Barr
    Keith L. Barr, Illinois State University, 104 Edwards Hall, Normal, IL 61761

VERMILLION: O´Mara
    P. Pinney, HC 61, Box 35, Whitney, NE 69367
WINNEBAGO: Prindels
    Mrs. Louis Broadley, 3010 NW Orchard St., Corvallis, OR 97330

---

## PAID ADVERTISING

Marie BRADY died 1890/95, aged, in Illinois; Mary TOTHAKER, her daughter, married first, COWAN, married second, TOTHAKER. Lillian COWAN, her daughter, married 1880 Fayette, Howard County, Missouri Fred Mason. Further information eagerly sought.
    John F. Mason, 240 Fisher Place, Princeton, NJ 08540

---

Want anything on Thomas COLE, married Louisa HAWKS 1827 Shelby; County, Ill. Children: Laurentine, Caroline who married James McKinley, Mary Electa Adeline who married Herginius LUDI, Joseph, Denima Ann who married Charles HOOD, Nancy Allen. Tom born Kentucky, died circa 1843, Iowa County, Iowa? Children lived in Jackson Co., Iowa later.
    David Cole, 1119 South Speed St., Santa Maria, CA 93454

---

## KINSHIP SEEKER

P.O. Box 1528, Alamogordo, NM 88310. Will help find your elusive kin. Send $1 per surname for a list of others searching your surname. Long SASE a must!

---

WHITE, Nathan, b. ca. 1815 NY, wife Esther BABCOCK, lived in Belvidere, Boone County, 1850-1870. Seeking date and place of death and burial information. BABCOCK, Hannah, b. ca. 1897 NY, mother of Esther BABCOCK WHITE, living in Belvidere, Boone County, 1850-1870. Seeking date and place of death and burial information.
    Barbara Hanley, 2714 Belmont Canyon Rd., Belmont, CA 94002

---

SEARCHING ILLINOIS ADVERTISING
        RATES
1 col. x 2, $10 for one time
1/4 page, $20 for one time
half page, $37.50 for one time
full page, $75 for one time.

County, surname queries published free. Query with maximum of 50 words published for $5.

NO BACK ISSUES AVAILABLE!

March April 1987

---

**INDIVIDUAL FAMILY NEWSLETTERS**

*PHILLIPS FAMILY FINDER*
*THE O'DELL DIGGIN'S*
*NICHOLS NOSTALGIA*

For Researchers Everywhere

**$15.00 per year**
Published Quarterly

**THE LEGACY**
Mrs. Kay O'Dell, Editor
P. O. Box 2040
Pinetop, AZ 85935

## SEARCHING ILLINOIS ANCESTORS
## INDEX TO VOLUME III, NUMBER III

Abbot, 57
Abbott, 73
Abernathy, 68
Able, 60
Adams, 64,73,74
Adock, 63
Agers, 59
Akers, 59
Akin, 65
Aldridge, 67
Aler, 62
Alexander, 63,75
Alger, 61
Allen, 58,62,67,76
Allison, 58,59
Allsback, 59
Amburn, 57
Anderson, 63,66,75
Ankle, 61
Anterbury, 57
Antol, 61
Armstrong, 68,75
Ashby, 73
Ashley, 64
Ashlock, 73
Ashmore, 59,60
Aspens, 73
Atwood, 61
Augburn, 63
Aughenbaugh, 62
Austin, 67
Auten, 65
Babcock, 77
Bagley, 61
Bain, 65
Baker, 57,63,65,68
Ballard, 75
Bange, 60
Bankson, 65,68
Barbee, 66
Barker, 66,68
Barlow, 66,67,75
Barr, 65,76
Bartlett, 68
Bashaw, 61
Bates, 62
Batty, 62
Baugher, 59
Bavha, 62
Baxter, 75
Bayler, 62
Bayles, 62
Bayless, 63
Beal, 75
Bealing, 63
Beaman, 68
Bean, 63
Bear, 73
Beaumont, 65
Beck, 65,68
Bell, 76
Bemis, 75
Benge, 59,60
Bennett, 59,60,65,68
Berlein, 63
Berry, 59,75
Bettis, 63
Betts, 66
Bigelow, 59
Biggerstaff, 67
Biggs, 65,76
Bingham, 60
Bird, 73
Birge, 65
Bish, 61
Bixby, 76
Blackman, 71
Blair, 64,73
Blake, 59,61
Blount, 57
Bogardus, 65
Bohers, 65
Boils, 64
Boling, 65
Bolton, 62
Bond, 65,66
Bone, 68
Booth, 76
Bost, 58
Boston, 75
Bowers, 60
Bows, 68
Boyce, 73
Boyer, 65
Boyles, 61
Bozarth, 58
Brady, 77
Brainard, 61
Brainer, 76
Brannon, 59,60
Braman, 68
Brents, 57
Brewst, 65
Brewster, 62
Bridges, 73
Briggs, 75
Brimbery, 59
Brinkerhoff, 61
Britman, 63
Brockman, 57
Brookins, 61
Broom, 68
Brown, 57,62,65
Browning, 65
Brownlee, 65
Bruner, 67
Bryson, 60
Buchanan, 59,60
Budgley, 64
Budlong, 76
Bullington, 70
Bullock, 68
Burbanks, 61,65
Burkill, 65
Burnett, 66
Burnfield, 63
Burns, 65
Burton, 66,67
Butler, 62
Butterfield, 76
Byerly, 62
Cain, 60,62,65
Caldwell, 64
Cale, 64
Call, 67
Calloway, 63
Camerer, 64
Cameron, 64
Campbell, 64
Canady, 64
Cann, 65
Cannon, 64
Cantrell, 65
Carpenter, 57,61
Carr, 68
Carroll, 64
Carruthers, 62
Carson, 75
Carter, 59,63,65
Carty, 62
Casaney, 65
Casey, 70
Cassaday, 63
Cassady, 64
Casterline, 73
Cauthin, 71
Chambers, 68
Chapman, 63,67
Charles, 73
Chastain, 64
Chenoweth, 62
Chestnut, 63
Chittenden, 61
Chronic, 64
Chronick, 63
Churchill, 69
Clapp, 64
Clark, 57,60,62,63,64,65,67,68
Clemens, 61
Cline, 63,75
Clinton, 64,65
Coblson, 66
Cockcroft, 64
Coffey, 65,75
Coin, 66
Cole, 62,77
Coleman, 64
Colgrove, 61
Collard, 67
Collins, 60,64,65,66

| | | | |
|---|---|---|---|
| Colvin, 64 | Compton, 60 | Comstock, 62,64 | Condit, 60 |
| Cone, 61 | Conkey, 63 | Conklin, 62 | Conlon, 57 |
| Connar, 65 | Conrey, 64 | Cook, 63,65 | Coons, 76 |
| Cooper, 61,63,64 | Copas, 75 | Copple, 58 | Cosby, 68 |
| Coslet, 64 | Cotter, 66 | Council, 75 | Courtright, 61 |
| Covington, 64 | Cowan, 64,77 | Cowrey, 63 | Cox, 63,64,66,68,76 |
| Craddock, 67 | Craft, 65 | Craig, 64,75 | Crane, 64 |
| Crawford, 64,66 | Crim, 65 | Crisel, 67 | Crisp, 65 |
| Crocker, 68,73 | Crocket, 64 | Croslin, 65 | Cross, 57,67 |
| Crownover, 76 | Cullins, 67 | Cullum, 75 | Cummings, 69 |
| Cunningham, 64 | Curnute, 63 | Curnutt, 64 | Curry, 63 |
| Curtis, 60,63,64 | Custer, 64 | Daily, 66 | Damon, 66 |
| Darnell, 61 | Darst, 63 | Date, 75 | Daub, 63 |
| Davenport, 65 | David, 64 | Davidson, 63,65 | |
| Davis, 60,64,65,70,71,73,76 | | Dawson, 63 | Delaney, 60 |
| DeNolf, 76 | Denton, 57,62,63 | | Derby, 62 |
| Derillo, 63 | Derr, 76 | Devere, 60 | Devoll, 61 |
| Dew, 64 | Dewey, 61 | Dewitt, 63 | Dickenson, 64 |
| Dickerson, 58,65 | Dickson, 58 | Dimmick, 65 | Dingle, 73 |
| Dobbin, 61 | Dodds, 60 | Doherty, 59 | Donden, 59 |
| Doolittle, 61 | Dorman, 63 | Dorris, 65 | Dove, 69 |
| Downs, 76 | Drake, 67 | Driskell, 66 | Drum, 75 |
| Drury, 62 | Dubois, 64 | Duckworth, 66,67 | Dudley, 63 |
| Dun, 73 | Dunbough, 75 | Duncan, 65,68 | Dunkerson, 57 |
| Dunkin, 68 | Dunlap, 73 | Dunn, 60 | Durbin, 57,66 |
| Durham, 65 | Durvin, 65 | Eastman, 61 | Easton, 59 |
| Ebby, 60 | Eddy, 65 | Edmiston, 62 | Edwards, 70,73 |
| Eggers, 60 | Elkins, 63 | Elledge, 64 | Elliott, 57,60 |
| Ellsworth, 61 | Ennis, 68 | Enochs, 73 | Erickson, 61 |
| Ernst, 65 | Esary, 66 | Eskew, 65 | Essex, 76 |
| Estes, 64 | Etheridge, 75 | Evans, 70,75 | Ewing, 60 |
| Fairbanks, 61 | Faris, 64 | Farnham, 64 | Farrar, 68,76 |
| Farrell, 63 | Fear, 69 | Ferguson, 63 | Ferry, 76 |
| Field, 65 | Fields, 66 | Fifer, 61 | Fike, 68 |
| Filson, 60 | Fisher, 68,76 | Fitch, 61 | Flannigan, 65 |
| Fleming, 58 | Floyd, 68 | Foley, 63,65 | Forcum, 60 |
| Ford, 75 | Forster, 65 | Fox, 61 | Frad,Fread,Fred, 75 |
| Frailey, 65 | Francis, 64 | Franklin, 62,63 | Fuller, 59,61,63 |
| Fullerton, 61 | Fullmore, 68 | Furgason, 60,73 | Gaines, 64 |
| Gaither, 63 | Garren, 57 | Garrison, 59 | Gasgill, 68 |
| Gayetty, 60 | Gelvin, 63 | Gibbs, 62 | Gideon, 62 |
| Gilbreath, 68 | Gifford, 61 | Gilleland, 60 | Gilliam, 76 |
| Glass, 73 | Goff, 65 | Goodin, 59,60 | Goodwin, 76 |
| Gordon, 59,60,75 | Grammon, 61 | Graves, 63 | Greaver, 64 |
| Gregg, 76 | Gregory, 67 | Griffin, 62 | Griswold, 66 |
| Groves, 67 | Gruen, 65 | Grup, 58 | Guin, 67 |
| Gurgle, 75 | Gwaltney, 66 | Hacket, 59,60 | Haentschel, 76 |
| Haford, 57 | Hagerman, 68 | Halbrook, 60 | Hale, 68 |
| Hall, 62,70 | Hamilton, 65 | Hamontree, 66 | Handley, 67 |
| Hanger, 73 | Hanley, 75 | Hannah, 63 | Hardabeck, 76 |
| Hardesty, 67 | Harmell, 62 | Harper, 75 | Harrawood, 67 |

| | | |
|---|---|---|
| Harris, 57,65 | Harrison, 57,61,62,65 | Harrold, 62,63 |
| Hart, 59 | Haster, 67  Hawkins, 59 | Hawks, 77 |
| Haynes, 75 | Hays, 57,65  Hayward, 57,58 | Head, 68 |
| Heart, 60 | Hefty, 60  Helme, 75 | Hendricks, 75,76 |
| Hendrix, 60 | Henry, 61  Hensley, 58 | Henson, 75 |
| Herdman, 57 | Hermis, 61  Hickman, 63,65 | Hicks, 66 |
| Higgins, 73 | Highsmith, 58,59  Higley, 60 | Hildearbrant, 60 |
| Hill, 65,68 | Hinkley, 61  Hitchcock, 76 | Hittle, 75 |
| Hoerner, 58 | Hoffman, 63  Hoge, 60 | Hogle, 63 |
| Holcomb, 68 | Holland, 66  Holley, 61,64 | Holt, 73 |
| Hood, 77 | Hook, 73  Hootes, 73 | Hoover, 60 |
| Hopkins, 65 | Hornada, 69  Hough, 61 | Houston, 59 |
| Howard, 60,65 | Howe, 61  Hubbard, 65 | Hubbell, 62 |
| Hudson, 63,65 | Huffstatler, 66  Hughes, 73,75 | Hull, 60,62 |
| Hume, 76 | Hungate, 67,68  Humphrey, 64 | Hurst, 57 |
| Hutchinson, 63 | Hutson, 65  Hutton, 68 | Hyde, 75 |
| Ingram, 64,67 | Irvin, 76  Itiff, 61 | Jackson, 57,63 |
| Jacobs, 57,76 | Jainlee, 57  James, 57,64 | Jameson, 66 |
| Jarnigan, 57 | Jeffrey, 57  Jenkins, 57 | Jennings, 66 |
| Jernold, 65 | Johnson, 57,65,66,67,68,75,76 | Johnston, 59,76 |
| Joles, 61 | Jones, 57,59,62,63,65,67,68,76 | Jordan, 57,61,65 |
| Journey, 68 | Joy, 57  Judd, 62 | Judge, 61 |
| Judy, 75 | Junkin, 57  Kane, 65 | Kanfield, 57 |
| Karcher, 67 | Karns, 67  Kavanaugh, 65 | Keiger, 58 |
| Keith, 58 | Kellams, 58  Keller, 58 | Kelley, 57,63,65,70 |
| Kellogg, 65 | Kelly, 58,61,62  Kelso, 58 | Kenmerer, 58 |
| Kemp, 58 | Kenedy, 58  Kennedy, 66 | Kennett, 60 |
| Kennington, 75 | Kenny, 60,75  Kensell, 59 | Keohoe, 76 |
| Ketcham, 57,58 | Kiger, 60  Killam, 70 | Kinery, 60 |
| King, 57,58,62,63,64,65 | Kinney, 59,62,73 | Kipper, 57 |
| Kirkpatrick, 58,65,68 | Kise, 59 | Kiser, 58 |
| Klinefelter, 57 | Kneadler, 62  Knee, 58 | Knight, 58 |
| Knott, 58 | Kouth, 61  Kreeps, 75 | Kuntz, 60 |
| Kurts, 59 | Lagon, 59  Laing, 61 | Lake, 60 |
| Lampkin, 66 | Land, 76  Lane, 67 | Langston, 68 |
| Lansdown, 60 | Lantz, 58  Laskins, 66 | Latham, 66 |
| Laudes, 75 | Lawrence, 63  Lawson, 68 | Layman, 65 |
| Laymon, 75 | Leach, 73  Leathers, 68 | Lee, 65 |
| Leitch, 61 | Lemen, 65  Lemon, 62 | Lewis, 59,64,75 |
| Link, 65 | Liter, 61  Livington, 61 | Long, 63 |
| Longenbaugh, 70 | Longfellow, 64  Lorton, 68 | Lott, 63 |
| Loyd, 66 | Lowe, 66  Lucas, 62,75 | Ludi, 77 |
| Lynch, 63 | Lyndon, 73  Lyons, 67 | McAlhaney, 62 |
| McAlister, 60 | McCaffee, 58  McCann, 75 | McCaragan, 63 |
| McCarrel, 76 | McClelland, 64  McClerrin, 63 | McClintock, 65,73 |
| McCollum, 65 | McComas, 59  McCormack, 60 | McCoy, 59,60 |
| McCracken, 68 | McDonald, 58,62,73  McFann, 76 | McFarland, 62,63 |
| McFarren, 64 | McGilvery, 61  McGee, 62 | McGough, 62 |
| McGregor, 65 | McGuire, 61  McHenry, 73 | McIntyre, 65 |
| McJenkins, 75 | McKinley, 77  McKinzie, 67 | McKnight, 75 |
| McLanield, 67 | M'Laughlin, 65  McMahon, 63 | McMickle, 58 |

McMurray, 62　McNear, 76　McNett, 61　McNown, 63
Maddox, 68　Maddux, 65　Madison, 68　Maitlett, 63
Maller, 60　Mallory, 65　Malony, 62　Marcy, 61
Marrs, 62　Marsh, 63　Marshall, 65　Martin, 59,60,62,63,75
Marvel, 65　Maryman, Merriman, Merrymen, 75　Mason, 65,77
Masters, 76　Matheny, 65　Mathews, 57,58,63　Mattison, 61
Mattocks, 76　Mauzy, 57　Maxwell, 75　Mayberry, 67
Maynard, 60　Mayo, 64　Mecumb, 62,63　Mencimer, 60
Mendinall, 75　Metcalf, 60　Mezo, 66,67　Middlehoff, 58
Middlemas, 61　Middlesworth, 69　Middleton, 68
Miller, 57,60,61,62,63,65,73　Million, 73　Minson, 68
Mitchell, 65　Mitten, 61　Moffett, 60　Moldenhaur, 63
Montgomery, 59　Montonye, 76　Moody, 62　Mooney, 68
Mooneyham, 65　Moore, 65,66,67,68,76　Moorman, 68
Moreley, 62,63　Morgan, 61,63,75　Morrison, 62,63,65
Mowry, 64　Moyers, 65　Mulkey, 65　Mullin, 61
Mundell, 60　Muns, 75　Munson, 69　Murphy, 57,63
Myers, 66　Nation, 58　Neal, 65　Nearen, 73
Neer, 61　Newbanks, 60　Newcomb, 63　Newman, 68
Newton, 76　Nicholas, 60,61　Nichols, 68,76,77　Nicholson, 62
Noe, 61　Nordyke, 76　North, 62　Nuckolls, 58
O'Dell, 77　Odum, 65　Ogborn, 62　Ogle, 73
Oglesby, 67　O'Larry, 62　Oliver, 60　O'Mara, 77
Orendorff, 75　Orr, 61,65　Osborn, 62　Otwell, 64
Owens, 73　Paisley, 75　Palmer, 61　Parker, 59
Partridge, 61　Patason, 73　Patch, 61　Patten, 76
Patterson, 62　Paul, 75　Payne, 65　Pea, 68
Pearce, 63,65　Pearson, 59　Peck, 68,76　Peeples, 64
Pemberton, 60　Penell, 66　Peppard, 63　Perkins, 75
Petty, 68,75　Phares, 62　Pharis, 64　Phelps, 59
Phillips, 63,65,73,77　Phipps, 60　Pierce, 57,61
Piper, 75　Pitt, 59　Pittman, 66　Plasters, 68
Plyler, 76　Poindexter, 65,67　Pool, 60
Poorman, 60　Porter, 61,62,63,66　Potter, 60,61
Prickett, 65　Prindels, 77　Proctor, 70　Proud, 62,63
Pullen, 57　Pullin, 58　Purcell, 75　Quinlisk, 61
Quirk, 63　Radeke, 60　Ralph, 75　Rampff, 63
Ramsey, 60,75　Rankin, 65　Ratcliff, 63　Rea, 65
Reagan, 76　Rece, 59　Redfern, 60　Redmon, 64
Reed, 60,61,64,67　Reeder, 75　Reidkey, 63　Renfro, 75
Reynolds, 65　Rhodes, 59,60,67,75　Rice, 60
Richards, 62,63　Richardson, 67　Richhart, 76　Rickey, 75,76
Riddle, 68　Riggor, 68　Riley, 63　Rivenburg, 76
Roach, 67　Robb, 63　Robertson, 68　Robinson, 60,65,67
Roman, 73　Root, 61　Rosenbauger, 57　Rosenthal, 60
Ross, 60,62,65　Rotramel, 65　Rounds, 63　Rowdon, 68
Rowmans, 57　Royall, 65　Rubado, 60　Rubart, 76
Rusk, 57　Russel, 57　Russell, 60,68　Ryon, 75
Sacrider, 59　St. Clair, 65　Sampson, 63　Samson, 60
Sanders, 57　Savadge, 68　Savage, 68　Sayre, 60
Scales, 57　Scate, 63　Schaniel, 76　Schmidt, 63

| | | | |
|---|---|---|---|
| Schrader, 63 | Scott, 68,73 | Seaman, 61 | Seeley, 61 |
| Selby, 58 | Sell, 59 | Serene, 61 | Severs, 67 |
| Sharp, 67 | Shaver, 76 | Shelton, 68 | Shepard, 67 |
| Sheridan, 61 | Sherman, 61 | Shields, 65,67,68 | Shipley, 75 |
| Shoemaker, 75 | Short, 63 | Shrader, 63,64 | Shuman, 63 |
| Shuster, 67 | Simons, 67 | Simpson, 61,73 | Sims, 65 |
| Sinks, 66 | Sittler, 69 | Skaggs, 69 | Skemp, 60 |
| Skiffy, 57 | Skinner, 58,61 | Sleeth, 69 | Sloan, 67 |
| Smeldell, 59 | Smith, 57,61,63,65,66,67,69,70,71,76 | | |
| Smock, 70 | Smyser, 70 | Snow, 70 | Solomon, 63 |
| Sothard, 67 | Souther, 70 | Spain, 66,71 | Spann, 73 |
| Sparkida, 75 | Speer, 57 | Spencer, 65,71 | Spiller, 65 |
| Spitsnas, 76 | Spraker, 71 | Sprigg, 65 | Stabler, 63 |
| Stables, 71 | Stamps, 71 | Stansbery, 69 | |
| Stark Co., Ill. Civil War Regiment NOT INDEXED, 72 | | | |
| Starkey, 68 | Starnes, 65 | Statton, 63 | Stearns, 61 |
| Steel, 65 | Stevens, Stephens, 75 | | Stettnisch, 75 |
| Stevenson, 59 | Stewart, 61,63 | Stidman, 68 | Stine, 76 |
| Stocker, 67 | Stockwell, 59 | Stone, 60 | Stout, 75 |
| Stovall, 64 | Street, 63 | Stubbens, 65 | Stubblefield, 65 |
| Stump, 64,76 | Sullivan, 65,66 | Summer, 75 | Summers, 65 |
| Swain, 65 | Swann, 68 | Swarthout, 61 | Swisher, 66 |
| Table, 58 | Tabler, 58 | Taft, 57 | Tanby, 69 |
| Tapp, 76 | Tate, 73 | Tatem, 67 | Taylor, 66,76 |
| Tefft, 60 | Terry, 73 | Thistlewait, 60 | Thomas, 63,70,73 |
| Thompson, 64,65,66 | | Thornton, 65,66 | Threkeld, 66 |
| Thurmond, 66 | Tippett, 60 | Todd, 66 | Tolly, 76 |
| Tothaker, 77 | Trapp, 61 | Trauber, 57 | Tripp, 61 |
| Trombla, 61 | Trowbridge, 61 | Trusler, 70 | Tucker, 71 |
| Turner, 66 | Twiss, 73 | Underwood, 61 | Upchurch, 66 |
| V?se, 66 | Valder, 61 | Vanderinder, 59 | Vandigrif, 73 |
| VanEchantly, 76 | VanOrder, 61 | VanSickle, 61 | VanValzer, 61 |
| Vanwinkle, 68 | Vaughn, 76 | Vermillion, 76 | Virden, 70 |
| Virtue, 60 | Wakefield, 68 | Walcott, 57 | Walgrove, 63 |
| Walker, 61,65 | Wallace, 61,71 | Waller, 60 | Ward, 65,66 |
| Ware, 76 | Warner, 62 | Warnock, 65 | Washburn, 66 |
| Washington, 63 | Wayman, 60 | Weamers, 60 | Webb, 65,66 |
| Weger, 59 | Weeks, 57 | Weiss, 63 | Welker, 73 |
| Wells, 63 | Weltzenaker, 60 | Wenkel, 76 | Werman, 58 |
| West, 60,61,63,73 | Wharton, 60 | Wheeler, 64 | Whiden, 66 |
| White, 67,68,77 | Whiteside, 64,65 | | Wilcox, 61,66 |
| Willey, 60 | Williams, 60,63,66,67,75 | | Willis, 66 |
| Wills, 65 | Wilson, 60,63,66,75 | | Winkler, 60 |
| Winn, 63 | Winston, 63,75 | Winters, 60,65 | Wohlfurt, 60 |
| Wolf, 60 | Wolshimer, 59 | Wood, 63 | Woodard, 60 |
| Woods, 73 | Woolley, 60 | Wouldridge, 67 | Wright, 60,61,75 |
| Wynn, 63 | Yates, 67 | Yeaman, 63 | Young, 70,76 |
| Youngblood, 66 | Ziegler, 59 | Zobel, 76 | |

# SEARCHING ILLLINOIS ANCESTORS

## VOLUME III NO. 4

May June 1987

INDEXED IN GENEALOGICAL PERIODICAL INDEX

Issued bi-monthly by Helen Cox Tregillis. Publication and advertising offices: Box 392, Shelbyville, IL 62565. Current single copy price, $2 plus 69 cents postage. Yearly subscription, $12. Send check or money order payable to: Helen Cox Tregillis, Box 392, Shelbyville, IL 62565. Surnames, articles appearing in publication are indexed in GENEALOGICAL PERIODICAL INDEX. Postage paid at Shelbyville, IL. Send address changes, queries, advertising to above address.

ISSN 0886 - 7763

PAYMENT MUST ACCOMPANY SUBSCRIPTION, QUERY AND ADVERTISING

NO BACK ISSUES AVAILABLE

FREE QUERY with county, surname only
$5 for maximum 50 word query
Check query section for format

## TABLE OF CONTENTS
## VOLUME III NO. 4
### SEARCHING ILLINOIS ANCESTORS

| | |
|---|---|
| Alexander County | |
|     Unpaid taxes for the year 1847 | 83 |
| Christian County | |
|     Early marriages, 1839-1866 | 83 |
| Clark County | |
|     Unpaid taxes for the year 1841 | 85 |
|     Unpaid taxes for the year 1843 | 85 |
| Coles County | |
|     Dead letter list for 1841 | 85 |
| Cumberland County | |
|     Unpaid taxes for the year 1843 | 86 |
|     Unpaid taxes for the years 1844,1845 | 86 |
| Douglas County | |
|     Genealogical Sources, Help | 87 |
| DuPage County | |
|     Genealogical Sources, Help | 87 |
| Edgar County | |
|     Early marriage records | 88 |
|     Unpaid taxes for the year 1844 | 88 |
| Edwards County | |
|     Genealogical Sources, Help | 88 |
| Ford County | |
|     Genealogical Sources, Help | 89 |
| Franklin County | |
|     Genealogical Sources, Help | 89 |
|     Unpaid taxes for the years 1846,1848 | 90 |
| Jackson County | |
|     Unpaid taxes for the year 1846 | 90 |
| Jefferson County | |
|     Unpaid taxes for the year 1848 | 91 |
| Moultrie County | |
|     Unpaid taxes for the year 1843 | 91 |
| Perry County | |
|     Unpaid taxes for the year 1850 | 92 |
| Union County | |
|     Unpaid taxes for the year 1847,1848 | 92 |
| Shelby County | |
|     Miscellaneous records | 93 |
| Pedigree Chart | |
|     Lineage of the editor | 95 |
| SEARCHING ILLINOIS ANCESTORS | |
|     Queries, advertising | 98,99 |
| Index | 99 |

Unpaid Taxes for 1847 for Alexander County, Illinois
Microfilm Number 1-285/M9B
Illinois State Historical Library, Springfield
Abstract from the CHESTER REVEILLE, Randolph County, Ill.

List of land and real estate situated in the county of Alexander, state of Illinois, on which taxes are due and unpaid for the year 1847.

Levi Hughes, John Daughtery, Heirs of Viex, Heirs of A. Synder, William Kinney, H.W. Billings, Heirs of Geo. Cloud, Thomas Forker, George Baumgard, Bray & Bancroft, J.B. Bowles, H.L. Webb, Robert A. Small, Benjamin McCool, Joseph Shields, Miles A. Gilbert, Heirs of H. Rhodes, J. Murphy, Owen Sullivan, Willis Lyttle, Willis Willard, John O. Gordon, Caroline Hull, Heirs of J.H. Piatt, Daniel Wood, Heirs of Jo'n McCravens, Adam Beaty, William Massey, Heirs of J. Massey, David Braken, Peter Miller, J.W. Baldwin, William Hutchinson, John R. Bakman, A.M. Fonlain. A.W. Anderson, collector. March 8th, 1848.

---

Christian County, Ill. Early Marriages
Book I, County Clerk, Taylorville, Ill.

Alenson LUCAS and Lucinda HAYREX, page 1
E.T. LEIGH and Mary Ann HILL, page 4
Abraham LIGHTS and Elizabeth RADFORD, page 5
James M. LOGSDON and Susannah DURBIN, page 7
Peter LOID and Precilla STRICKLAND, page 8
John C. LANGLEY and Mary WADIC, page 8
John A. LEACHMAN and Mary E. HESSER, page 12
William LANCASTER and Ann DAVIS, page 13
Joseph LOGSDON and Susan MEADS, page 19
Jesse LANGLEY and Elizabeth CRUMPTON, page 21
William T. LANGLEY and Louisa J. SPRIGHTS, page 21
Reuben L. LILLIS and Nancy MIDDLETON, page 23
John A. LEIGH and Margaret GEORGE, page 24
Elisha LOGSDON and Maria RALLS, page 27
John LETHERSHOES and Susan WARNICK, page 31
Elisha LOGSDON and Susannah DURBIN, page 32
William LEE and Jeminah DONNELLY, page 35
Edward LUSK and Jane A. AUGUR, page 37
James LANGLEY and Sarah J. ALLISON, page 38
James L. LAUGHLIN and Martha N. SCOTT, page 42
Daniel B. LEIGH and Julia Ann PAYNE, page 47
Isaac Henry LEMON and Louisa LAMBRIAL, page 49
William LANGLEY and Sarah HANON, page 50
G.W. LONG and Sarah C. STOCKTON, page 51
John LARIMORE and Sarah Ann BENTON, page 54
John LEATHERHOS and Levina RAWLS, page 60
James M. LANGLEY and Lucinda VANDEOUR, page 62
Edwin F. LARKHAM and Sarah J. PARKHURST, page 69
James M. LACKEY and Elizabeth E. RYAN, page 76
Robert P.J. LANGLEY and Irena L. CLARK, page 77

Edward LEIGH and Mary CURRIE, page 83
Richard LEE and Lucinda CROCKER, page 84
David LEACH and Martha E. LOGAN, page 85
John E. LOCKER and Nancy J. WILSON, page 89
George LAWTON and Emily J. CHASTAIN, page 92
Ridakiah LEWIS and Eliza Jane LUCKEY, page 97
G.W. LOIT and Sarah Jane LAMBERT, page 103
James M. LINN and Emelia DAVIS, page 109
William P. LORTON and Ellen ELLIS, page 112
Josiah LARD and Emily FUNDERBURK, page 112
Christopher LEHMAN and Mary LARGE, page 114
Benjamin F. LELLS and Mary J. BANKSON, page 115
Isaac LOCKWOOD and Sarah WESTFALL, page 115
Elisha LOGSDON and Mary C. DURBIN, page 118
Tiophill LARNENT and Eminia LONET, page 120
Hugh LAFLAN and Mary SHURDON, page 121
Benjamin LAMBERD and Isabel DEMARS, page 121
Theophilas LARRNENT and Augenstine LOARETS, page 123
Isaminger LURRING and Allex TYATT, page 124
Ivory H. LIBBEY and Sarah E. SHUTTLE, page 127
Stephen T. LILLEY and Mary E. GAINES, page 128
Marion LARPT and Sarah HINSLEY, page 125
James LAW and Lytitia CHURCHMAN, page 125
Hiram S. LUDWICK and Sarah C. SPINDLE, page 130
William H.H. LEIGH and Mary J. GLASS, page 132
Thos R. LAWRENCE and Mary VICE, page 134
James L. LAMB and Mary M. SHIVERS, page 135
James W. LAW and Nancy STEPHENS, page 137
James M. LEWIS and Emily C. RICKS, page 143
Clark I. LOCKWOOD and Minerva DOAK, page 144
Charles W. LANGLEY and Sophia GORE, page 144
Thomas J. LORTON and Harriet E. MORRIS, page 145
Westley L. LYONS and Caroline A. CREEGER, page 147
Mathew C. LONG and Mary BALLIETT, page 152
Abram B. LAWRENCE and Nancy BYLEW, page 157
John E. LOCKER and Sarah E. HARRISON, page 158
Abram K. LEMON and Nancy J. McHOTTON, page 160
Levi S. LUDWICK and Jane A. SPINDLE, page ?
Thomas W. LONG and Martha A. BUGG, page 163
Benjamin F. LONG and Anna E. RICE, page 164
Adolphus LAMBERT and Mary PRINCE, page 166
John H. LUTGENHIZER and Ann E.W. KEMERER, page 169
Samuel C. LORTON and Irene A. RIDLEN, page 171
Ofenoshe LOMBARD and Josev PUMEA, page 172
Randolph LEE and Sarah G. SEXTON, page 172
Jesse M. LONGSTREET and Louisa BROCKMAN, page 175
Thomas N. LAKIN and Rebecca HUNTER, page 176
William T. LITTICK and Margaret S. GREEN, page 177
Willis LEE and Laura J. HOLLAND, page 177
Thomas J. LEMON and Frances S. CROWN, page 179
George W. LAMB and Frances J. HELSOE, page 187

Unpaid Taxes for Clark County, Illinois
Due and unpaid for year 1841
The Courier, Charleston, Ill. March 28, 1844
Newspaper Microfilm from Illinois State Historical Library

Tax sale/ a list of lands and other real estate situated in Clark and state of Illinois on which taxes remain due and unpaid for the year 1841.

James C. Hillebart, James McAvoy, Henry Dougherty, O. Bumham, George Armstrong, Elijah Handy, John Craig, Charles White, Josiah Black, Joohn L. Mounts, James Baird, R. Richardson, Enoch Lee, William A. Brown, E.W. Brown, A. Stewart, John Moore, C & T Dullett, Jacob Decker, Samuel Peevy, Joseph Eudus, Jesse Eary, Joseph Willard, Ralph Hasket, Thomas Johnson, Andrew Caldwell. Calvin Boyd, Col. Clark County.

ALSO FROM SAME MICROFILM ROLL
The Courier, Charleston, Ill. 13 March 1844
Taxes Unpaid for Year 1843, Clark Co., Ill.

Robert C. Brown, Heirs of Wm. Black, Levi Beancham, Estate of Amos Biby, Bigod and Patridge, Horace M. Bazier, J.P. Cooper, Peter Garrott, Fayett Cole, William Cullom, James Draper, Joseph Duncan, James Ennis, Sylvester Faris, William Hullambeck, Jonathon Hicklin, James How, Michael Hendly, Samuel Johnson, Joseph C. Jones, Samuel Jenkins, Henry Killiam, Harden Kidwell, Stephen Kidwell, Andrew Lowery, Stephen Lee, John Lycon, Abraham Lindley, William Low, James R. Low, John O. Mattews, R.B. M'Cowen, Yorick M'Gillipin, Thomas Moore, Edwin W. Madison, James M. Miller, Rawly and Davidson, Simon D. Rarar, Stephen Runnels, Isa B. Ross, John Sams, Archibald C. Stark, Abner Stark, Jacob Shetler, William Watson, Silas Whitehead, Isaac Walden, William Walker, Wheeler & Co. James R. Anderson, Col. Clark County.

---

Post Office List of Coles County, Illinois
The Courier, Charleston, Ill. Saturday, July 10, 1841
Newspaper Microfilm, Illinois State Historical Library

List of letters at the post office at Coles Courthouse on 1 July 1841

Matilda Adams, Moses Alford, Benjamin Austin, Mrs. Deborah Allen, Nathan Austin, Emmett Balch, Alfred Balch, Elisha C. Brewster, John B. Barker, Isaac Bundell, Richard Carver, John Connelly, Daniel Caldwell, Benjamin and Wm. Dunn, Edmond Dickson, R.S. Dickson, John Ellis, John Eddington, Ely Ford, Henry ?, Hix Gifford, Josiah R. Gilham, L.R. Hutchason, James F. Hoskins, Daniel H. Hermer, Josiah Hoots, Wm. Hare, S.A. Hodgeman, Arthur Montgomery Ingrum, Adam Jacobs, George Kellogg, Charles H. Kemper, Lavier Linder, Esq., Benjamin Land, Adam Latner, William Megahan, John Merrell, James Myres, James Martin, James Miner, R.M. Newport, G. Ourer, Benjamin C. Ross, Isaac Rundall, Michael Rawlings, Philip Shepler, Hiram Shane, Thomas Sconce, Hiram Tucker, E.W. Trew, J.b. Veach, Joseph Wade or William Wade, Miss Nancy Wilson, Henry Wilson, Marcus Wilson, B.R. Wishard, George Wilson, Truman E. Andrews, Dr. R. H. Allison, John

Aperson, John Ashly, Gowin Adkins, Richard Barker, Mr. Burch, John Barrick, William Blakney, John C. Baldwin, John W. Crusan, G.W. Camper, Samuel Clam, Robert Dawks, Mr. Duncan, William Durham, Wm. Duty, Wm. Ewing, Susan Frost, Joseph Fowler, Robert Gray, W.W. Goodwier, Jun., Andrew Hensley, John Hannah, John Hutton, Frederick Hamp, Henry Haughan, Joseph Hawley, Zachariah Johnson, William or Tho. Jeffries, Sarah Kemper, James Kelly, Jacob Larue, Samuel Lester, Robert Moore, Thomas A. Marshall, Miss Ellen Marshall, Daniel Mitchell, Israel Moofort, N. Parker, James F. Rolson, James Roberts, John Rogers, John Shipp, George Stewart, Anthony K. Shores, Jonathon Tipton, Charles E. Vaughn, Thomas J. Wright, William Williams, James W. Walker, John Waltrip, B.W. White, Mr. Wankiesa. H.C. Dunbar, P.M.

---

Unpaid Taxes for year 1843 Cumberland Co., Ill.
The Courier, Charleston, Ill. April 4, 1844
Newspaper Microfilm, Illinois State Historical Library

Lists of lands and other real estate, situated in the county of Cumberland and state of Illinois, on which the taxes remain due and unpaid for the year 1843.

Enos Kennedy, Ely Nees, Levi Gritton, Daniel Funk, Jonathon Graham, Aaron Ferguson, Charles S. Marion, William Halbatt, Daniel Troubell, Morgan Dryden, Daniel Clary, Evans Cisna, John Wall, John Dryden, Byron Fancher, Henry Ammons, John C. Williams, Lewis Riley, John Haughn, Joseph Wilson, William D. Wilson, Peter Allgood, Joseph Evartt, Alfred Evertt, H.C. Thayer, Ezra Baker, L.T. Coone, Robert Kelsey, Clark Cushman, John W. Vance, Thomas Rolland, John Cogshell, Miles Magree, Robert H. Publes, Joseph Griffith, Daniel T. Allen, Jas. Madonal's heirs, John Lard.

SAME MICROFILM ROLL
Unpaid Taxes for years 1844 and 1845, Cumberland County, Ill.
The Courier, Charleston, Ill. Saturday, Sept. 5, 1846

A List of lands and other real estate situated in Cumberland and state of Illinois on which the taxes remain due and unpaid for the years 1844 and 1845.

D.T. Allen, John Armstrong, Moses Blocksom, John Bennett, John Byrd, George Bauglive, John Dowham, William Brooks, Heirs of Samuel Cisna, James Cutright, John G. Conner, E. Clapp, Heirs of C.G. Chowney, Peter Cushner, E. Capps, John Dryden, John Dickson, John Dures, Nathan Ellington, Buel Earman, Aaron Ferguson, Calvin Griffith, David Gillmore, John Giddis, Nicholas Haughn, D.Y. Hughes, Daniel Linder, Benjamin Land, John Lee, John Larde, Heirs of T. Mouser, Charles L. Moore, Wesley Moore, Heirs of J. Mitchell, Byrd Monroe, Thomas Melvin, Samuel Owings, Jane Poulson, James Prentice, David Pugh, Samuel Prichard, H. Linenbaugh, Allen Patterson, Joseph Russell, Hewet Ruffner, Samuel Rogers, Mitchell Roberts, M. Simpson, Dugan Sanders, John Smith, Mat Shaw, Enough thompson, J. Whitstone, Assigne of Wm. W. Wilson, Heirs of E. Workman, Henry Worthy, Jacob Winkler, William J. Wilson, Joseph Wilson, Elijah Kalb, Ephraim Cates, Allen Trigg, Joseph Kirkpatrick, Wm. C. Mitchell, D.T. Allen, Moses Blosum.

## DOUGLAS COUNTY, ILLINOIS
### Genealogical Sources, Help

County created 8 Feb. 1839 from parent county of Coles. Named for Stephen A. Douglas. County seat at Tuscola, IL 61953 has vital, land records (county clerk, 217-253-2411) and circuit court records (217-253-2352). Courthouse open Monday through Friday, 8:30 - 4:30. Illinois genealogical society that covers this county is Douglas County Genealogical Society, 504 E. Main St., Arcola, IL 61910.

### Sources

<u>1929 Roll of Honor: Record of Burial Places of Soldiers, Sailors, Marines and Army Nurses of All Wars of the United States Buried in the State of Illinois.</u> Springfield, Ill. Shows burials of soldiers in Albin, Arcola, Arthur, Broadus, Cartwright, Chesterville, Deer Creek, Fairfield, Hugo, Quinn, Murdock, Nelson, Newman, Pleasant Ridge, Tuscola, Van Voorris, and Villa Grove Cemeteries in Douglas County, Illinois.

<u>1860, 1870 Census of Douglas County.</u> Douglas County Genealogical Society.

<u>Every Name Indexes to 1884 History and 1910 History.</u> Douglas County Genealogical Society.

<u>Index to Probate Records, 1859-1963, Douglas County.</u> Douglas County Genealgocial Society.

<u>Male Marriage Index, 1859-1879.</u> Douglas County Genealogical Society.

Check with the society for other genealogical help.

---

## DUPAGE COUNTY, ILLINOIS
### Genealogical Sources, Help

County created 9 Feb. 1839 from parent county of Cook. Named for DuPage River. County seat at Wheaton, IL 60187 has vital, land records (county clerk, 312-682-7034) and court records (circuit clerk, 312-682-7100). Courthouse hours, Monday through Friday, 8 - 4:30. Illinois genealogical society that covers this county is DuPage County Genealogical Society, P.O. Box 133, Lombard, IL 60148.

### Sources

<u>1929 Roll of Honor: Record of Burial Places of Soldiers, Sailors, Marines and Army Nurses of All Wars of the United States Buried in the State of Illinois.</u> Springfield, Ill. Shows burials of soldiers for Arlington, Bloomingdale, Bronswood, Calvary, Cass, Catholic, Concordia, Downers Grove, Elmhurst, Elm Lawn, Fair View, Forest Hill, Forrest Home, Freedens, Fullersburg, Glen Ellyn, Glen Oak, Greenridge, Hinsdale, Jewell, Lace, Little Woods, Lombard, Mt. Carmel, Mt. Emblem, Naperville, Oak Forest, Oakridge, Oakwood, Pleasant Hill, St. John's, St. Mary's, St. Peter and Paul, Torode, Waldheim, Warrenville, Wayne Center, West Side, Wheaton, Winfield, York and Zion Lutheran Cemeteries.

There are several sources for this county. Check with the society for other genealogical help.

## EDGAR COUNTY, ILLINOIS
### Early Marriage Records, County Clerk

Jan. 4, 1849 Hiram CASSELL and Eliza CUSICK
Jan. 27, 1849 Henry D. CONNELLY and Susan CAMPBELL
Feb. 22, 1849 Daniel M. CAMERER and Dica Ellen BROWN
Aug. 7, 1849 Isaac CHILDERS and Elizabeth MADDOCK
Aug. 20, 1849 James CLARK and Nancy BURR
Aug. 22, 1849 Joseph COONS and Mary Ann EDWARDS
Sept. 5, 1849 David J. CONNELY and Nancy B.C. REDMON
Oct. 11, 1849 Isaac H. CURTIS and Rachel N.J. LAWRENCE
Jan. 1, 1850 Joseph CUMMINS and Sarah PURCELL
Jan. 4, 1850 Benjamin CROW and Elizabeth Ann RAY
March 4, 1850 Niles COLLINS and Sarah J. WILLIAMS
March 16, 1850 Virgil COLLINS and Fanny L. MILLER
March 26, 1850 Elam COOK and Elizabeth HOLDEN
May 25, 1850 Moses CONNER and Mary C. THOMPSON
Aug. 6, 1850 William B. CALLOWAY and Margaret CALDWELL
Oct. 19, 1850 James W. CRAIG and Mariah L. MILLER
Oct. 26, 1850 Josiah W. CLARK and Margarett BUSH
Oct. 26, 1850 Archilbald CALLAWAY and Harriett W. WEAR
Nov. 6, 1850 Benjamin CONNER and Betsey Jane JONES
Nov. 8, 1850 James W. CLARK and Emily BURT
Jan. 6, 1851 Oregon CASSMON and Elizabeth SPRINGER
Jan. 8, 1851 Charles CARRY and Mary Jane HUNTER
Jan. 23, 1851 Robert L. CAMIRON and Elizabeth Jane CASH
Jan. 24, 1851 Franklin CHILDRESS and Sarah MOCK
Feb. 24, 1851 Isaac COMSTOCK and Mary F. BRYANT

---

### UNPAID TAXES FOR 1844 in EDGAR COUNTY, ILLINOIS
Microfilm: The Reporter, Charleston, Ill. April 4, 1845

Taxes unpaid and due for the year 1844 in Edgar County, Illinois

J. Caldwell, Jr., James Kimbrough, Laranus Baker, Naron's Heirs, James Tweedy, Robt. Shields' Heirs, Lewis West's Heirs, Myron Merchant, Thomas Forster, Allen Martin, Abram Stotts, Nancy Curry, J.A. Kimbrugh, Jesse Ogle, John Jones, Alexander McBath, John Jones, James Garrett, G. Mattey's Heirs, James Murphy, Sam'l Littlefield, James Dinwiddle, Patrick McDonald, William Raney, James Kidwell, Joel Moores, William Newlon, James Ingram, William Gillman, Thomas McCorkle, Wm. Hoffman's Heirs, Geo. W. Roberts, Daniel Durnall, Lewis Wayne, Leonard Bell, A.E. Brockway, Robert Matson. Town lots: Daniel Darnall, James Murphy, Myron Merchant, Eli Poulter, John Goodman, John C. Bradley. James Gordon, collector of Edgar County.

---

### EDWARDS COUNTY, ILLINOIS
### Genealogical Sources, Help

County created 28 Nov. 1814 from parent counties of Madison and Gallatin. Named for Gov. Ninian Edwards. County seat at Albion, IL

62806 has vital, land records (county clerk, 618-445-2115) and court records (circuit clerk, 618-445-2016). Courthouse hours, Monday through Friday, 8-4. Illinois genealogical society that covers this county is Edwards County Historical Society, P.O. Box 205, Albion, IL 62805.

### Sources

Birkbeck, Morris. Notes on a Journey in America from the Coast of Virginia to the Territory of Illinois. 3d ed of 1818.
Decatur Genealogical Society. Cemetery Inscriptions, Vol. I.
Edwards County Historical Society:
    1820-1840 Censuses of Edwards County, Ill.
    1830 Federal Census of Edwards County, Ill.
    1860 Census of Edwards County, Ill.
    1870 Census of Edwards County, Ill.
    A History of Edwards County, Ill. Reprint.
    1815-1844 Marriage Records of Edwards County, Ill.
1850 Census of Edwards County, Ill. Heritage House, 1972.
Illinois State Archives. Original Land Sales in Edwards County, Ill. beginning in 1814. 1983.
Combined History of Edwards, Lawrence and Wabash Counties, Ill. 1883. Reprinted 1981.
1880 Census of Edwards County, Ill. Richland County Genealogical Society, 1981.

---

## FORD COUNTY, ILLINOIS
### Genealogical Sources, Help

County created 17 Feb. 1859 from parent county of Clark (Probably should be Vermilion or Champaign Counties.) Named for Gov. Thomas Ford. County seat at Paxton, IL 60957 has vital, land records (county clerk, 217-379-2721) and court records (circuit clerk, 217-379-2641). Courthouse hours, Monday through Friday, 8-4. Check with adjoining county genealogical societies.

### Sources

Combined Landowner Atlases, 1884-1901-1916. Repr. 1976.
Gardner, E.A. History of Ford County to 1908. 2 volumes.
Lake City Pub. Co. Portrait and Biographical Record of Ford County, 1892.
Prairie Farmer's Directory of Ford County, Ill. 1917. Repr. 1982.

---

## FRANKLIN COUNTY, ILLINOIS
### Genealogical Sources, Help

County created 2 January 1818 from parent counties of White and Gallatin. Named for Benjamin Franklin. County seat at Benton, IL 62812 has vital, land records (county clerk, 618-438-3221) and court records (circuit clerk, 618-439-2011). Courthouse hours, Monday through Friday, 8-4. Illinois genealogical society that covers this county is Frankfort Area Genealogical Society, 2000 East St. Louis, West Frankfort, IL 62896.

Sources

Davis, Cloe and Ruby Henderson. Franklin Co., Ill. Cemetery
   Inscriptions.
Frankfort Area Genealogical Society:
   Cemetery Inscriptions. About five volumes.
War History, 1832-1919. Indexed.
Goodspeed Pub. Co. History of Gallatin, Saline, Hamilton, Franklin
   and Williamson Co., Ill. 1887.
Check with the society for other genealogical help.

----------

FRANKLIN COUNTY, ILLINOIS
Unpaid taxes for year 1846
Chester Reveille, Chester, Ill. Feb. 10, 1849
Newspaper Microfilm, Illinois State Library

Lists of land and other real estate situated in the county of Franklin and state of Illinois, on which taxes remain due and unpaid for the year 1846.

Sylvester Adams, Allen D. Burton, David Blocher, Z. Casey and J. Pace, Calvin M. Clark, A.Y. Claggett, Wm. B. Driden, A.J. Dickison, H. Eddy and J.A. McClermand, H. Eddy and D.J. Baker, O.B. Harrison, David L. Peacock, Benjamin Roberts, Thomas Ruddick, Henry J. Sulser, Nelson Wade, S.W.D. Chare, Lucy Corgan, William Hincheliff, Robert Martin, Sion H. Mitchell, Adm'r Meshack Morris, deceased., Robt. Montgomery, L. Montgomery, Abraham North, Samuel McElwain, N.b. Robinson, Thomas Romine, Israel Sheldon, Henry J. Sulser, D.T. Scraunir, J.C. Sloo, Peter Teel, J.S. Walker. George W. Akin, collector, Benton, Feb. 1, 1849.

Same County
Unpaid Taxes for 1848
The Chester Herald, Randolph County, Ill. May 4, 1850
Newspaper Microfilm, Illinois State Library

Unpaid taxes for Franklin County, Ill. for 1848
   D. Baugh and J. Pace, A. Clayett, A.J. Dickinson, H. Eddy and A. Kirkpatrick, A.B. Hawkins, D.D. Hemperman, William Night, David L. Peacock, Thomas Romnius, D.T. Scranner, Nelson Wade, Robert Martin, Clendening Adison & Co., Henry D. Brown, Tilmon Brooks, J. Para and Baugh, C.M. Clark, E.H. Ridgway, R. Castles Estate, Isham Tiner, James C. Sloo, Grippin Whipple, Thomas Wellington, Adam Yantrey.

----------

JACKSON COUNTY, ILLINOIS
Unpaid Taxes for the year 1846
The Chester Reveille, Chester, Ill. Aug. 9, 1849
Newspaper Microfilm, Illinois State Library

Lists of lands and other real estate situated in county of Jackson and state of Illinois, on which taxes remain due and unpaid for the year 1846.

William Morrison, Wm. McIntosh, S. M'Clintock, Charles Garner, Joshua Davis, Thomas Leviers, Heirs S. Manville, Peter Keiffer, Henry

Bannford, Jas. Fulkerson, Hason Brush and Jenkins, A.M. Jenkins, Wm. Richards, Jas. O'Harrow, John A. Heaps, J.M. Duncan, Jos. B. Denning, M. Lemrick, Henry Bug, Sydney Breese, Alex. Jenkins, Heirs of Isaac Aldridge, S.H. Kimmell and A.M. Jenkins, Kimball and Breese, James Gill, Joseph culley, John J. Henry, Wm. Bilderback, Pierre Menard, Elias Cumming, John Synder, Jas. Thompson, Jas. Taylor, Joe Duncan, Heirs J.T. Johnston, Heirs J. Sweet, Estate J. Sweet. John Elmore, collector, Murphysboro, Aug. 3, 1849.

---

## JEFFERSON COUNTY, ILLINOIS
### Unpaid Taxes for the year 1848
The Chester Herald, Randolph Co., Ill. May 4, 1850
Newspaper Microfilm, Illinois State Historical Library
(NOTE: ALL NEWSPAPER MICROFILM IS ON FILE AT THE ILLINOIS STATE HISTORICAL LIBRARY NOT THE STATE LIBRARY.)

John Hooks, Thomas McCullough, John Hudlow's Heirs, Charles Jennings, William Raddle, James C. Martin, John Afflack, Stephen S. Cutts, Thomas Burrow's Heirs, Richard Bullock's Heirs, Henry Eddy, Daniel King, A.S. Merritt, W.H. Stoops, Goerge M. Rutlege, Mary J. Eddy, Heirs of Wm. Eyers, Solomon K. Robinson, David Dow, Heirs Rad Wilbanks, John Flesner, Mathew Davis, Samuel Boswell's Heirs, Susan Wallis, George J. Baltzwell, Amy Casey's Heirs, H.H. Baldwin, Downing Baugh, John H. Rahn, Heirs of A.J. Hudlow, Heirs of Richard K. Hams, William Stickney, Thomas Bird, James Stone, M.L. Johnson, John D. Wood, Heirs of James Breeze, Jeptha Hardin, Edmund R. Larvis, Heirs of A.R. White, John S. Robinson, Heirs of Henry Eddy, H.G. Hooks' Heirs, Benjamin Monroe, Jaems T. Swearingen, W.H. Stoops, Benton Y. Lyttell, Heirs of David Dow, Moses Neal Exec. of Rad Willbanks. Elijah Piper, Sheriff and collector of said county, April 29, 1850.

---

## MOULTRIE COUNTY, ILLINOIS
### Unpaid taxes for the year 1843
The Courier, Charleston, Ill. March 28, 1844
Newspaper Microfilm, Illinois State Historical Library

Lists of lands and real estate situated in the county of Moultrie and state of Illinois on which taxes remain due and unpaid for the year 1843.

Benjamin Budlong, Thos. T. Blythe, Thomas Curry, John Crouch, Frederick Daws, John H. Duncan, James and M. Elder, James Fruit, Jonathon Graham, David Hoffman, David Hood, Josiah L. Hale and Walter R. Jones, Philo Hale, Francis G. Hill, Joseph Howell, Reuben P. Harper, Andrew Johnson, Heirs of Thos. Lee, Mathew S. Marsh, Randolph Miller, Franklin Overstreet, Granvill S. Patterson, George Parkinson, Robert Rutherford, John Rucker, Moses Story, J.T.B. Stapp, Michazah Sadler, Mathew Thompson, Charles Tetrick, Alfred Wood, Elizabeth Walker, Heirs of S. Walker, Alexander M. Wilson, Daniel B. Williams, David B. Williams, David Welborn, Saml. Wilson, Evan Wallace, John T. Kennedy, H.S. Apple, Thomas Cary, John True, Joseph N. Lewis. Isaac Walker, col. Moultrie Co. March 23, 1844.

PERRY COUNTY, ILLINOIS
Unpaid Taxes for the year 1850
The Chester Herald, Randolph Co., Ill. May 3, 1851
Newspaper Microfilm, Illinois State Historical Library

Lists of lands delinquent for 1850 in the county of Perry, Ill.
Blackstock Walker, James M. Reynolds, E. Seymour and J.T. Hope, Isaac Hatcher, Robt. B.M. McGlasson, H.H. Reeves, G.W. Tegg, Rolan Wittleman, John Collville, Samuel Hawkins, John Colville, E.M. Thompson, Samuel Benson, George Lype, Noah Washburn, Edon Laferty, William Balch, J.M. Campbell, C.A. Keyes, Titus Hale, William Huchings, C.T. Pyle, Amos Andeson, Mathew Jones, M. Baldridge, J.F. Metten, Alex Anderson, John Lynch, William Williams, S.M. Woodside, William McIntosh, F. Yearean, William McDonald, John D. Barketlow, Jo Lindley, David Baldridge, M. Baldridge, George Franklin, J.H. Franklin, Isaac Brown, James Steel, Robert Woodside, John Milligan, Samuel Woodside, William D. Osburne, Joel Craine, Nelson McDowal, A. Hood, Mathew Niel, David Ferries, William Gamble, H. Kirkpatrick, Mary Kirkpatrick, Samuel Elliott, James Gillespie, John Brooks, John Worth, Alexander Campbell, Samuel H. Eaton, William Moyer, J.T. Moyer, J.T. Jackson, Lewis Moyer, Josiah Wells, Timothy Barber, Charles Owens, Richard Greene, William Brown, Thomas Brinkley, Avery Chapman's Heirs, John Carswell, Josiah R. Hughey. J.W. Piatt, sheriff and collector for Perry Co.

---

UNION COUNTY, ILLINOIS
Chester Reveille, Randolph Co., Ill. March 3, 1849
Newspaper Microfilm, Illinois State Historical Library

Lists of lands and other real estate situated in the county of Union and state of Illinois on which taxes remain due and unpaid for the year 1847 and 1848
Morris Gurley, John T. McGinnis, Henry McGinnis, James Carver etal., Nancy A. Davis, Heirs Jno. Albright, Heirs of Benj. Crise, Wm. Penninger Jr., Heirs of Henry Kellar, Heirs of Wiley Cope, Newton Pierce, Heirs of Isaac Beggs, James Guthrie, Heirs of John Lingle, Henry Penroe, Heirs of J. Burman, Heirs of Thos. Sams, Wiley Mowrey, Heirs of Saml. Miller, Heirs of Mathias Penninger, Caleb Sitter, Heirs of James Thompson, Heirs of Mathias Zimmerman, Heirs of Saml. Moland, Joseph Smith, Henry Kro?, Heirs of Jno. Freeman, Elizabeth Crips, Heirs of Thos. Wright, Herman Wimbermolen, Heirs of Eliel Freeman, David Dobson, Heirs of Samuel Lewis, John W. Warralls 1847 and 1848, Heirs of Ed. Conoway, Heirs of Wm. H. Madden, Wm. Armstrong, Alfred Cotner, Philip Kimmel, Caleb Casper, Heirs of J. G. Wilkins, Simeon H. Poe, Thomas and William Johnson, James O'Harra, John H. Henderson, Thomas Hamilton, William Garner, Jacob H. Neely, John J. Spence, Jacob William, Joshua B. Lee, Heirs of Zachariah Walker, H. B. Harlow, Hiram Pennroyer. Andrew Deardorff, sheriff and collector, Feb. 23, 1849.

SHELBY COUNTY, ILLINOIS
Miscellaneous Record Books
Shelby County, Ill. Clerk's Office
MRB=book number and page following

NOTE: Miscellaneous records can also include records from other counties or countries if individual owner non-resident.

Moyer, Jacob
   Of Vermilion County, Ill. Land no. 5369, 10 Aug. 1838. MRB 215, page 492

Munson, Joel
   Estate and heirs of Moultrie Co., Ill. Died 16 Jan. 1921. MRB 215, pp. 551-558.

Mose, James H.
   Will and estate of Christian Co., Ill. 1912. MRB 189, p.281-285.

Murdock, Alexander
   Died 21 Jan. 1879 Baltimore Co., MD. MRB 189, pp. 36-45.

Munger, Frank E.
   Of Rawlins Co., Kansas. MRB 189, p. 58.

Munger, Elijah S.
   Died Watertown, Jefferson Co., NY. MRB 189, p. 52-53.

Murphy, James
   Land no. 23622, Fla. War, 1854. MRB 143, p. 159.

Murray, David E.
   Affadavit, heirs of Wm. S. Davis. MRB 172, p. 226.

Myers, Berkey
   Heirs of. MRB 157, p. 635.

Myers, Henry F.
   Heirs of, died 1860. MRB 163, p. 451-452.

Myers, Peter
   Heirs of. MRB 189, pp.323-325.

Nance, Mary A.
   Heirs of. MRB 178, p. 184.

Nance, N.J.
   Heirs of 1899. MRB 178, p. 616.

Needham, Jerusha
   Heirs of. MRB 189, p. 162.

Neff, George
   Heirs of 1877. MRB 193, p. 431.

Nehring, Gottlieb
   Heirs of, d. 1884. MRB 189, p. 431.

Neighbor, Silvanus W.
   Estate of Cumberland Co., Ill. died 18 Dec. 1904. MRB 215, pp. 433-434.

Neil, James L.
   Will and estate of Macon Co., Ill. died 25 May 1891. MRB 215, pp. 578-585.

Neil, John
   Heirs of. MRB 193, p. 390.

Neil, Peter
   Died 1843, heirs of. MRB 163, p. 319.

Newman, Henry
    Affadavit of Tulare Co., CA; heirs of John C. Newman of Springfield, Ill. MRB 172, p. 412.

Nichols, Benj.
    Land no. 29116, 1854. MRB 157, p. 557.

Nichols, Green F.
    Heirs of 1862. MRB 189, p. 300.

Nieman, Bernadina
    Heirs of Effingham Co., Ill. MRB 157, pp. 420-421.

Niles, David
    Land no. 65026. MRB 193, p. 208.

Noecker, Wm.
    Heirs of Piatt Co., Ill. MRB 163, pp. 397-426.

Noland, Hiram
    Land no., 1838. MRB 215, p. 343.

O'Brien, Patrick
    Heirs of 1902. MRB 215, p. 168.

Ohler, Jonathon
    Pvt. Capt. Owsely's Co., Kentucky Mil. 1812. Land no. 23189 assigned to John P. Albert. MRB 236, pp. 104-105.

Oliver, Eliza
    Affadavit of, heirs of Wm Prentice, died 1852. MRB 172, p. 471.

Olson, Ola
    Heirs of and estate of Piatt Co., Ill. died 1913. MRB 189, pp. 463-483; MRB 200, pp. 58-68, 75.

Opel, Henry
    Heirs of Cook Co., Ill. MRB 157, pp. 628-631.

O'Rourke, Patrick
    Will of St. Clair Co., Ill. MRB 163, pp. 261-265.

Osborn, Alanson
    Heirs of. MRB 143, p. 639.

Ott, John
    Heirs of, Marion Co., Ill. died 1914. MRB 189, pp. 484-485; MRB 193, pp. 92-97, 273-276.

Otto, August
    Will and estate of Macon Co., Ill. died 20 June 1927. MRB 234, pp. 532-534.

Owens, Wm. P.
    Heirs of. MRB 163, p. 359.

Page, Elizabeth
    Heirs of 1882. MRB 189, p. 164.

Page, John James
    Land no. 9845, 1840. MRB 215, p. 575.

Parish, H.C.
    Affadavit, MRB 157, p. 567; heirs of, MRB 193, p. 181.

Parker, Lemuel
    Heirs of. MRB 163, p. 382.

Parkinson, Leonard
    Heirs of, died 25 Feb. 1911 Denver Co., CO. MRB 189, pp. 541-542.

Parks, George
    Land no. 6966, 1839. MRB 236, p. 289.

## PEDIGREE CHART OF THE EDITOR

1. Helen COX Tregillis, b 8 May 1944 Shelby Co., IL
    m and div Harry Robert Tregillis
2. James Harvey COX, b 22 Nov 1919 Macon Co., IL, m 19 Sept 1942
3. Lena May STONEBURNER, b 13 Feb 1925 Shelby Co., IL, d 23 Oct. 1982
4. James Henderson COX, b 18 Sept 1883 Sullivan Co., TN, m 1910 Macon Co., IL, d 22 May 1958 Macon Co., IL
5. Emma May HAYES, b 17 April 1883 Perry Co., IN, d 27 Feb 1961 Macon Co, IL
6. Laurence A. STONEBURNER, b 8 July 1902 Shelby Co., IL, m 26 Feb 1924 Christian Co., IL, d 14 April 1965 Shelby Co., IL
7. Goldie A. SPRACKLIN, b 8 April 1904 Shelby Co., IL, d 3 April 1983 Christian Co., IL
8. James Harvey COX, b 4 Feb 1859 Washington Co., TN, m 1880 TN, d 2 March 1936 Sullivan Co., TN
9. Emmaline WORLEY, b 1853 Sullivan Co., TN, d June 1893 near Gainesville, TX
10. William HAYES, b 27 June 1821 Ross Co., OH, m 23 Nov 1871 Tippecanoe Co., IN, d 14 March 1901 Piatt Co., IL
11. Charlotte Emily KELLOGG, b 23 July 1842 Tippecanoe Co., IN, d 9 Oct 1915 Piatt Co., IL
12. Linzie O. STONEBURNER, b 2 March 1876 Morgan Co., OH, m 1900 Shelby Co., IL, d 3 Aug 1944 Shelby Co., IL
13. Ella A. MILLER, b 8 Oct 1883, d 4 July 1934 Shelby Co., IL
14. George E. SPRACKLIN, b 14 July 1881 Shelby Co., IL, m 26 March 1903 Shelby Co., IL, d 2 June 1964 MORGAN CO., IL
15. Grace Belle AUSTIN, b 5 Sept 1884 Howard Co., MO, d 1972 Champaign Co., IL
16. John H. COX, b 1818 TN, m 17 Feb 1839 Washington Co., TN, d aft Feb 1870 TN
17. Hannah Edna COPAS, b 1819 TN
18. Isaac WORLEY, b 1832 Sullivan Co., TN, m 1849 TN
19. Margaret Jane SPROLES, b 20 Jan 1833 Washington Co., VA, d 8 Feb 1885 Sullivan Co., TN
20. Samuel HAYES, b 5 July 1790 Baltimore Co., MD, m 20 Aug 1810 Brook Co., W VA, d 8/12 March 1857 Pike Co., OH
21. Elizabeth MEEK, b 11 Sept 1792 W VA, d 26 Feb 1857 Pike Co., OH
22. Seth Judd KELLOGG, b 27 May 1811 Montgomery Co., OH, m 10 March 1836 Tippecanoe Co., IN, d 16 Dec 1902 White Co., IN
23. Rebecca BLUE, b 6 May 1818 Hampshire Co., VA, d 19 May 1847 Tippecanoe Co., IN
24. John M STONEBURNER, b 31 Jan 1847 Morgan Co., OH, m 11 March 1869 Muskingum Co., OH, d 9 April 1930 Shelby Co., IL
25. Margaret MOHLER, b 1853 Muskingum Co., OH, d 1935 Shelby Co., IL
26. Benedict MILLER, b 1841 IN, m 9 June 1877 IN, d c 1917
27. Lucie SPOCKWELL
28. Marvin SPRACKLIN, b 1847 Hardin Co., OH, m 13 Oct 1870 Shelby Co., IL, d 1932 Shelby Co., IL
29. Mary Elizabeth DEAL, b 1855 VA, d 1933 Shelby Co., IL
30. Belfield Kirtley AUSTIN, b 10 Aug 1856 Madison Co., VA, m 28 Oct 1883 Howard Co., MO, d 15 March 1943 Shelby Co., IL

31. Gertrude Wilma RHODUS, b 13 Oct 1863, d 29 Feb 1899 Shelby Co., IL
32. John HULSE, b 1779/88 Berkley Co., VA, d c 1867 Sullivan Co., TN
33. Sarah COX, b 1779 Sullivan Co., TN, d aft 1870 TN
34. Thomas COPAS
35. Hannah Edna JOBE
36. Hendry WORLEY, b 1 April 1796 TN, d 26 Oct 1832 Sullivan Co., TN
37. Rachel RANGE, b 27 Oct 1800, d 18 Nov 1891 Sullivan Co., TN
38. Jonathon SPROLES, b 1804 VA
39. Jane ?, b 1810 VA, d 1888 Sullivan Co., TN
40. Joseph HAYES, b 1739 Newcastle Co., DE, m 1761, d 1789/90 Baltimore Co., MD
41. Sarah ?
42. Samuel MEEK, b 1757 VA, d bef 1838 Brooke Co., W VA
43. Polly WELLS, d bef 1838 Brooke Co., W VA
44. Ethol KELLOGG, b 27 Oct 1781 Winsted, CT, m 22 Aug 1805 Montgomery Co., OH, d 20 Aug 1858 Tippecanoe Co., IN
45. Charlotte MUNGER, b 3 Oct 1783 Guilford, CT, d 2 Oct 1846 Tippecanoe Co., IN
46. Isaac BLUE, b 9 Jan 1785 Berkley Co., VA, m 1810
47. Jane BLUE
48. Robert STONEBURNER, b 3 Sept 1819 Morgan Co., OH, m 1842, d 4 Aug 1898 Morgan Co., OH
49. Margaret LANDERMAN, b 1815 PA
50. Adam MOHLER, b 1828 Muskingum Co., OH, m 1851
51. Caroline DOZIER, b 1830 Muskingum Co., OH
52. Jacob MILLER, b 1796, m 1818
53. Elizabeth ?, b 1818
56. George SPRACKLIN, 7 Feb 1814 Somerset Co., ENG, m 9 April 1840 Knox Co., OH, d 3 June 1902 Shelby Co., IL
57. Arloa Turner MINOR, b 1824 OH, d 11 July 1892 Shelby Co., IL
58. Elias DEAL, b 3 July 1820 Rappahanock Co., VA, m 1850, d 22 Jan 1910 Shelby Co., IL
59. Frances Elizabeth BROYLES, b 1834 Madison Co., VA, d 1866 Shelby Co., IL
60. John H. AUSTIN, b 1824 Madison Co., VA, m 1854/55, d 1863 Henry Co., MO
61. Louisa J. BROYLES, b 6 Feb 1837 Madison Co., VA, d 6 Feb 1889 Shelby Co., IL
64. William HULSE, b 1753, d aft 1833 Sullivan Co., TN
66. John COX, b 1755, d 1837 Sullivan Co., TN
68. William COPAS, b 1744, d aft 1833 Sullivan Co., TN
72. John WORLEY, b 1772 VA
73. Nancy HENDRY
74. Peter RANGE, b 1749, d 1817 Washington Co., TN
75. Elizabeth HIERONYMUS
80. Jonathon HAYES, b 1685, d 1770
81. Elizabeth ELLIOTT, b 1690, d 1761
84. Robert MEEK, b 1732, d 1838
85. Elizabeth ALEXANDER
88. Seth KELLOGG, b 8 Feb 1740 Norwalk, CT, m 6 Sept 1761 Danbury, CT, d 26 June 1819 Montgomery Co., OH

89. Eunice JUDD, b 11 Feb 1733 CT, d aft June 1819 Montgomery Co., OH
90. Jonathon MUNGER, b 30 Nov 1755 Guilford, CT, m 9 Oct 1783 CT, d 9 Nov 1837 Montgomery Co., OH
91. Elizabeth LAWRENCE, b 20 April 1760 Norfolk, CT, d 6 June 1830 Montgomery Co., OH
92. Micheal BLUE, b 1742 Berkley Co., VA, d 25 Aug 1821 Fayette Co., OH
93. Mary HERRIOTT, b 1757 VA, d 6 March 1826 Fayette Co., OH
96. John Peter STONEBURNER, b 16 Jan 1790 Loudoun Co., VA, m 1810, d 17 April 1855 Morgan Co., OH
97. Catherine VINCEL, b 19 Sept 1785, d 10 Oct 1865 Morgan Co., OH
100. Peter MOHLER, b 1791
101. Hannah ?, b 1791
102. John DOZIER, b 1810 OH
103. Margaret ?
104. Edward MILLER, b 1753, m 1787, d 1836
105. Rebecca COLVILLE, b 1771
112. Peter SPRACKLIN, 20 Dec 1774 Co Somerset, ENG, m 11 Aug 1794 Co Somerset, ENG, d 26 Oct 1845 Hardin Co., OH
113. Elizabeth ANDREWS, b 6 June 1771 Co Somerset, ENG, d 13 Nov 1860 Hardin Co., OH
118. Garriott K. BROYLES, b 1810 Madison Co., VA, m 22 Dec 1831 Madison Co., VA, d 28 April 1895 Shelby Co., IL
119. Eunice V. WAYMAN, b 1815 VA, d 6 Feb 1889 Shelby Co., IL
120. Willis AUSTIN, b 1796 Albemarle Co., VA, m 1824, d aft 1850 VA or MO
121. Jane MALONE, b 1805 VA
122. Garriott K. BROYLES, b 1810 Madison Co., VA, m 22 Dec 1831 Madison Co., VA, d 28 April 1895 Shelby C., IL
123. Eunice V. WAYMAN, b 1815 VA, d 6 Feb 1889 Shelby Co., IL
148. Noah RANGE, b 1713
149. Elizabeth COONS
160. Jonathon HAYES, b England
168. John MEEK, b 1687, d 1760
176. Deacon John KELLOGG, b 1701 Norwalk, CT, m 1 March 1729/30, d 17 April 1740 Norwalk, CT
177. Ann COLEY, b 1 Aug 1709 Fairfield, CT, d aft 1740
178. William JUDD, m 14 March 1723 CT, d 1 Sept 1741 Farmington, CT
179. Ruth LEE, b 14 June 1703 Farmington, CT
180. Reuben MUNGER, b 28 March 1725 Guilford, CT, m 18 June 1748, d 1808 Norwalk, CT
181. Elizabeth DUDLEY, b 24 Dec 1727 Norfolk, CT
182. Samuel LAWRENCE      183. Elizabeth BIGELOW
184. John BLUE        185. Margaret KEYSER
192. Peter STONEBURNER        193. Susanna COMPHER
204. George DOZIER     205. Mary ?
208. Jacob MILLER
210. Andrew COLVILLE    211. Mary CRAIG
236. Moses BROYLES   237. Susan BROYLES
240. Henry AUSTIN    241. Nancy WATT
244. Moses BROYLES   245. Susan BROYLES
ADDITIONAL LINEAGE AVAILABLE

## PAID ADVERTISING

Seeking information and/or descendants of the following who lived in Pope County, IL in 1870: HOLT, Wesley, Eliza, Mary, Nancy. HOLT, Allen, Mary, Martha, Matilda, William. HARROLD/HARRELL, Isaac, Susan, George, Charlotte, Parthenia. HARRELL, Robert, Nancy, Sarah, Catherine, Kansas, David, Robert, Vina.
    Alice Blevins, 3235 Jay St., Wheat Ridge, CO 80033

------------

NOTE: THIS PERIODICAL is being indexed in the <u>Genealogical Periodical Index</u>. Individuals who find particular entries of interest need only address the editor for information in past issues. Query, first, with SASE for number of pages and cost of 50 cents per page.

------------

### SEARCHING ILLINOIS ANCESTORS
County, Surname, Person Searching

LIVINGSTON: Geer, Patterson, Slater, Mollison, Hill
    Ginger M. August, 32 Stetson Way, Princeton, NJ 08540
MASON: Rogers-Rodgers-Roggers, Putt; MACOUPIN: Rogers, Hensley
    Martha A. W. White, Rte 5, Box 193, Fayette, AL 35555
ROCK ISLAND, HENRY, TAZEWELL, MCCLEAN, PEORIA, KANKAKEE, JERSEY, MACOUPIN, ST CLAIR, MORGAN, FAYETTE, COLES, LASALLE: Surnames not given
    Lucia R. Collins, 7026 Valley Greens Cir. No. 16, Carmel, CA 93923
ADAMS, HANCOCK, HENDERSON: Surnames not given
    Maxine Gleason Hertrick, 2417-185h St., Santa Monica, CA 90405
CLARK: Blankenbaker
    Donna T. Bowen, P.O. Box 2092, Grass Valley, CA 95945
COUNTY UNKNOWN: Puckett, Sanders
    Berta Green, Rte 1, Texico, IL 62889
HENDERSON, KNOX: Hurd
    Jean Hurd Jones, 406 E. Whaley - B, Longview, TX 75601
KANKAKEE: Emmott
    Marilyn E. Benda, 5215 S. Parkside Ave., Chicago, IL 60638
GALLATIN: Hubbs
    Pat Graham, 3159 So. 3075 E, Salt Lake City, UT 84109
COUNTY NOT GIVEN: Bolen, Boyd, Hatchet, Dodson, Fagala, Shirley, Kington, Carlton
    Betty Lou Kington, 4723 N. Edgewood Drive, Peoria, IL 61615

------------

### ADVERTISING RATES
1 col x 2 "...$5 one time; 1/4 page....$10 one time; half page...$17.50 one time; full page...$35 one time. Deadlines: Feb. 21, April 21, June 20, Aug. 22 and Oct. 24. Black on white only! 8 x 11 1/2 format. FULL PAYMENT REQUIRED WITH COPY.

------------

Check with the editor for other publications.

INDEX TO MAY JUNE 1987
VOLUME III NUMBER 4

| | | | |
|---|---|---|---|
| Adams, 85,90 | Adison, 90 | Adkins, 86 | Afflack, 91 |
| Akin, 90 | Albright, 92 | Aldridge, 91 | Alexander 96 |
| Alford, 85 | Allen, 85,86 | Allgood, 86 | Allison, 83,85 |
| Ammons, 86 | Andeson, 92 | Anderson, 83,85,92 | Andrews, 85,97 |
| Aperson, 86 | Apple, 91 | Armstrong, 85,86,92 | Ashley, 86 |
| Augur, 83 | Austin, 85,95,96,97 | | Baird, 85 |
| Baker, 86,88,90 | Bakman, 83 | Balch, 85,92 | Baldridge, 92 |
| Baldwin, 83,86 | Balliett, 84 | Bancroft, 83 | Bankson, 84 |
| Bannford, 91 | Barber, 92 | Barker, 85,86 | Barketlow, 92 |
| Barrick, 86 | Baugh, 90,91 | Bauglive, 86 | Baumgard, 83 |
| Bazier, 85 | Beancham, 85 | Beaty, 83 | Beggs, 92 |
| Bell, 88 | Bennett, 86 | Benson, 92 | Benton, 83 |
| Biby, 85 | Bigelow, 97 | Bigod, 85 | Bilderback, 91 |
| Billings, 83 | Bird, 91 | Black, 85 | Blakney, 86 |
| Blankenbaker, 98 | Blocher, 90 | Blocksom, 86 | Blosum, 86 |
| Blue, 95,96,97 | Blythe, 91 | Bolen, 98 | Boswell, 91 |
| Bowham, 86 | Bowles, 83 | Boyd, 85,98 | Bradley, 88 |
| Braken, 83 | Bray, 83 | Breese, 91 | Brewster, 85 |
| Brinkley, 92 | Brockway, 84,88 | | Brooks, 86,90,92 |
| Brown, 88,85,90,92 | | Broyles, 96,97 | Brush, 91 |
| Bryant, 88 | Budlong, 91 | | |
| Bug, 91 | Bugg, 84 | | |
| Bullett, 85 | Bullock, 91 | | |
| Bumham, 85 | Bundell, 85 | | |
| Burch, 86 | Burman, 92 | | |
| Burr, 88 | Burrow, 91 | | |
| Burt, 88 | Burton, 90 | | |
| Bush, 88 | Bylew, 84 | | |
| Byrd, 86 | Caldwell, 85,88 | | |
| Callaway, 88 | Camerer, 88 | | |
| Camiron, 88 | Campbell, 88,92 | | |
| Camper, 86 | Capps, 86 | | |
| Carlton, 98 | Carry, 88 | | |
| Carswell, 92 | Carver, 85,92 | | |
| Cary, 91 | Casey, 90 | | |
| Cash, 88 | Casper, 92 | | |
| Cassell, 88 | Cassmon, 88 | | |
| Castles, 90 | Cates, 86 | | |
| Chapman, 92 | Chare, 90 | | |
| Chastain, 84 | Childers, 88 | | |
| Childress, 88 | Chowney, 86 | | |
| Churchman, 84 | Cisna, 86 | | |
| Claggett, 90 | Clam, 86 | | |
| Clapp, 86 | Clark, 83,88,90 | | |
| Clary, 86 | Clayett, 90 | | |
| Cloud, 83 | Cogshell, 86 | | |
| Cole, 85 | Coley, 97 | | |
| Collins, 88 | Collville, 92 | | |

**PROFESSIONAL GENEALOGICAL RESEARCH**

At the Salt Lake City Genealogical library. Seven day service on smaller projects, two to four weeks on major research efforts. For free brochure send long self addressed stamped envelope to:

**DAVID S. BARSS**

Attn: 132 • P.O. Box 174
North Salt Lake, UT 84054

| | | | |
|---|---|---|---|
| Colville, 97 | Compher, 97 | Comstock, 88 | Connelly, 85,88 |
| Conner, 86,88 | Conoway, 92 | Cook, 88 | Coone, 86 |
| Coons, 88,97 | Cooper, 85 | Copas, 95,96 | Cope, 92 |
| Corgan, 90 | Cotner, 92 | Cox, 95,96 | Craig, 85,88,92.,97 |
| Craine, 92 | Creeger, 84 | Crise, 92 | Crocker, 84 |
| Crouch, 91 | Crow, 88 | Crown, 84 | Crumpton, 83 |
| Crusan, 86 | Culley, 91 | Cullom, 85 | Cumming, 91 |
| Cummins, 88 | Currie, 84 | Curry, 88,91 | Curtis, 88 |
| Cushman, 86 | Cushner, 86 | Cusick, 88 | Cutright, 86 |
| Cutts, 91 | Daughtery, 83 | Davidson, 85 | Davis, 83,84,90,91,92 |
| Dawks, 86 | Daws, 91 | Deal, 95,96 | Deardorff, 92 |
| Decker, 85 | Demars, 84 | Denning, 91 | Dickinson, 90 |
| Dickison, 90 | Dickson, 85,86 | Dinwiddle, 88 | Doak, 84 |
| Dobson, 92 | Dodson, 98 | Donnelly, 83 | Dow, 91 |
| Dozier, 96,97 | Draper, 85 | Driden, 90 | Dryden, 86 |
| Dunbar, 86 | Duncan, 85,86,91 | Dunn, 85 | Durbin, 83,84 |
| Dures, 86 | Durham, 86 | Durnall, 88 | Duty, 86 |
| Earman, 86 | Eary, 85 | Eaton, 92 | Eddington, 85 |
| Eddy, 90,91 | Edwards, 88 | Elder, 91 | Ellington, 86 |
| Elliott, 92,96 | Ellis, 84,85 | Elmore, 91 | Emmott, 98 |
| Ennis, 85 | Eudus, 85 | Evartt, 86 | Ewing, 86 |
| Eyers, 91 | Fagala, 98 | Fancher, 86 | Faris, 85 |
| Ferguson, 86 | Ferries, 92 | Flesner, 91 | Fonlain, 83 |
| Ford, 85 | Forker, 83 | Forster, 88 | Fowler, 86 |
| Franklin, 92 | Freeman, 92 | Frost, 86 | Fruit, 91 |
| Fulkerson, 91 | Funk, 86 | Funderburk, 84 | Gaines, 84 |
| Gamble, 92 | Garner, 90,92 | Garrett, 88 | Garrott, 85 |
| Geer, 98 | George, 83 | Giddis, 86 | Gifford, 85 |
| Gilbert, 83 | Gilham, 85 | Gill, 91 | Gillespie, 92 |
| Gillman, 88 | Gillmore, 86 | Glass, 84 | Goodman, 88 |
| Goodwier, 86 | Gordon, 83,88 | Gore, 84 | Graham, 86,91 |
| Gray, 86 | Green, 84,92 | Griffith, 86 | Gritton, 86 |
| Gurley, 92 | Guthrie, 92 | Halbatt, 86 | Hale, 91,92 |
| Hamilton, 92 | Hamp, 86 | Hams, 91 | Handy, 85 |
| Hannah, 86 | Hanon, 83 | Hardin, 91 | Hare, 85 |
| Harlow, 92 | Harper, 91 | Harrell, 98 | Harrison, 84,90 |
| Hasket, 85 | Hatcher, 92 | Hatchet, 98 | Haughn, 86 |
| Hawkins, 90,92 | Hawley, 86 | Hayes, 95,96,97 | Hayrex, 83 |
| Heaps, 91 | Helsoe, 84 | Henperman, 90 | Henderson, 92 |
| Hendly, 85 | Hendry, 96 | Henry, 91 | Hensley, 86,98 |
| Herner, 85 | Herriott, 97 | Hesser, 83 | Hicklin, 85 |
| Hieronymus, 96 | Hill, 83,91,98 | Hillebart, 85 | Hincheliff, 90 |
| Hinsley, 84 | Hodgeman, 85 | Hoffman, 88,91 | Holden, 88 |
| Holland, 84 | Holt, 98 | Hood, 91,92 | Hooks, 91 |
| Hoots, 85 | Hope, 92 | Hoskins, 85 | How, 85 |
| Howell, 91 | Hubbs, 98 | Huckings, 92 | Hudlow, 91 |
| Hughes, 83,86 | Hughey, 92 | Hull, 83 | Hullambeck, 85 |
| Hulse, 96 | Hunter, 84,88 | Hurd, 98 | Hutchason, 85 |
| Hutchinson, 83 | Hutton, 86 | Ingram, 88 | Ingrum, 85 |
| Jackson, 92 | Jacobs, 85 | Janes, 92 | Jeffries, 86 |
| Jenkins, 85,91 | Jennings, 91 | Jobe, 96 | Johnson, 85,86,91,92 |

| | | |
|---|---|---|
| Johnston, 91 | Jones, 85,88,91,92 | Judd, 97 |
| Kalb, 86 | Keiffer, 90 | Kellar, 92 | Kellogg, 85,95,96,97 |
| Kelly, 86 | Kelsey, 86 | Kemerer, 84 | Kemper, 85,86 |
| Kennedy, 86,91 | Keyes, 92 | Keyser, 97 | Kidwell, 85,88 |
| Killiam, 85 | Kimball, 91 | Kimbrough, 88 | Kimmell, 91,92 |
| King, 91 | Kington, 98 | Kinney, 83 | Kirkpatrick, 86,90,92 |
| Kro?, 92 | Lackey, 83 | Laferty, 92 | Laflan, 84 |
| Lakin, 84 | Lamb, 84 | Lamberd, 84 | Lambert, 84 |
| Lamerial, 83 | Lancaster, 83 | Land, 85,86 | Landerman, 96 |
| Langley, 83,84 | Lard, 84,86 | Large, 84 | Larimore, 83 |
| Larkham, 83 | Larnent, 84 | Larpt, 84 | Larue, 86 |
| Larvis, 91 | Latner, 85 | Laughlin, 83 | Law, 84 |
| Lawrence, 84,88,97 | | Lawton, 84 | Leach, 84 |
| Leachman, 83 | Leathershoes, 83 | Lee, 83,84,85,86,91,92,97 | |
| Lehman, 84 | Leigh, 83,84 | Lells, 84 | Lemon, 83,84 |
| Lemrick, 91 | Leviers, 90 | Lewis, 84,91,92 | Libbey, 84 |
| Lights, 83 | Lilley, 84 | Lillis, 83 | Linder, 85,86 |
| Lindley, 85,92 | Linenbaugh, 86 | Lingle, 92 | Linn, 84 |
| Littick, 84 | Littlefield, 88 | Loarets, 84 | Locker, 84 |
| Lockwood, 84 | Logan, 84 | Logsdon, 83,84 | Loid, 83 |
| Loit, 84 | Lombard, 84 | Lonet, 84 | Long, 83,84 |
| Longstreet, 84 | Lorton, 84 | Low, 85 | Lowery, 85 |
| Lucas, 83 | Luckey, 84 | Ludwick, 84 | Lurring, 84 |
| Lusk, 83 | Lutgenhizer, 84 | Lycon, 85 | Lynch, 92 |
| Lyons, 84 | Lype, 92 | Lyttell, 91 | Lyttle, 83 |
| McAvoy, 85 | McBath, 88 | McClernand, 90 | M'Clintock, 90 |
| McCool, 83 | McCorkle, 88 | M'Cowen, 85 | McCravens, 83 |
| McCullough, 91 | McDonald, 88,92 | McDowal, 92 | McElwain, 90 |
| M'Gillipin, 85 | McGinnis, 92 | McGlasson, 92 | McHotton, 84 |
| McIntosh, 90,92 | Madden, 92 | Maddock, 88 | Madison, 85 |
| Madonal, 86 | Malone, 97 | Manville, 90 | Marion, 86 |
| Marsh, 91 | Marshall, 86 | Martin, 85,88,90,91 | Massey, 83 |
| Matson, 88 | Mattews, 85 | Mattey, 88 | Meads, 83 |
| Meek, 95,96,87 | Megahan, 85 | Melvin, 86 | Menard, 91 |
| Merchant, 88 | Merrell, 85 | Merritt, 91 | Metten, 92 |
| Middleton, 83 | Miles Magree, 86 | Miller, 83,85,88,91,92,95 | |
| Milligan, 92 | Miner, 85,96 | Mitchell, 86,90 | Mock, 88 |
| Mohler, 95,96 | Moland, 92 | Mollison, 98 | Monroe, 86,91 |
| Montgomery, 90 | Moofort, 86 | Moore, 85,86 | Moores, 88 |
| Morris, 84,90 | Morrison, 90 | Mose, 93 | Mounts, 85 |
| Mouser, 86 | Mowrey, 92 | Moyer, 92,93 | Munger, 93 |
| Munson, 93 | Murdock, 93 | Murphy, 83,88,93 | Myers, 93 |
| Myres, 85 | Nance, 93 | Naron, 88 | Neal, 91 |
| Needham, 93 | Neely, 92 | Nees, 86 | Neff, 93 |
| Nehring, 93 | Neighbor, 93 | Neil, 93 | Newlon, 88 |
| Newman, 94 | Newport, 85 | Nichols, 94 | Niel, 92 |
| Nieman, 94 | Night, 90 | Niles, 94 | Noecker, 94 |
| Noland, 94 | North, 90 | O'Brien, 94 | Ogle, 88 |
| O'Harra, 92 | O'Harrow, 91 | Ohler, 94 | Oliver, 94 |
| Olson, 94 | Opel, 94 | O'Rourke, 94 | Osborn, 94 |
| Osburne, 92 | Ott, 94 | Otto, 94 | Ourer, 85 |

Overstreet, 91   Owens, 92,94     Owings, 86       Pace, 90
Page, 94         Para, 90         Parish, 94       Parker, 86,94
Parkhurst, 83    Parkinson, 91,94 Parks, 94        Patridge, 85
Patterson, 86,91,98  Payne, 83    Peacock, 90      Pearce, 92
Peevy, 85        Penninger, 92    Pennroyer, 92    Penroe, 92
Piatt, 83,92     Piper, 91        Poe, 92          Poulson, 86
Poulter, 88      Prentice, 86     Prichard, 86     Prince, 84
Publes, 86       Puckett, 98      Pugh, 86         Pumea, 84
Purcell, 88      Pyle, 92         Raddle, 91       Radford, 83
Rahn, 91         Ralls, 83        Randall, 92      Raney, 88
Range, 96,97     Rarar, 85        Rawlings, 85     Rawls, 83
Rawly, 85        Ray, 88          Redmon, 88       Reeves, 92
Reynolds, 92     Rhodes, 83       Rhodus, 96       Rice, 84
Richards, 91     Richardson, 85   Ricks, 84        Ridgway, 90
Ridlen, 84       Riley, 86        Roberts, 86,88,90  Robinson, 90,91
Rogers, 86,98    Rolland, 86      Rolson, 86       Romine, 90
Romnius, 90      Ross, 85         Rucker, 91       Ruddick, 90
Ruffney, 86      Rundell, 85      Runnels, 85      Russell, 86
Rutherford, 91   Rutlege, 91      Ryan, 83         Sadler, 91
Sams, 85,92      Sanders, 86,98   Sconce, 85       Scott, 83
Scraunir, 90     Seymour, 92      Sexton, 84       Shane, 85
Shaw, 86         Sheldon, 90      Shepler, 85      Shetler, 85
Shields, 83,88   Shipp, 86        Shirley, 98      Shivers, 84
Shores, 86       Shurdon, 84      Shuttle, 84      Simpson, 86
Sitter, 92       Slater, 98       Sloe, 90         Sloo, 90
Small, 83        Smith, 86,92     Snyder, 83       Spence, 92
Spindle, 84      Spockwell, 95    Spracklin, 95,96,97  Sprights, 83
Springer, 88     Sproles, 95      Stapp, 91        Stark, 85
Steel, 92        Stephens, 84     Stewart, 85,86   Stickney, 91
Stockton, 83     Stone, 91        Stoneburner, 95,96,97
Stoops, 91       Story, 91        Stotts, 88       Strickland, 83
Sullivan, 83     Sulser, 90       Swearingen, 91   Sweet, 91
Synder, 91       Taylor, 91       Teel, 90         Tegg, 92
Tetrick, 91      Thayer, 86       Thompson, 86,88,91,92
Tiner, 90        Tipton, 86       Tregillis, 95    Trew, 85
Trigg, 86        Troubell, 86     True, 91         Tucker, 85
Tweedy, 88       Tyatt, 84        Vance, 86        Vandeour, 83
Vaughn, 86       Veach, 85        Vice, 84         Viex, 83
Vincel, 97       Wade, 85,90      Wadic, 83        Walden, 85
Walker, 85,86,90,91,92            Wall, 86         Wallace, 91
Waltrip, 86      Wankiesa, 86     Warnick, 83      Warralls, 92
Washburn, 92     Watson, 85       Watts, 97        Wayman, 97
Wayne, 88        Wear, 88         Webb, 83         Welborn, 91
Wellington, 90   Wells, 92,96     West, 88         Westfall, 84
Wheeler, 85      Whipple, 90      Whitehead, 85    Whitney, 92
Whitstone, 86    Wilbanks, 91     Wilkins, 85      Willard, 83,85
William, 92      Williams, 86,88,91,92             Wilson, 84,85,86,91
Wimbermolen, 92  Winkler, 86      Wishard, 85      Wittleman, 92
Wood, 83,91      Woodside, 92     Workman, 86      Worley, 95,96
Worth, 92        Worthy, 86       Wright, 86,92    Yantrey, 90
Yearean, 92      Zimmerman, 92

NEW PUBLICATION BY EDITOR SCHEDULED: <u>Runaway Notices and Certificates of Freedom Found in Illinois Sources</u>.  Reserve your copy now for $20. After publication, $25. Address on cover page.

SEARCHIN ILLLINOIS ANCESTORS

VOLUME III NO. 5

July August 1987

INDEXED IN GENEALOGICAL PERIODICAL INDEX

Issued bi-monthly by Helen Cox Tregillis. Publication and advertising offices: Box 392, Shelbyville, IL 62565. Current single copy price, $2 plus 69 cents postage. Yearly subscription, $12. Send check or money order payable to: Helen Cox Tregillis, Box 392, Shelbyville, IL 62565. Surnames, articles appearing in publication are indexed in GENEALOGICAL PERIODICAL INDEX. Postage paid at Shelbyville, IL. Send address changes, queries, advertising to above address.

ISSN 0886 - 7763

PAYMENT MUST ACCOMPANY SUBSCRIPTION, QUERY AND ADVERTISING

NO BACK ISSUES AVAILABLE

FREE QUERY with county, surname only
$5 for maximum 50 word query
Check query section for format

## TABLE OF CONTENTS
## TO VOLUME III, NUMBER 5

| | |
|---|---|
| Book Reviews | 103 |
| Christian County, Ill. Marriages | 105 |
| Cumberland County, Ill. Newspaper Abst. | 106 |
| Edgar County, Ill. Delinquent Taxes, 1845, 46 | 107 |
| Fulton County, Ill. Genealogical Sources | 108 |
| Gallatin County, Ill. Genealogical Sources | 108 |
| Jackson County, Ill. Black Hawk War Unit | 111 |
| Lawrence County, Ill. Black Hawk War Unit | 110 |
| Macon County, Ill. Black Hawk War Unit | 111 |
| Moultrie County, Ill. Delinquent Taxes, 1849 | 109 |
| "   "   Delinquent Taxes, 1846 | 110 |
| Peoria County, Ill. Black Hawk War Unit | 109 |
| Putnam County, Ill. Genealogical Sources | 110 |
| Randolph County, Ill. Genealogical Sources | 111 |
| "   "   Black Hawk War Unit | 111 |
| Richland County, Ill. Genealogical Sources | 112 |
| Rock Island County, Ill. Genealogical Sources | 113 |
| Shelby County, Ill. Miscellaneous Records | 114 |
| SEARCHING ILLINOIS ANCESTORS | 103, 116 |

## SEARCHING ILLINOIS ANCESTORS
### QUERY, SURNAME, COUNTY, PERSON SEARCHING

McDONOUGH: Nicole, Perham; JoDAVIESS: Ludi, Brown
    David L. Cole, 1119 South Speed Street, Santa Maria, CA 93454
SHELBY: Piatt
    Roy Nichols, Box 30544, Columbus, OH 43230
MASON: Joseph Lockwood Hunt
    Dette Brymer, P.O.B. 2868, Harbor, OR 97415
DuPAGE, COOK: Lamb, Curphy
    Patricia Schuster, R 1, Box 46B, Livermore, IA 50558
COUNTY NOT GIVEN: Pearson, Ahlee, White
    Dr. Ian M. Johnston, 3246 Pepperhill Road, Lexington, KY 40502
ST CLAIR: Robert and Charles Keller; SANGAMON: Miles Scott;
MONTGOMERY: Louisa Zimmerman Scott
    Mrs. Marlowe J. Meyers, 1026 Kirkham, Glendale, MO 63122
MACON: Benjamin Shirk
    Greg Shirk, 315 W. Walnut St., Argos, IN 46501
COUNTY NOT GIVEN: Bush, Gould
    Barbara Bush, 202 Heritage Court, Mt. Pleasant, MI 48858
POPE, JOHNSON, MASSAC: surnames not given
    Janise Bader, 9060 Boygil, Starwood, MI 49346
KANKANKEE: Emmott
    Marilyn E. Benda, 5215 S. Parkside Ave., Chicago, IL 60638

------------

### Prairie Pioneers of Illinois
Volume I
Illinois State Genealogical Society, 1986

Pioneers Listed in the Volume: Contact the Society for more information at Box 157, Lincoln, IL 62656

    Acom, Thomas, Jr. Settled 1840 Morgan Co., Ill.
    Adams, John M. Settled 1844 Coles Co., Ill.
    Adams, Robert Stewart Sr. Settled 1837 Whiteside Co., Ill.
    Adrian, Evans Settled 1837 Lee Co., Ill.
    Ahlfield, Frederick Settled 1859 Edwards Co., Ill.
    Allen, George Settled 1845 McHenry Co., Ill.
    Allwardt, Christoph Settled 1879 Peoria Co., Ill.
    Ames, George Robinson Settled 1847 Bureau Co., Ill.
    Amundson, Erik Settled 1875 Cook Co., Ill.
    Amundson, Olava Settled 1870 Cook Co., Ill.
    Andersdotter, Johann Settled 1868 Rock Island Co., Ill.
    Anderson, Henry Clay Settled 1844 Coles Co., Ill.
    Anthony, Abraham Settled 1817 Bond Co., Ill.
    Armantrout, Phillip Settled 1831 Moultrie Co., Ill.
    Armstrong, Aaron Settled 1809 Madison Co., Ill.
    Armstrong, John II Settled 1836 Bond Co., Ill.
    Arnspiger, Stephen Settled 1835 Champaign Co., Ill.
    Atterbury, Melchizedek Settled 1835 Greene Co., Ill.
    Aurand, Henry Settled 1844 Stephenson Co., Ill.
    Axon, Elias Briant Settled 1822 Randolph Co., Ill.

Ayres, Ludlum B. Settled 1845 Lee Co., Ill.
Baccus, Enoch Settled 1820 Crawford Co., Ill.
Bader, Henry Settled 1847 Cumberland Co., Ill.
Bacon, Joseph S. Settled 1814 Whiteside Co., Ill.
Baer, Jacob Settled 1845 St. Clair Co., Ill.
Bain, Daniel Settled 1805 White Co., Ill.
Baker, James Alexander Settled 1839 Ogle Co., Ill.
Baker, Katherine Featherly Settled ca1850 Whiteside Co., Ill.
Baldridge, Joseph SEttled 1832 Marion Co., Ill.
Ball, James R. Settled 1849 DuPage Co., Ill.
AND MANY MORE NAMES THROUGH THE ALPHABET

FOR EACH individual listed in this volume, there is a brief modified family group sheet with descendants to submitter of information who obtained a certificate indicating ancestor was early pioneer to the state of Illinois. There are 1000 entries and an index is included to cross reference all the other surnames. EDITOR'S NOTE: Some places and dates do not seem to coincide with the geographaic chronology of the state of Illinois. For example, Shelbyville, Ill. did not exist in 1805, but was created in 1827. Check ILLINOIS PLACE NAMES by James N. Adams and William W. Keller, editors, published in 1968.

---

WAU-BUN: THE EARLY DAY IN THE NORTHWEST by Juliette A. Kinzie.

Recently reprinted by Hertiage Books, 3602 Maureen Lane, Suite 400, Bowie, MD 20715. (1855,1930) reprint, 395 pp., index, illus., paper, $20.00 T.

Juliette A. Kinzie was the wife of John H. Kinzie, a fur trader and sub-Indian Agent at Fort Winnebago, and an associate of Lewis Cass, the first Governor of Wisconsin. John H. Kinzie was the son of John Kinzie, one of the first white settlers of Chicago, andhad lived a wild frontier life throughout the Northwest Territory before marrying Juliette in 1830. She, on the other hand, was a well educated descendant of the Wolcott family of Connecticut.

The value of the present edition has been further enhanced by the addition of an every-name index.

---

SHELBY COUNTY BOOK, 1986 by Helen Cox Tregillis, Box 392, Shelbyville, Ill. 62565 Soft cover, indexed, $10.

This volume contains biographies submitted by individuals who have ancestors in the county given. The biographies contain several generations in some cases. The second part of the book contains family reunion writeups from the month of August 1937 from the local newspaper.

Check with the this editor for biographies and reunions contained therein by sending a SASE.

---

IF YOU HAVE an Illinois connected genealogical book that you would like to have reviewed, send it to:

The Editor, Searching Illinois Ancestors, Box 392, Shelbyville, IL 62565. Reviews will be published as soon as possible, and books will be donated to the Illinois State Historical Library. Be sure to include name, place and price of book with copy.

Christian County, Illinois
Early Marriages, Index from Book I 1839-1866

Lambert, Xavier and Philamine Prince, page 188
Logan, Samuel S. and Elmira W. Conner, page 188
Long, Thomas W. and Harriet Logan, page 188
Lamond, Phileas C. and Adeline Percments, page 190
Long, Martin V. and Martha J. Robertson, page 191
Lewis, Joseph D. and Emily C. Harris, page 192
Lillard, William B. and Betty George, page 192
Lemanon, Nathaniel M. and Mary J. Hum, page 195
Langley, Wm. F. and Caroline Brents, page 195
Lagarlan, Wm. S.F. and Isabell Moore, page 198
Ludwick, Levi S. and Mary E. Hunt, page 198
Lambird, James K. and Eliza A. Springer, page 199
Lacharite, David and Elenore Lambert, page 200
Little, James W. and Mary E. Dalley, page 203
Leach, Charles and Adelia Brents, page 204
Logan, ? and Sarah S. Black, page 208
Lancaster, Wm. H. D. and Ann Nation, page 209
Langley, T.J. and Mary M. Allers, page 214
Langley, Alfred C. and Cordelia P. Thompson, page 214
Landers, William and Nancy J. Offidd, page 216
Levanture, Joseph and Mary Duchni, page 218
Logsdon, ? and ? Durbin, page ?
Layman, Jacob and Elizabeth J. Hayes, page 224
Libbey, Ivroy H. and Amanda F. Jernigan, page 236
Lavigne, Noath and I. Turgeon, page 232
Liberman, John A. and Logsdon, James M. see "D"
Martin, Meredith and Susan Harvey, page 1
McCrary, William Y. and Ann Simon, page 5
McKinzie, Samuel and Martha Peters, page 5
Moore, William S. and Nancy A. Locker, page 9
Myer, Fredrick and Elizabeth Leachman, page 10
Mathews, James K. and Nancy Young, page 11
Murphey, William and Louisa A. Crosthwait, page 11
Masterson, James and Margaret Copenbarger, page 14
Moore, John W. and Elizabeth Wigger, page 14
Morton, William and Margaret W. Morris, page 19
Meads, Thomas and Margaret Durbin, page 20
Moore, William and Susan A. Stokes, page 20
Maxwell, Jacob and Sarah Porter, page 21
Macy, Jeptha and Emma Ann Sharrock, page 22
Morgan, John and Lucinda Allen, page 25
Myers, Sennett and Pantine Hanon, page 30
Milligan, Wm. F. and Eliza Jane Keizer, page 30
Miller, Levi and Sarah Bearden, page 30
McCarry, William Y. and Teressa Hanon, page 31
Mills, Gibson and Margaret Dyson, page 32
Murphy, George T. and Margaret E. Gessner, page 34
Maxedy, John and Rebecca Bundy, page 36

McKenzie, John and Charity Davis, page 37
Melugen, James and Nancy Clark, page 38
Martin, Moses and Mary Jane Crull, page 39
Martin, Eli and Elizabeth Manary, page 39
Mathews, Aaron V. and Sarah Sharp, page 43
McCay, William and Delila I. Sargeant, page 44
McKenzie, John and Nancy Durbin, page 45
Munhum, John and Matilda Whitteman, page 47
Miller, Martin and Mary Hayward, page 50
Morell, Jesse A. and Mary Ann Stephens, page 52
Minnis, Thomas J. and Aline B. Mason, page 53
Moore, John and Elizabeth DeCamp, page 54
Martin, Aaron H. and Lutitia Ann Giger, page 55
Mathew, Silas C. and Elizabeth N. Woods, page 5?
McKenzie, George and Nancy Verdin, page 59
McDonald, Henry C. and Mary A. Young, page 59
Morgan, James W. and Amanda M. Runyon, page 60
Myers, Sinnet and Jane Rabe, page 64
Mutterspaugh, John and Mary C. Olinger, page 65
Mathews, William R. and Nancy J. Wilson, page 71
May, Albert N. and Ann Eliza Smith, page 72
Miller, Francis M. and Rebecca M. Powers, page 73
Mathew, John M. and Mary Ann Scott, page 74
Madison, William H. and Nancy Iler, page 75
McKenzie, Eli and Eliza A. Honald, page 77
McColwin, Alexander and Laura A. Slinker, page 77
Miller, George W. and Mary E. Chick, page 77
Melugin, Thomas and Joanna Smith, page 79
Morrison, James C. and Elizabeth H. Young, page 79
Meads, Elijah and Margaret Durbin, page 83
Menary, Jesse and Susan George, page 85
Morgan, Levi S. and Sarah J. Reed, page 85
Monroe, William J. and Rachael Hawk, page 88
Mathews, Martin W. and Susan Collenburger, page 89
Marvin, John L. and Marinda K. Hardey, page 90
Mull, Henry L. and Mary Hunter, page 91
McDowell, William and Nancy J. Wadkins, page 91
McDonald, Hiram M. and Mary E. Richardson, page 91
Morganthall, Jacob and Harriet Laneghe, page 95
Murphey, John and Harriet W. Danner, page 95
Mathews, Elijah H. and Hannah M. Lane, page 99
Maxwell, Jacob and Evaline S. Funk, page 97

---

Cumberland County, Illinois
Newspaper Abstracts
Cumberland Democrat, volume 3, Majority Point
6 Jan. 1870
    Circuit Court, May term 1871
    Fanny Shores vs. Bishop A. Shores and Benjamin Olmstead, Injunction and divorce
    Administrators Sale: To sell on 13th day of Feb. 1871, dower

interest of Kisiah Fletcher, late widow of Carroll Kayhoe, deceased. NE NW quarter section 10 T 10 N R 8 E. George Thornton, administrator, Sept. Term Circuit Court 1870.

Sheriffs Sale: Leonidus L. Logan vs. John Edwards, in favor of Logan to sell property, Edward Baumgardner, sheriff.

Petition for Dower: Malinda Radley vs. John S. Radley and Daniel A. Radley, May court term 1870. Daniel A. Radley, a non-resident of state/ also filed at same time foreclosure of mortgage by Malinda Radley vs. same individuals.

Petition to sell real estate: January term of Cumberland Co., Ill. Jan. 1871. Benjamin Aleshire, administrator of estate of William Sanders, deceased, vs. Sally Sanders, Alves Sanders, Susan Dudley, Elizabeth McKinney, Polly Chews, Richard Chew, Wiley Sanders Jr., Martha Warner, Franklin Warner, John D. Sanders, Mason Sanders, Dikases Holmes?, Susan Elder, Martin Holmes, Nancy Holmes, John Underwood and Thompson Allen. Filed 10 Dec. 1870.

Administrators notice dated 23 Dec. 1870: Maron R. Lee, administrator of estate of Vincent Scott, deceased of Cumberland Co., Ill.

January 20, 1870

Petition to sell land to pay debts/dated 13th Jan. 1871/March term. Clinton Swickard, administrator of estate of Philander Parr, deceased vs. Lucretia Parr, James L. Parr, Philander Parr, Mary Parr and Moses L. Parr.

Petition to sell land to pay debts. Leonidas L. Logan, administrator of estate of James Swift, deceased, vs. John Gilliham and unknown heirs of James Swift, deceased.

Executors notice: W. Barrett, executor for estate of Ellen Kelly, deceased, late of Cumberland Co., Ill. dated 12 Jan. 1871.

Administrators notice: Wm. R. Hubbard, administrator for estate of Rachel Hubbard, deceased, late of Cumberland Co., Ill. dated 12 Jan. 1871.

---

Edgar County, Illinois
Delinquent Taxes for years 1845-46
The Illinois Globe, Charleston, Il. Saturday, Sept. 5, 1846
Newspaper Microfilm, Illinois State Historical Library

G.M. Shinn, Absalom Davis' heirs, William Edwards, Isaac Esrey, Wm. H. Blanfor, John Welsh, Rachel Cahall, ? Hampton, Jonathon Moore, G. Jourdan, William Hamas, William Wallace, Sarah Buchanan, Shield's heirs, J.B. Madison, Alexander Love, William Love, Lewis West's heirs, J.H. Cash, Owen's heirs, E. Parker, Allen Martin, John Tade, Maria Shoaff, George Whitaker, Liberty Wilson, Robert Partridge, John McNulty, J.A. Kimbrough's heirs, Josiah Wollard, D.W. Starkes Jr., Tandy B. Brown, Abraham Smith, Jesse Ogle, Patrick Garmon, Joshua Sigemore, Thomas Meyers, Reuben McDaniels, Eliza Callaway, Edward's heirs, Francis Stump, Arthur Foster, John Mitchell, A.H. Whitley, J. Ellington, Jesse Earey, James Bodine, George S. Collum, William Clarke, H.J. Manning, Patrick Cowan, Thomas Day, William Redden, Nancy Curry, E. Hobbs, C.R. Ward, Nancy Collins, Abraham Connerey

Joseph Stephenson, Nathan Lane, H.S. Jonson, J.B.M. Call, R.E. Taylor, Everett Boyer, E. Parker, William Young, John Bowell's heirs, Elijah Fleming, Joel Moores, Asabel Davis, Robert Stewart, Harvey Mullens, Hutchison Braden, Isaac Rogers, J.Z.W. Eddy, Abraham Williams, William Clarke, Barret Smith, Daniel Treadwell, W.S. Dennison, William Ingles, J.W. Whipple, John C. Frame, Richard Frame, John Lindsay, Samuel Blevins, John F. Olmstead, J.W. Brown, Wayne's heirs, C. Reed, George Bord, Thomas Buitt, Samuel Mundall, Adreil Harsey, Isaiah Roberts, Wm. Jarvis's heirs, Lewis Wayne, Nathaniel Wayne, Thomas Craig's heirs, Isaac Lankford, Leonard Bell, John K. Doak, Scammon Cox, Robert Matson, John Rogers, James Tawdry, John Wilson, Price D. Johnson, John C. Bradley, Luther Conrey, Eli Porter, Samuel Craig, Thomas Craig, Wm. Jarvis's heirs. James Gordon, collector.

---

## Fulton County, Illinois
## Genealogical Sources, Help

County created 28 Jan. 1823 from parent county of Pike. Named for Robert Fulton. County seat at Lewistown, IL 61542 has vital, land records (county clerk, 309-547-3041) and court records (circuit clerk, 309-547-3041). Courthouse hours, Monday through Friday, 8 - 4. Illinois genealogical society that covers this county is Fulton County Historical and Genealogical Society, 45 N. Park Dr., Canton, IL 61520.

Fulton was known as the military tract. This area was set aside by the government so each soldier of the War of 1812 could have 160 acres and Lewiston was organized as a town in 1822.

### Sources
History of Fulton County, Sketches of its Cities. Chapman, 1879.
Portrait and Biog. Album of Fulton Co. Biog. Publ. Co. 1890.
Plat Book of Fulton Co. Ogle, 1895
History of Fulton Co. and Its Townships. Lewiston Republican, 1897.
Hist. Encycl. of Ill. & Hist. of Fulton Co. Jesse Heylin, 1908.
Standard Atlas of Fulton Co., Ill. Ogle, 1912.
This Fulton County. John Drury, 1954.
Morning Star Cemetery Inscriptions. Doris W. Welker.
Fulton Co. Hist. & Gen. Soc. 10 volumes of Cemetery Inscriptions.
Prairie Farmer Fulton County Directory. 1916.

Check with the society for other information, help.

---

## Gallatin County, Illinois
## Genealogical Sources, Help

County created 14 Sept. 1812 from parent county of Randolph. Named for Albert Gallatin. County seat at Shawneetown, IL 62984 has vital, land records (county clerk, 618-269-3025) and court records (circuit clerk, 618-269-3140). Courthouse hours, Monday through Friday, 8 - 4. Illinois genealogical society that covers this county is Genealogical Society of Southern Illinois, c/o John A. Logan College, Carterville, IL 62918.

The birth records begin with the year 1879; the deaths, 1880; the marriages, 1830; and court records, 1860. Remember that records were not mandatory until after the turn of the century for vital statistics. Census records begin with 1818. This county was known as the gateway to Illinois because of the ferry service on the river.

The Illinois State Archives, Springfield, Ill., has the following years of Gallatin county's board minutes: 1807-1829; 1840-1846; 1860-1941.

## Sources

History of Gallatin, Saline, etc. Cos. Goodspeed, 1887, rept. 1967.
Marriages in Gallatin Co. 1813-38. Mrs. L. Bender, 1938.
Early Gallatin County. 5 vols. L.R. Bender, 1936.
Gallatin Co., Gateway to Illinois. L. Lawler, 1968.
1850 Federal Census. Tri-City Genealogical Society, 1972.
1860 Federal Census. John V. Murphy, 1982.
Prairie Farmer's Reliable Dtry, 1920. Repr with index, 1982.

---

## Moultrie County, Illinois
### 1849 Delinquent Taxes
Charleston Courier, Newspaper Microfilm, Springfield, Ill.
Illinois State Historical Library

A list of lands and town lots, 1849: John Carmean, Jacob DeHaven, Charles DeHaven, Joseph Dehaven, Robert Rutherford, Mrs. Hamilton, Phelps & Boling, Coller and Others, Margaret Gittes. Joseph Thomason, collector of taxes. Saturday, Aug. 3, 1850 Courier.

### Cholera Note:
Charleston Courier, Saturday, Aug. 2, 1851

Cholera abatting: the following is a list of those who have been harried off from among us by this disease -- Stephen Nott, Mrs. Hawkins, Steth Kelley, John Merrifield, Mrs. Hart, F.J. Van Deren, Mrs. Perkins, Mrs. Goodrich, Mrs. Walker and her daughter, Mrs. Helen Miller, J.H. Harris, Christian Mock and Mrs. Gray.

The cholera is said to have broken out in the family of Mr. Furry, living in or near the Goosenest Prairie. Several members of that family it is said to have died.

Glasgow, Mo. is abandoned on account of the cholera -- the people have fled to the woods to avoid the disease.

---

## Capt. Abner Ead's Company
### Black Hawk War, Peoria County, Ill.
### Enrolled at Peoria 23 April 1832

Capt. Eads; First Lt. William A. Stewart; Second Lt. John W. Caldwell; Sgts. Aquilla Wren, Hiram M. Curry, Edwin S. Jones, John Hinkle; Coprs. William Wright, John Stringer, John Hawkins, Thomas Webb; Pvts. John E. Bristol, Harrison Brown, Jeremiah Cooper, John Clifton, Stpehen Carle, Joseph H. Conner, Jefferson Cox, John Cox, Ebenezer Clarke, Hiram Cleveland, Alexander Caldwell, James Doty, John D. Dodge, William Eads, Elias Love, Alvah Moffat, Jacob Moats, Sylvanus Moore, Harris Miner, John C. Owen, Joseph Phillis, George Reddick, David Ridgeway, Lucas Roof, David Ross, John Ross, Thomas B.

Reed, Simon Reed, Francis Sharp, Rice Smith, Jefferson Talifero, William D. Trial, Johnson T. Thurman, Henry Thomas, William L. Wood.

---

## Detachment of Capt. Barns' Company
## Black Hawk War, Lawrence Co., Ill.
## Enrolled May 5, 1832

Second Lt. Daniel Morris; Sgts. John L. Bass 1st, Tho. McDonald, 2d; Corp. Jas. Buchanan, 2d; Pvts. Archibald Berton, Richard Bass, James Crews, Joseph M. Christy, Samuel Dunlap, Bonapart Gallaher, James Gaddy, John Livingstone, Edward Moor, John Montgomery, Peyton Moaler, Benjamin McCleave, Daniel Organ, Thomas T. Lewis, James W. Pollard, Joshua Richards, Thomas I. Turner, John Turner, E.D.M. Turner, George W. Taylor, John Walden.

---

## Moultrie County, Illinois
## The Illinois Globe, Newspaper Microfilm
## Illinois State Historical Library
## Charleston, Ill. 4 Sept. 1847

Delinquent taxes for 1846: John Carmean, Frederick Dawse, Mathew Cay, Mathew J. Marsh, David Hood, E.D. Cleveland, Collier and Others, Thomas J. Blythe, Randolph Miller, James H. Northcutt, James H. Money, Benjamin Budlong, Arthur Scott, Henry S. Apple, Andrew Gamel, William Walker, John Walker, Isaac Walker, Rufus Pierce, George M. Handson, Thomas Curry, G.S. Pattison, Thomas Wiley, Philip Vadakin, John G. Purvis, Hugh M. Elder, John Goldsby, Heirs of D. Lord, Aurealius Richardson, Isaac Munson, Philip Apple.

---

## Putnam County, Illinois
## Genealogical Sources, Help

County created 13 Jan. 1825 from parent county of Fulton. Named for Gen. Isael Putnam. County seat at Hennepin, IL 61327 has vital, land records (county clerk, 815-925-7129) and court records (circuit clerk, 815-925-7016). Courthouse hours, Monday through Friday, 8 - 4:30.

County birth and death records begin with 1879; marriage and court records, 1831; circuit court, 1825, and census records, 1830. Reemember that vital statistics were not mandatory until after the turn of the century. Illinois State Archives at Springfield has the county board minutes from 1831 to 1922.

### Sources
History of Putnam and Marshall Co. E.A. Ford, 1860.
Ellsworth's Records of Old Putnam & Marshall Cos. 1880.
Plat Book of Marshall and Putnam Co. Ogle, 1890.
Biog. Record of Bureau, Marshall & Putnam Co. Clarke, 1896.
Standard Atlas of Marshall & Putnam Cos. Ogle, 1911.
1850 Federal Census. Maxine Wormer, 1972.
Best Town in Illinois by a Dam Site. Helen Raffensperger.

## Capt. William Warnick's Company
## Black Hawk War, Enrolled 4 June 1832
## Macon County, Illinois

Capt. William Warnick; First Lt. J.C. Pugh; Second Lt. E. Freeman; Sgts. F.G. Paine, J.H. Johnson, A.M. Wilson, R. Law; Corps. J. Smith, A. Travice, J. Brown, J. Miller; Pvts. A. Arnold, Thomas Alsup, N. Burrell, M. Brown, E. Butler, T.G.D. Church, H. Cunningham, J. Cunningham, J. Davis, J. Edwards, J. Farris, A. Hall, D. Howell, W. Hooper, A. Hemdline, D. Hall, I. Ingram, R. Johnson, L. Jackson, J. Lowry, S. Mounce, I.H. McMennamy, D. Newcomb, T. Owen, M. Paine, Mason Paine, J. A. Piatt, A.W. Smith, S. Sinnett, J. Stevens, Benjamin Slatten, F. Travis, S. Widick, William Ward, T.F Wilson, James Warnick, J. Warnick, J. Walker, R. Wheeler.

---

## Randolph County, Illinois
## Genealogical Sources, Help

County created 5 Oct. 1795 from parent county of St. Clair and northwest territory. Named for Edmund Randolph. County seat at Chester, IL 62233 has vital, land records (county clerk, 618-826-2510) and court records (circuit court, 618-826-3116). Courthouse hours, Monday through Friday, 8 - 4:30.

Birth and death records begin 1877; court records, 1804; marriages, 1809; circuit court 1825, and census, 1810. Illinois State Archives at Springfield, Ill. has county board minutes for years 1802-1806; 1810-1814; 1824-1838.

### Sources
Dtry and Hist. of Randolph Co. E. J. Montague, 1859.
Hist. Atlas of Randolph Co. Brink, 1875.
Combined Hist. of Randolph, Monroe & Perry Co. McDonough, 1883.
Port. & Biog. Record of Randolph, Jackson, Perry & Monroe Co. 1894.
Ill. & Randolph Co. Hist. Soc. Journal Vol. 2 1918.
Randolph Co. Notes. J.W. Allen, 1944.
Randolph & Kaskaskia Island, 1859. E.J. Montague.
Rev. War Soldiers Buried in Randolph Co. Mrs. L. Campbell.
The Illinois Regiment (SAR Yearbook) J.T. Long.
1825 Census of Randolph Co. Mrs. Hardin B. Taylor, 1972.
Records of Randolph Co., Ill. Early marriages, probate. Mrs. Hardin
    B. Taylor, 1973.
1850 Federal Census. Yakima Valley Genealogical Soc. 1976.

---

## Capt. Alex. M. Jenkins Co.
## Black Hawk War, Enrolled 12 July 1832
## Jackson & Randolph Counties

Capt. Alexander M. Jenkins; First Lt. James Herald; Second Lt. Silas Hickman; Sgts. Milton Ladd, John D. Owings, Mathias Hagler, Aaron Quillman; Corps. Binningson Boone, Daniel House, John Logan, Jacob Schwartz; Cornet, Wm. M. Bowning; Pvts. David Burkeley, James Blacker, David Blacker, Henry Casey, John Casey, Squire Crum, Hiram

Creath, John G. Clark, James Camron, James A. Deason, William Deason, John Delaplain, Joseph Davis, Ralph Davis, Samuel Davis, James Etherton, Robert H. Gardner, Geo. F. Griffith, Paul Hagler, O.M. Huff, Nicholas Hanson, Edmond Hagler, John Holden, Alexander Ireland, James Logan, John M. Logan, Walker Lorrels, Alexander Lafferty, James F. Owings, William Orton, John Richards, James Sorrels, William Shumaker, James M. Timmons, Hezekiah Teague, Richard R. Taylor, Gilbert B. Vote, George Vansel, Nathan D. Walker, Wilson D. Wood.

---

## RICHLAND COUNTY, ILLINOIS
### Genealogical Sources, Help

County created 24 Feb. 1841 from parent counties of Clay and Lawrence. Named for a county in Ohio. County seat at Olney, IL 62450 has vital, land records (county clerk, 618-392-3111) and court records (circuit clerk, 618-392-2151). Courthouse hours, Monday through Friday, 8-4.

The birth and death records begin with 1877; marriages, 1844; court records, 1841; and census with 1845. The public library in Olney is the Carnegie Library, 401 East Main St., Box 97, Olney, IL 62450. 1-618-392-3711.

Among the early pioneers were the Evans brothers, Thaddeus Morehouse, Hugh Calhoun and son, Thomas Gardner, James Parker, Cornelius DeLong, James Gilmore and Elijah Nelson.

In 1820 there were but 30 families in the district. The first frame houses—the Nelson and Morehouse homesteads—were built in 1821, and some years later, James Laws erected the first brick house.

The pioneers traded at Vincennes, but in 1825, a store was opened at Stringtown by Jacob Hay; and the same year, the first school was opened at Watertown, taught by Isaac Chauncey.

The first church was erected by the Baptists in 1822, and services were conducted by William Martin, a Kentuckian. For a long time, the mails were carried on horseback by Louis and James Beard, but in 1824, Mills and Whetsell established a line of four-horse stages.

The principal road, known as the "trace road", leading from Louisville to Cahokia, followed a buffalo and Indian trail about where the main street of Olney now is. A Mr. Lilly built the first house there. [1917 HISTORIC ENCYCLOPEDIA OF ILLINOIS.]

Civil War soldiers from Richland County, Illinois number 1,577, and comprised these regiments: 8th, Co. D; 60th, Co. F; 63rd, Co. A,C,E,I; 98th, Co. B,G,H; 130th, Co. H; 136th, Co. C,G; and 155th, Co. E. The Illinois State Archives at Springfield, Ill. has the records.

The archives also has the county board minutes from 1841 to 1917; county and state census for 1850,1855,1860,1865,1870,1880; historical sketch for 1936-1942, and inventory made of records, 1936-1942.

Only county newspaper that is preserved on microfilm available from the Illinois State Historical Library is that of Olney for various different years ranging from 1849 [a single issue] to current date.

## Sources

1850 Federal Census. Don A. Craddock, no date.
Cemetery Inscriptions. Barbara J. Craddock. 1969. Not indexed.
1884 Counties of Cumberland, Jasper and Richland.
1893 Portrait & Biographical Record of Effingham, Jasper & Richland Counties.
1894 Biographical & Rem. History of Richland, Clay & Marion Counties. B. Bowen.
1901 Atlas of Richland County with Directory. Ogle.
1909 History of Richland, Clay and Marion Counties. Bowen.
1850,60,70,80,1900,10 Censuses of Richland County. Richland County Genealogical Society.

---

## Rock Island County, Illinois
### Genealogical Sources, Help

County created 9 Feb. 1831 from parent county of Jo Daviess. Named for an island. County seat at Rock Island, IL 61201 has vital, land records (circuit clerk, 309-786-4451) and court records (circuit clerk, 309-786-4451). Courthouse hours, Monday through Friday, 8-5. Illinois genealogical society that covers this area is Rock Island Public Library, Rock Island, IL 61201.

There are also public libraries at: Andalusia, Township Library, Box 365, Andalusia 61232; Coal Valley, Robert R. Jones Public Library District, 2210-1st Street, Box 114, Coal Valley 61240; Cordova Township Library, 402 Main Avenue, Box 37, Cordova 61242; East Moline, Public Library, 740-16th Ave., Box 777, East Moline 61244; Hampton, Public Library, Box 347, Hampton 61256; Hillsdale, Moore Memorial Library, 509 Main St., Box 143, Hillsdale 61257; Moline, Public Library, 504 17th St., Moline 61265; Port Byron, Township Library, 106 N. High St., Box 10, Port Byron 61275, and Silvis, Public Library, 105-8th St., Silvis 61282.

County has birth and death records from 1877; marriages, 1833; court records, 1833, and census, 1835.

In 1816 the government built a fort on Rock Island (an island in Mississippi), naming it Fort Armstrong. It has always remained a military post, and is now the seat of an extensive arsenal and workshop. [This was written in 1917.]

In the spring of 1828, settlements were made near Port Byron by John and Thomas Kinney, Archibald Allen and George Harlan. Other early settlers, near Rock Island and Rapids City, were J.W. Spencer, J.W. Barriels, Benjamin F. Pike and Conrad Leak; and among the pioneers were Wells and Michael Bartlett, Joel Thompson, the Simmes brothers and George Davenport.

The country was full of Indians, this being the headquarters of Black Hawk. [Note: the Sac and Fox Indians had their FARMS along the Rock River, and were forced to leave them.]

In 1831, Rock Island then called Stephenson was made the county seat. Joseph Conway was first county clerk and Joel Wells, Sr., the first treasurer. [1917 HISTORIC ENCYCLOPEDIA OF ILLINOIS.]

The Civil War solders from Rock Island County number 2,473, and comprised the following regiments:

11th, Co. d; 13th, Co. D; 37th, Co. A,H; 43rd, Co. E; 45th, Co. H; 51st, Co. H; 58th, Co. K; 69th, Co. F; 71st, Co. D; 89th, Co. F; 93rd, Co. A; 102nd, Co. C; 126th, Co. E,E,G,H,I; 129th, Co. K; 132nd, Co. H; 140th, Co. F,H,I; and 155th, Co. K. Calvary, 4th, Co. M and 9th, Co. A. The Illinois State Archives has the records.

The state archives also has county board minutes, 1833-1936; and censuses for 1850,55,60,65,70 and 80.

County newspapers preserved on microfilm available from the Illinois State Historical Library are those of East Moline, Milan, Moline, Port Byron, Reynolds, Rock Island, and Stephenson. Check with the editor for more particulars.

### Sources

1877 Past & Present of Rock Island County. Kett.
1885 Portrait & Biographical Album of Rock Island County.
1894 Plat Book of Rock Island County. Ogle.
1897 Biographical Record of Rock Island Co. Clarke.
1905 Atlas of Rock Island County with Directory. Iowa Pub.
1905 Early Rock Island and Moline History. W.A. Meese.
1908 History of Rock Island County from Earliest Period. Kramer.
1914 History of Rock Island County. Bateman.
Directories of Rock Island, 1855,56,57,58-60,58-59. Various editors.

---

### Shelby County, Illinois
### Miscellaneous Records, County Clerk's Office

Editor's Note: Miscellaneous records in any given location usually provide information from other geographic areas.

Pratt, Henry A.
    Will of, MRB 157, pp.608-609.
Prentice, William
    Heirs of, MRB 178, p. 160.
Patton, James H.
    Heirs of, died 13 March 1873. MRB 236, p. 60.
Pegan, Isiah
    Heirs of, died 1 Feb. 1911. MRB 236, pp.184-186.
Penwell, David A.
    Heirs of, died 25 Dec. 1864. MRB 236, p. 163-166.
Penwell, Frank & George
    Estate of Vermilion County. Frank died 19 June 1920. MRB 236, pp. 230-240.
Perryman, James
    Land, died 21 April 1910. MRB 189, pp.404-405.
Phelps, Nathan
    Heirs of, died 26 March 1920 Coles County, Ill. MRB 234, pp.436-459.
Pierce, Arthur S.
    Will and estate of 1907. MRB 236, p. 17-20.
Poe, Elizabeth
    Heirs of, died 11 Nov. 1924. MRB 236, p. 419.
Prescott, Ezekiel
    Land no. 22076, 1854. MRB 143, p. 483.

Pretlow, George F.
    Will of Montgomery County, Ill. 1854. MRB 189, pp.110-112.

Price, Joseph P.
    Will and Estate of Montgomery County, Ill. MRB 178, pp.104-105.

Provost, Benjamin B.
    Land no. 24193. MRB 143, p. 60.

Pugh, John
    Land no. 3113, 1838. MRB 234, p. 531.
    Heirs of, died 1892. MRB 234, pp.300-301.

Pugh, Robert
    Heirs of, MRB 163, p. 606.

Pugh, William H.
    Heirs of, died 1857. MRB 236, pp.167-169.

Quarles, George L.
    Pvt. in Capt. Earley's Co. Col. Leftwicks Reg. Va. Mil. 1812, land no. 2893. Assigned to M.D. Gregory, 1854. MRB 193, p. 420.

Quigley, James H.
    Heirs of, 1882. MRB 172, p. 380.

Ragan, William H.
    Affidavit, heirs of Mary D. Gallagher. MRB 172, p. 546.

Ramsey, Elizabeth Corley
    Will and Estate of 1929 of Montgomery Co., Ill. MRB 236, pp.557-568.

Randall, Alice C.
    Heirs of. MRB 163, p. 626.

Rasor, William H.
    Affidavit, heirs of Joseph Neel, died 1851. MRB 172, p. 32.

Raymond, Thomas
    Pvt. in Capt. Smith's Co. Maine Mil. 1812. Land no. 49474 assigned to Peter P. Scott, 1853. MRB 193, p. 426.

Read, George W.
    Heirs of Christian County, Ill. MRB 163, pp. 622-625.
    Will of Christian County, Ill. MRB 143, pp. 535-536;604-607.

Read, James
    Of Suffolk Co., Mass. Land no. 3077. MRB 215, p. 576.

Reber, Charles Van
    Of Franklin County, Ohio; land no. 8495; 8494; 8498; 9121; MRB 215, pp. 585,586,617,618.

Rector, Mary A.
    Affadavit of, heirs of William M. Osborn. MRB 172, p. 249.

Mulverhill, Dennis
    Heirs of, MRB 172, p. 77.

Moyer, William
    Estate of McLean County, Ill. MRB 193, p. 149.

Reed, Allen B.
    Land no. 15692, 1850. MRB 215, pp.295-296.

Reed, Amos V.
    Land no. 15542, 1850. MRB 193, p. 421.
    Land no. 10684, 1853. MRB 163, p. 216.

Renfro, William B.
> Heirs of 1855, Montgomery County, Ill. MRB 215, pp. 573-574. Individuals listed in affidavit: Joshua and Phereby Renfro; widow, Elizabeth C.; Margaret Kirk; Rhoda Denton (William); Elsaby Merryman (Kyatting or Wm. R.); John; Hiram; James. Grandchildren?: William Armstrong, Washington Armstrong, Salle Armstrong who married Elisha Merryman; John Armstrong Jr., Catherine Armstrong and David Armstrong. (Editor's Note: Washington Armstrong married Delila Renfro 23 Jan. 1845 in Shelby County, Ill. All this in a miscellaneous record.)

---

## SEARCHING ILLINOIS ANCESTORS
### COUNTY, SURNAME, PERSON SEARCHING

ST. CLAIR: Ott, Merkel, Tribbel/Triffel/Trippel, Rutz, D/Rothmund, Armbrust, Crossley, Germaine, Hauswirth, Alberter, Boehrn
> Audrey Tait, 1009 W. Tudor Road, Anchorage, AK 99503

ADAMS, UNION: Duncan, Howell
> Mary Jones Ziegler, 606 Cooper Drive, Placentia, CA 92670

CRAWFORD: no surname given
> Charlotte Meredith, Pineview Road, Custer, MT 59024

BOND, MARION, FAYETTE: White, Pugh, Neal, Hathaway
> Ms. M. "Jane" White Price, Box 106, Webb City, MO 64870

---

### PAID QUERY

Seeking information and/or descendants of David and Isabella Gould Bush. They arrived in Adams or Brown County in 1832 from Virginia. The children were Aaron, Calvin, David and Aletha.
> Barbara Bush, 202 Heritage Ct., Mt. Pleasant, MI 48858

---

TAZEWELL: Shay, Blue
> Lois M. Laird, Box 441, Dighton, KS 67839

ST. CLAIR, WASHINGTON, JEFFERSON, MARION: Foster, Lively
> Lela Gunning, 4062 Sara No. 8C, Granite City, IL 62040

WILLIAMSON, MARION: Klope/Clope, Carter, Crosslin
> William Klope, 278 Crestwood Ave., Ventura, CA 93003

SHELBY COUNTY: Durst, Shanholtzer, Rouse, Peterson
> David A. Zabriskie, 1100 South Boulevard, Evanston, IL 60202

EDGAR: Glass, Calvin
> Robert Weston, 112 Beeson Rd., Niles, MI 49120

DUPAGE: Geer
> Ginger M. August, 32 Stetson Way, Princeton, NJ 08540

ADAMS: Cunningham, Duffy, Weaver, Lierle/Lyerly
> Ruth Coward Cunningham, 5100 John D. Ryan Blvd. Apt. 735, San Antonio, TX 78245

COUNTY NOT GIVEN: Singleton, Fielder
> Wilda Singleton, 845 N. Jackson, Bushnell, IL 61422

SOUTHERN ILLINOIS: County and surname not given
> Margaret Sherman, R. 1, Box 287, Gerald, MO 63037

# INDEX TO JULY AUGUST 1987
## SEARCHING ILLINOIS ANCESTORS

Acorn, 103
Adams, 103
Adrian, 103
Ahlee, 103
Ahlfield, 103
Alberter, 116
Aleshire, 107
Allen, 103,105,107,113
Allers, 105
Allwardt, 103
Alsup, 111
Ames, 103
Amundson, 103
Andersdotter, 103
Anderson, 103
Anthony, 103
Apple, 110
Arnantrout, 103
Armbrust, 116
Armstrong, 103,116
Arnold, 111
Arnspiger, 103
Atterbury, 103
Aurand, 103
Axon, 103
Ayres, 104
Baccus, 104
Bacon, 104
Bader, 104
Baer, 104
Bain, 104
Baker, 104
Baldridge, 104
Ball, 104
Barrett, 107
Barriels, 113
Bartlett, 113
Bass, 110
Baumgardner, 107
Beard, 112
Bearden, 105
Bell, 108
Berton, 110
Black, 105
Blacker, 111
Blanfor, 107
Blevins, 108
Blue, 116
Blythe, 110
Bodine, 107
Bochrn, 116
Boling, 109
Boone, 111
Bord, 108
Bowell, 108
Bowning, 111
Boyer, 108
Braden, 108
Bradley, 108
Brants, 105
Bristol, 109
Brown, 103,107,108,109,111
Buchanan, 107,110
Budlong, 110
Buitt, 108
Bundy, 105
Burkeley, 111
Burrell, 111
Bush, 103,116
Butler, 111
Cahall, 107
Caldwell, 109
Calhoun, 112
Call, 108
Callaway, 107
Calvin, 116
Camron, 112
Carle, 109
Carmean, 109,110
Carter, 116
Casey, 111
Cash, 107
Cay, 110
Chauncey, 112
Chews, 107
Chick, 106
Christy, 110
Church, 111
Clarke, 106,107,108,109,112
Cleveland, 109,110
Clifton, 109
Collenburger, 106
Coller, 109
Collier, 110
Collins, 107
Collum, 107
Conner, 105,109
Connerry, 107
Conrey, 108
Conway, 113
Cooper, 109
Copenburger, 105
Cowan, 107
Cox, 108,109
Craig, 108
Creath, 112
Crews, 110
Crossley, 116
Crosslin, 116
Crosthwait, 105
Crull, 106
Crum, 111
Cunningham, 111,116
Curphy, 103
Curry, 107,109,110
Dalley, 105
Dane, 106
Danner, 106
Davenport, 113
Davis, 106,107,108,111,112
Dawse, 110
Day, 107
Deason, 112
Decamp, 106
Dehaven, 109
Delaplain, 112
Delong, 112
Dennison, 108
Denton, 116
Doak, 108
Dodge, 109
Doty, 109
Duchni, 105
Dudley, 107
Duffy, 116
Duncan, 116
Dunlap, 110
Durbin, 105,106
Durst, 116
Dyson, 105
Eads, 109
Earey, 107
Eddy, 108
Edwards, 107,111
Elder, 107,110
Ellington, 107
Emmott, 103
Esrey, 107
Etherton, 112
Farris, 111
Fielder, 116
Fleming, 108
Fletcher, 107
Foster, 107,116
Frame, 108
Freeman, 111
Funk, 106
Furry, 109
Gaddy, 110
Gallaher, 110
Gamel, 110
Gardner, 112
Garmon, 107
Geer, 116
George, 105,106
Germaine, 116
Gessner, 105
Giger, 106
Gilliham, 107
Gilmore, 112
Gittes, 109
Glass, 116
Goldsby, 110
Goodrich, 109
Gordon, 108
Gould, 103,116
Gray, 109
Griffith, 112
Hagler, 111,112
Hall, 111
Hamas, 107
Hamilton, 109
Hampton, 107
Hanon, 105
Handson, 110,112

Hardey, 106        Harlan, 113         Harris, 105,109   Harsey, 108
Hart, 109          Harvey, 105         Hathaway, 116     Haunwirth, 116
Hawk, 106          Hawkins, 109        Hayes, 105        Hayward, 106
Hendline, 111      Herald, 111         Hickman, 111      Hinkle, 109
Hobbs, 107         Holden, 112         Holmes, 107       Honald, 106
Hood, 110          Hooper, 111         House, 111        Howell, 111,116
Hubbard, 107       Huff, 112           Hum, 105          Hunt, 103,105
Hunter, 106        Iler, 106           Ingles, 108       Ingram, 111
Ireland, 112       Jackson, 111        Jarvis, 108       Jenkins, 111
Jernigan, 105      Johnson, 108,111                      Jones, 109
Jonson, 108        Jourdan, 107        Kayhoe, 107       Keizer, 105
Keller, 103        Kelley, 109         Kelly, 107        Kimbrough, 107
Kinney, 113        Kinzie, 104         Kirk, 116         Klope, 116
Lacharite, 105     Ladd, 111           Lafferty, 112     Lagarlan, 105
Lamb, 103          Lambert, 105        Lambird, 105      Lamond, 105
Lancaster, 105     Landers, 105        Laneghe, 106      Langley, 105
Lankford, 108      Lavigne, 105        Law, 111          Laws, 112
Layman, 105        Leach, 105          Leachman, 105     Leak, 113
Lee, 107           Lemanon, 105        Levanture, 105    Lewis, 105,110
Libbey, 105        Liberman, 105       Lierle, 116       Lilland, 105
Lilly, 112         Lindsay, 108        Little, 105       Lively, 116
Livingstone, 110   Locker, 105         Logan, 105,107,111,112
Logsdon, 105       Long, 105           Lord, 110         Lorrels, 112
Love, 107,109      Lowry, 111          Ludi, 103         Ludwick, 105
McCarry, 105       McCay, 106          McCleave, 110     McColwin, 106
McCrary, 105       McDaniels, 107      McDonald, 106,110 McDugan, 106
McDowell, 106      McKinney, 107       McKenzie, 105,106 McMennamy, 111
McNulty, 107       Macy, 105           Madison, 106,107  Manary, 106
Manning, 107       Marsh, 110          Martin, 105,106,107,112
Marvin, 106        Mason, 106          Masters, 105      Mathews, 105,106
Matson, 108        Maxedy, 105         Maxwell, 105,106  May, 106,112
Meads, 105,106     Melngin, 106        Menary, 106       Merkel, 116
Merrifield, 109    Merryman, 116       Meyers, 107
Miller, 105,106,109,110,111            Milligan, 105     Mills, 105,112
Miner, 109         Minnis, 106         Mitchell, 107     Moaler, 110
Moats, 109         Mock, 109           Moffat, 109       Money, 110
Monroe, 106        Montgomery, 110     Moor, 110         Moore, 105,106,107,109
Moores, 108        Morehouse, 112      Morell, 106       Morgan, 105,106
Morganthall, 106   Morris, 105,110     Morrison, 106     Morton, 105
Mounce, 111        Moyer, 115          Mull, 106         Mullens, 108
Mulverhill, 115    Mundell, 108        Munhum, 106       Munson, 110
Murphy, 105,106    Mutterspaugh, 106   Myer, 105         Myers, 105,106
Nation, 105        Neal, 116           Nelson, 112       Newcomb, 111
Nicole, 103        Northcutt, 110      Nott, 109         Offidd, 105
Ogle, 107          Olinger, 106        Olmstead, 106,108 Organ, 110
Orton, 112         Ott, 116            Owen, 107,109,111 Owings, 111,112
Paine, 111         Parker, 107,108,112                   Parr, 107
Partridge, 107     Pattison, 110       Patton, 114       Pearson, 103
Pegan, 114         Penwell, 114        Perchments, 105   Perham, 103
Perkins, 109       Perryman, 114       Peters, 105       Peterson, 116
Phelps, 109,114    Phillis, 109        Piatt, 103,111    Pierce, 110,114

| | | | |
|---|---|---|---|
| Pike, 113 | Poe, 114 | Pollard, 110 | Porter, 105,108 |
| Powers, 106 | Pratt, 114 | Prentice, 114 | Prescott, 114 |
| Pretlow, 115 | Price, 115 | Prince, 105 | Provost, 115 |
| Pugh, 115,116 | Purvis, 110 | Quarles, 115 | Quigley, 115 |
| Quillman, 111 | Rabe, 106 | Radley, 107 | Ragan, 115 |
| Ramsey, 115 | Randall, 115 | Rasor, 115 | Raymond, 115 |
| Read, 115 | Reber, 115 | Rector, 115 | Redden, 107 |
| Reddick, 109 | Reed, 106,108,110,115 | | Renfro, 116 |
| Richards, 110,112 | | Richardson, 106,110 | |
| Ridgeway, 109 | Roberts, 108 | Robertson, 105 | Rogers, 108 |
| Roof, 109 | Ross, 109 | Rothmund, 116 | Rouse, 116 |
| Runyon, 106 | Rutherford, 109 | Rutz, 116 | Sanders, 107 |
| Sargeant, 106 | Scott, 106,107,110 | | Schwartz, 111 |
| Shanholtzer, 116 | Sharp, 106,110 | | Sharrock, 105 |
| Shay, 116 | Shield, 107 | Shinn, 107 | Shirk, 103 |
| Shoaff, 107 | Shores, 106 | Shumaker, 112 | Sigmore, 107 |
| Simmes, 113 | Simon, 105 | Singleton, 116 | Sinnett, 111 |
| Slatten, 111 | Slinker, 106 | Smith, 106,107,108,110,111 | |
| Sorrels, 112 | Spencer, 113 | Springer, 105 | Starkes, 107 |
| Stephens, 106 | Stephenson, 108,113 | | Stevens, 111 |
| Stewart, 108,109 | Stokes, 105 | Stringer, 109 | Stump, 107 |
| Swickard, 107 | Swift, 107 | Tade, 107 | Talifero, 110 |
| Tawdry, 108 | Taylor, 108,110,112 | | Teague, 112 |
| Thomas, 110 | Thomason, 109 | Thompson, 105,113 | Thornton, 107 |
| Thurman, 110 | Travice, 111 | Travis, 111 | Treadwell, 108 |
| Trial, 110 | Triffel, 116 | Turgeon, 105 | Turner, 110 |
| Underwood, 107 | Vadakin, 110 | Van Deren, 109 | Vansel, 112 |
| Verdin, 106 | Vote, 112 | Wadkins, 106 | Walden, 110 |
| Walker, 109,110,111,112 | | Wallace, 107 | Ward, 107,111 |
| Warner, 107 | Warnick, 111 | Wau Bun, 104 | Wayne, 100 |
| Weaver, 116 | Webb, 109 | Wells, 113 | Welsh, 107 |
| West, 107 | Wheeler, 111 | Whetsell, 112 | Whipple, 108 |
| Whitaker, 107 | White, 103,116 | Whitley, 107 | Whitteman, 106 |
| Widick, 111 | Wigger, 105 | Wiley, 110 | Williams, 108 |
| Wilson, 106,107,108,111 | | Wollard, 107 | Wood, 110,112 |
| Woods, 106 | Wren, 109 | Wright, 109 | Young, 105,106,108 |

---

NOW TAKING PRE-PUBLICATIONS ORDERS FOR
Illinois and the Fugitive Slave, 1816-1850: Runaway Notices and Certificates of Freedom Found in Illinois Sources

Order now and save $5--$20. --- $25 after publication tentatively scheduled for latter part of 1988. The final work will contain an introduction on the fugitive slave laws and the effect on the state of Illinois. The bulk of the work will be actual newspaper quotations of runaway notices found in Illinois newspapers. The certificates of freedom are found in county deed records where the resident owner released his property and recorded the transaction similar to that of real estate. Data such as physical descriptions, styles of clothing, geographical locations, individuals' ages and names or aliases, and much more clarify for the reader the prevailing attitudes of society during those years that slavery was in existence.

Send payment now to the editor, Box 392, Shelbyville, IL 62565.

SEARCHING ILLINOIS ANCESTORS

VOLUME III NO. 6

September October 1987

INDEXED IN GENEALOGICAL PERIODICAL INDEX

Issued bi-monthly by Helen Cox Tregillis. Publication and advertising offices: Box 392, Shelbyville, IL 62565. Current single copy price, $2 plus 69 cents postage. Yearly subscription, $12. Send check or money order payable to: Helen Cox Tregillis, Box 392, Shelbyville, IL 62565. Surnames, articles appearing in publication are indexed in GENEALOGICAL PERIODICAL INDEX. Postage paid at Shelbyville, IL. Send address changes, queries, advertising to above address.
ISSN 0086 - 7763
PAYMENT MUST ACCOMPANY SUBSCRIPTION, QUERY AND ADVERTISING

NO BACK ISSUES AVAILABLE

FREE QUERY with county, surname only
$5 for maximum 50 word query
Check query section for format

SEARCHING ILLINOIS ANCESTORS
VOLUME III NUMBER 6
SEPTEMBER OCTOBER 1987

| | |
|---|---|
| Christian County, Marriages | 121 |
| Clay County, Delinquent Taxes 1844 | 122 |
| Clinton County, Delinquent Taxes 1837 | 122 |
| Coles County, Cutler Entries | 123 |
| Effingham County, Delinq. Taxes 1844 | 124 |
| Fayette County, Delinquent Taxes 1838 | 128 |
| Gallatin County, Delinquent Taxes 1847 | 127 |
| Greene County Genealogical Sources | 124 |
| Illinois Biographies, 1910 | 125 |
| Illinois Mounted Volunteer Regiment, Black Hawk War | 128 |
| Illinois Mounted Regiment, War of 1812 | 131 |
| Johnson County, Delinquent Taxes 1845ff | 127 |
| Lawrence County, Delinquent Taxes 1838 | 127 |
| Perry County, Delinquent Taxes 1838 | 128 |
| Shelby County, Obituary Abstracts | 129 |
|     Cholera Era Victims | 131 |
| Williamson County, Biographies 1887 | 132 |
| SEARCHING ILLINOIS ANCESTORS QUERIES | 120, 126, 133 |

# SEARCHING ILLINOIS ANCESTORS
## County, Surname, Person Searching

### PAID QUERIES

William T. Day served Civil War, enlisted New Columbia, born Tennessee, wife Mary Anderson; William Foreman, wife Mary O'Brien, son John, his wife Anna Belle Day. Pope, Johnson or Massac Counties.
   Janise Baker, 9060 Boggie Dr., Stanwood, MI 49346

---

What Richardson had a daughter Emily that married James Smock? Her age was 22 years on 1850 Illinois Census for Carlinville, Macoupin Coiunty. She died of cholera in 1851.
   Ivaloo Smock, 610 22nd St., Apt. 13, Greeley, CO 80631

---

### FREE QUERIES

ADAMS: Cox
   Martin Cox, 205 New York, Wichita, KS 67214
St. CLAIR: Cox
   Alta Pinney, 3022 S. Wheeling Way, Aurora, CO 80014
COLES: Cox
   Lawrence Daniels, 4017 Welsley Ln, Bowie, MD 20715
WARREN: Cox
   Donna J. Buol, 512 20th St., Hawarden, IA 51023
CASS: Cox
   Alma Francis, 1512 Karen Ln, Iowa Park, TX 76367
St. CLAIR: Cox
   Shirley R. Bryant, 1305 State St., Charleston, MO 63834
STARK: Cox
   Bobbie Cox, 2205 Bonfoy Ave., Colorado Springs, CO 80909
WASHINGTON: Cox
   Karra J. Porter, Rt 1, Box 31A, Scranton, KS 66537
BROWN: Cox
   Jane Farmer, 1040 Ferry St. 202B, Eugene, OR 97401
PIKE: Cox
   Pauline M. McKinney, 4392 E. Sunrise Dr., Phoenix, AZ 85044
FULTON: Cox
   Gene E. Welch, 2872 W. Via Del Santo, Tucson, AZ 85741
JOHNSON: Cox
   Judith C. Whipple, 76439 Alston Rd., Rainier, OR 97048
MORGAN: Cox
   Katharine E. Manchester, 8621 Camden St., Alexandria, VA 22308
ROCK ISLAND: Cox
   Merrily N. Tunnicliff, 322 N. 18 St., Clarinda, IA 51632
SHELBY: Baldridge
   Margaret Gooding, 1406 W. Cushing St., Decatur, IL 62526
COUNTY UNKNOWN: Allston Rich
   Margaret Austin, 76 Goose Hill Rd., Chester, CT 06412
MERCER: Surname not given
   Mrs. L. Hawthorne, 2122 Kolomyia, West Bloomfield, MI 48033
SHELBY: Austin
   Edwin L. Thornton, Box 222, Robinson, KS 66532

CUMBERLAND, MACOUPIN: McCaskey, Howard, Cutright
    Lynette Schwartz, Box 3295, Munster, IN 46321
MARION: Hicks/Hix
    Audrey Hicks Bloznik, Rt 1, Box 192A, Collins, MO 64738
    EDITOR'S NOTE: S.G. Hicks, CW vet, died 1869 buried in East Lawn cemetery, Salem, Ill.
COOK: Schmidt
    Alma M. Barnum, Rt 2, Box 78E, Niangua, MO 65713
WAYNE: Gash
    Naomi E. Spinner, 4024 Dolbil Drive, Lemay, MO 63125
ST CLAIR: Rittmeyer, Spalt, Kessler
    Russell G. Mann, Jr., 1354 West Jarvis Ave., Apt. 1, Chicago, IL 60626
CASS: Cole, Nicholson
    Ruth Dillingham, Box 901, Stinnett, TX 79083

----------------

## BOOK REVIEWS

Illinois connected genealogies, histories and source record publications are welcomed for review in this magazine. Send a copy with price info, etc. to the publisher.

----------------

## CHRISTIAN COUNTY, ILLINOIS
### MARRIAGES, 1839-1866
### County Clerk

Moore, Joseph and Clemency Wilson, page 98
May, Clinton and Serena Roberts, page 99
Martin, A.S. and Mileah Bowman, page 99
McDonald, Hugh W. and Ellen E. Crosthwait, page 101
McKenee, Henry and Virginia Hatchett, page 102
Matthew, Thomas G. and Ann E. Pherigo, page 103
Michel, Joseph S. and Sarah Ann Hinklin, page 103
McConnall, James and Callasta Parish, page 105
McKinzy, Othnide and Maria E. Baber, page 106
Miller, James and Lucretia Carman, page 107
McCoy, James H. and Margaret A. Cheadis, page 108
Mathews, William D. and Martha A. Foor, page 109
Mason, Joseph and Hester A. M. Langley, page 111
Minnis, Ferdinand M. and Jane George, page 112
Milam, John and Nancy A. Taylor, page 114
Murry, John R. and Elizabeth McQuon, page 116
Miller, Charles and Mary Phenix, page 116
Morgan, Samuel and Eliza Pate, page 116
Masters, Samuel and Eliza Warren, page 119
McConkey, Granderson and Marian Richardson, page 120
Missen, William and Hannah Carpenter, page 121
Mount, John and Elizabeth Moore, page 122
Morris, Miles and Hannah Prichett, page 122
Mason, Seth and Syrena Hanon, page 123
Montel, David W. and Anna Smith, page 127
Milligan, James S. and Emma Dunn, page 127

Maxfield, A.J. and Hester A. Haines, page 129
Montgomery, John and Mary Reynolds, page 129
Misenbarger, Daniel and Julia Harris, page 130
Moore, John C. and Mary E. H. David, page 130
Michels, Joseph and Margaret Conter, page 131
Muer, John and Lavina A. Potts, page 132
Morris, Thomas F. and Catherine Hill, page 133
Moore, John W. and Margaaret A. Layman, page 13?
Malom, Jeremiah and Amanda Klinefelter, page 140
Maxfield, Jesse and Orilla Dowham, page 140
Miller, George D. and Hettie M. Heinlein, page 141
Moore, John D. and Susan Apple, page 141
Meads, Silas and Elizabeth Wolf, page 142
Mugin, Peter and Elizam Will, page 145
Mason, Joseph and Lucinda L. Taylor, page 148
Marshall, William and Rebecca Ellis, page 148
May, William and Sarah M. Pate, page 153
McQuon, William and Mary J. Braddley, page 153
Madox, John S. and Sarah E. Hollingsworth, page 153
Morgret, Jackson and Susannah Linn, page 153
Myer, William and Briska Miller, page 153

---

Clay County, Illinois
Delinquent Taxes for 1844
Baptist Helmet, Vandalia, Ill. April 10, 1845
Newspaper Microfilm

A list of lands and other real estate situated in county of Clay, state of Illinois, on wich tax remains due and unpaid for the A.D. 1844.

R. Scriber & Keys, heirs of Childers, John Wilson, Jeremiah Vincents, Hugh McDaniel, John McDaniel, Richard Penren, Adam Lee, David Lee, Adam Trinkle, Joseph Campbell, F.D. Waters, W. Kinney & Taylor, James Bishop, William Calbert, Zediah Parker, Richard Raffity, Jeremiah Collin, Calvin Davis, William Egbert, Jr., R.C. Watson, Martin Dukes, David Erwin, Sr., John Cherry, Nathaniel Cherry, Thomas Cherry, Calloway Celton, Jesse Hampton, Elmore J. Colman, Daniel Oldham, John O. Pearce, Reuben Washburn, B.W. Williams, Jacob Lemaster.

---

Clinton County, Illinois
Delinquent Taxes for the year 1837
Vandalia Free Press, Vandalia, Ill. Nov. 11, 1837
Newspaper Microfilm

A list of lands lying in the county of Clinton, state of Illinois, on which the taxes remain due and unpaid for the years and amounts herein set forth, both for state and county purposes in 1837.

Elijah Rittenhouse, William Middleton, Solomon Silkwood, John Edgar, Batte Abernathy, Pierre Menard, William Lewis, John D. French, James Mitchell, John Bradford, Wingate Maddox, William Riggs, John Adams, Calvin Larnes, Richard Vanarsdale, William Morrison, Harry Wilton, Stace Mc'Donough, Charles Slade, Jacob Crocker, Andrew Province, Rison H. Price, Thomas Slade, C. Barnes, John Strode, heirs of Abm. Daker, William Radfield Sr., Benjamin Taylor, William Kinsey,

Anne E. Cheeks, David Pierce, Samuel Brown, Calvin Barnes, Benjamin Tucker, John Whitten, Francis Webster Sr., William Dunn, Robert Chesney, Thomas Knight, Samuel Robinson, Chs. Clade, heirs of T.P. Huddard and Daniel V. Swearingen, Daniel Swearingen, David and Caleb Pierce, Theos. H. Nichols, Arthur Patterson, George Ward, Abijah Maddox, John Journey, Samuel Mitchell, James H. Halstead, Samuel L. Patterson, James Saunders, Samuel Robinson, Levi Morris, Anthony W. Casad, John Brown.

---

Coles County, Illinois
Grantor Index Book I, Cutler Land Transactions
County Clerk's Office, Charleston, Ill.

Jonathon Cutler and wife, to Thos. Hardin, 5 Sept. 1832, bk A, p. 105.
John Cutler and wife, to Chas. S. Morton, 27 Dec. 1832, bk A, p. 267.
John Cutler, to James Mitchell, 11 Nov. 1834, bk A, p. 367.
Jacob Cutler and wife, to Chas. S. Morton, 3 May 1834, bk B, p. 9.
Jacob Cutler and wife, to Nathan Ellington, 28 Oct. 1835, bk B, p. 231.
John Cutler and wife, to Robert Mitchell, 30 Nov. 1835, bk B, p. 315.
John Cutler and wife, to John Combs, 30 Nov. 1835, bk B, p. 316.
Jacob Cutler and wife, to Peter Miller, 2 Jan. 1836, bk B, p. 322.
Jacob Cutler and wife, to Peter Miller, 20 Jan. 1836, bk B, p. 328.
Jacob Cutler and wife, to Thomas D. Trower, 24 March 1836, bk B, p. 362.
John Cutler and wife, to Thomas Hardin, 9 Sept. 1835, bk B, p. 363.
Jacob Cutler and wife, to John H. Moderal, 3 March 1836, bk B, p. 376.
John Cutler and wife, to Hezekiah J. Ashmore, 7 May 1836, bk B, p. 419.
John Cutler and wife, to Gideon M. Ashmore, 12 Sept. 1836, bk C, p. 144.
John Cutler and wife, to John Mitchell, 16 March 1837, bk C, p. 579.
Jacob Cutler, to Ninian Steele, 28 Sept. 1837, bk C, p. 594.
John Cutler and wife, to Caleb Tutle, Jr., 12 Nov. 1838, bk D, p. 53.
Jacob Cutler and wife, to John Cutler, 15 Oct. 1839, bk E, p. 221.
Jacob Cutler and wife, to John Cutler, 4 Apr. 1840, bk F, p. 365.
John Cutler and wife, to B.F. Cutler, 12 Dec. 1846, bk K, p. 251.
John Cutler, to Thomas Lytle, 12 Dec. 1846, bk K, p. 313.
B.F. Cutler and wife, to James S. Clark, 8 Aug. 1848, bk L, p. 55.
   [Same land description from John Cutler, 12 Dec. 1846.]
EDITOR'S NOTE: The will of John Moffett, Sept. 30, 1834 is recorded in Deed Book D, p. 280. Often early wills were recorded in deed books if the individual was a non-resident and had relatives there; and or, if ownership to land was in question, then the individual's will would be recorded to clarify the fact.

## Effingham County, Illinois
### Delinquent Taxes for year 1844
### Baptist Helmet, Vandalia, IL 9 July 1845
### Newspaper Microfilm

A list of lands and other real estate situated in county of Effingham and state of Illinois on which taxes remain due and unpaid for the year 1844.

Wm. Linn and Gideon Blackburn, C.T. Aims, William Powell, William Brown, John Loy, William S. Clark, N.H. McCurdy, James M. Duncan, Prealy Pailee, Jonathon Hart, John Jane, Hudson L. Wrence, Martin K. Robinson, Samuel Defebaugh, John Funkhouser, William W. Jones, James Cartwright, John Maxfield, William Brockett, David Campbell, Jeremiah Abbott, John R. Griffith, William Turpin, W.E. Tamant, T.J. Gillinwarters, John Bingerman, Joseph Brookman, Henry Farmore, Jacob Slover, John Forth, Joseph Duncan.

---

## Greene County, Illinois
### Genealogical Sources, Help

County was created 20 January 1821 from parent county of Madison. Named for Gen. Nathaniel Greene. County seat at Carrollton, IL 62016 has vital, land records (county clerk, 217-942-5443) and court records (circuit clerk, 217-942-3421).

County birth and death records begin 1877; marriages, 1821; census, 1825. Greene County has public libraries at: Carrollton Public Library, South Main, Carrollton, IL 62016; Greenfield Public Library, West Chestnut, Greenfield, IL 62044; Roodhouse Public Library, 220 W. Franklin St., Roodhouse, IL 62082, and White Hall Twp. Library, 119 East Sherman St., White Hall, IL 62092.

County newspapers on microfilm at the Illinois State Historical Library are: Carrollton, Greenfield, Kane, Roodhouse and White Hall. Check with the editor for particulars.

The Illinois State Archives at Springfield, Ill. has the county board minutes for 1821 to 1849.

Probably the first English speaking settlers were David Stockton and James Whiteside, who located south of Macoupin Creek on June 1817. Smauel Thomas and others, Gen. Jacob Fry, followed soon afterward. Carrollton, the county seat, was laid off by Thomas Carlin in 1821.

Revolutionary Soldiers buried in Greene County were: Michael M. Baker, William Beman, Allen J. Bridges, John Clark, Jesse Conway, John Flatt, James Garrison, Adonijah Griswold, John Hewitt, Robert Lorton, Francis Miller, John A. Miller, Caleb Post, Thomas Richardson, Jonah Scroggins, Aaron Smith, William Thaxton, John Thompson and George Vinciner.

Civil war soldiers from the county numbered 1,940, and comprised the regiments, 14,D; 32,D,E; 59, G; 70,I; 91,G,I,K; and 122,C.

### Sources

Patriot Souvenir Edition, 1896. Charles Bradshaw, 1976. Reprint of 1896.

Individuals from
Historical Encyclopedia of Illinois
Bateman, Selby: 1916

Abbott, Edward
    served at Fort Vicennes during capture by Geo. Rogers Clark

Accault, Michael
    French explorer into Illinois country in 1680

Ackerman, William K.
    born NY city 29 Jan. 1832, still living 1900, railroad pres.

Adams, John LLD
    born Canterbury, CT 18 Sept. 1772; died Jacksonville, IL 24 April 1863; educator and philosopher

Adams, John McGregor
    born Londonderry, NH 11 March 1834; manufacturer

Adams, Dr. Samuel
    born Brunswick, ME, 19 Dec. 1806; died April 1877 Jacksonville, Ill.; physician and educator

Adams, George Everett
    born Keene, NH 18 June 1840; lawyer and ex-congressman

Adams, James
    born Hartford, CT 26 Jan. 1803; died 11 Aug. 1843 Springfield, IL; pioneer lawyer

Addams, John Hay
    born Sinking Springs, Berks Co., PA 12 July 1822; died 17 Aug. 1881 Stephenson Co., Ill.; legislator

Akers, Peter, DD
    born Campbell Co., VA 1 Sept. 1790; died 21 Feb. 1886 Jacksonville, Ill.; Methodist Episcopal clergyman

Akin, Edward C.
    born Will Co., Ill. 1852; lawyer and attorney general

Alcorn, James Lusk
    born near Golconda, Ill. 4 Nov. 1816; died 20 Dec. 1894; U.S. Congressman

Aldrich, J. Frank
    born Two Rivers, Wis. 6 April 1853; Congressman

Aldrich, William
    born Greenfield, NY 20 Jan. 1820; died 3 Dec. 1885 Fond du Lac, WI; merchant and congressman

Alexander, John T.
    born Western Virginia 15 Sept. 1820; died 22 Aug. 1876; agriculturalist and stock grower

Alexander, Milton K.
    born Elbert Co., GA 23 Jan. 1796; died 7 July 1856; pioneer

Alexander, Dr. William M.
    born ?; pioneer physician in southern Illinois; died ?

Allen, William Joshua
    born 9 June 1829 Wilson Co., Tenn.; died 26 Jan. 1901 southern Illinois; jurist, district US judge

Allen, Willis
    born Tenn.; died after 1859; Williamson Co., Ill. native, and father to William Joshua Allen

FOR ADDITIONAL names and information from this volume, contact the editor on the cover address.

---

## SEARCHING ILLINOIS ANCESTORS
### COUNTY, SURNAME, PERSON SEARCHING

SHELBY: Easye, Thornton
    David L. Heisenheimer, 140 E. Shore Dr., South Wind Estates, Maybank, TX 75147

SHELBY: Hart, Mathias, Hish
    Linda Daniel, 860 Maple, Virginia, IL 62691

SHELBY: Hooper, Jones, Inman
    Christopher H. Hooper, 3310 Bluebird Way, Pearland, TX 77584
       [Note: Address not correct as answer came back unforwardable.]

SHELBY: Cocannour, Smith, Lanning
    Zepha S. Major, 816 E. Second, Colorado Springs, CO 80907
       {Note: Address unforwardable on this person likewise.}

JODAVIESS: Morrissey, Le Poer, Hogan
    Richard Morrissey, 28056 Murrieta Rd., Sun City, CA 92381

LUND: Johnston
    Mrs. Wanda F. Buss, 14465 Rath Street, La Puente, CA 91744

COOK: Fiene, Radeker, Knief
    Marjorie D. Lukecart, 607 Cherry Ave., Albert Lea, MN 56007

LAKE: Henneman, Schoeneberger
    Gretchen Leisen, 1018 Riverside Dr. SE, St. Cloud, MN 56301

MACOUPIN: Barrow, Hodges
    Larry Barrow, 415 Monterey Drive, Aptos, CA 95003

HAMILTON: Trammell, Young
    Paulaja Trammel, 4401 Marraco Dr., San Diego, CA 92115

KANKAKEE: Parks
    James T. Graley, 727 Stolle Road, Lima, New York 14059

DUPAGE: Standish
    Dixon A. Larr, 104 Bob-o-Link Dr., Richmond, KY 40475

SHELBY: Hasworthy, McClain
    Diana Hart, c/o Salt Lake City Pub. Lib., 209 East 500 South, Salt Lake City, UT 84111

GRUNDY: How, Schneider
    W.H. Brewster, 40 Stonicker Dr., Lawrenceville, NJ 08648

IROQUOIS: Leggott, Platt
    Carol Tilson, 2725 South 106th St., Omaha, NE 68124

HENRY: Kalahar
    Douglas H. Kalahar, 5140 W. 7th St., Apt. 1, Winona, MN 55987

FULTON: Chaplin, Chatterton, Hainline
    Stephen Chaplin, Box 24, Yuma, CA 80759

SHELBY: Baker, Record, Neif
    Tina Nobriga, 410 Sherwood Dr., Brentwood, CA 94513

FRANKLIN: Reed, Blaymaker
    Mary Rasmussen, 1524 Bessie, Cape Girardeau, MO 63701

OGLE: Schoon
    Letty M. Schoon, 4745 4th Ave. So., Minneapolis, MN 55409

## GALLATIN COUNTY, ILLINOIS
### DELINQUENT TAXES FOR 1847
Southern Illinois Advocate, 27 April 1849
Newspaper Microfilm

A list of lands and town lots on which taxes remain due and unpaid for the year 1847.

Jonathon Brown, Caleb Carr, George Edwards, Eddy, Lane & Hardin, Isaac Hogan, John J. Hardin, Jefferson King, Kirkpatrick & Gatewood, Heirs of Humphrey Leech, Eph. B. Lane, Wm. McGehen's heirs, Richard Miles, George Sexton, Frederick Smith, John Seabolt's heirs, Jeremiah Splan, F.B. Southmaid, O.C. Vanlandingham, J. Heddon's heirs, Hargrave Carter, Gilson Peter, Calvin Gold, E.H. Gatewood, John Grove's heirs, Rebecca McGlone, David Goforth, H. Hatsell's heirs, J.P. Dudley, J. Buck, G. Scudmore's heirs, Wm. Garvin & Co., J.D. Potter, Owen Patrick, J. Heralson, Wm. Williams, Sarah Tite, Unity Dorsey, James H. Thacker, S.P. Larron, James Greer, T. Sahne's heirs, James S. Rudick, Mary Hargrave, Walter Carns, A. Kirkpatrick & ehirs of Wm. Hick, Mag. Thompson, John Willis, John Dorsey's heirs, John Fowler, A.W. Page, Calvin D. Morrison, George Smith, Benjamin Rice, Sampson Taurante, heirs of M. Gallagher, Zmri Perkins, Edmundson Taylor, D.F. Vinson, heirs of James Larker, Jeremiah Baker, Jesse Lewis, John Morris, Jesse Seegars, Crawford's heirs, Daniel Fields, Martha Pierce, Andrew Jameson, Samuel Blair, J.E. Hall, ex-sheriff & ex-officio collector Gallatin Co., Ill.

----------

## JOHNSON COUNTY, ILLINOIS
Delinquent Taxes for years 1845,46,47,48
Southern Illinois Advocate, April 20, 1849
Newspaper Microfilm

A list of lands and real estate situated in the county of Johnson and state of Illinois on which taxes remain due and unpaid for the years 1845,46,47,48.

Lewis R. Brewers, William Printy, E & J Forman, the heirs of Godfrey Muchler, Jeremiah White, Richard McGinnis, Bennet Jones, Joel Hobbs, Swe'man, C.G. Ladd. R.S. Gray, collector.

----------

## LAWRENCE COUNTY, ILLINOIS
Delinquent Taxes for the year 1838
Vandalia Free Press and Illinois Whig, 27 Dec. 1838
Newspaper Microfilm

A list of lands lying in Lawrence County, due and unpaid for the year on 1st day of Sept. 1838

James Bryant, James Little, Gerald V Cauchran, John Radsittlet, Adam Lakey Jr., John Allinson, Adam Corrie, John Wilson, William Kinkade, W. Franch and T. Rogman, John Law, Joel Wise, Cornelius Delong, James P. Cunningham, Daniel Rawlings, Jess B. Corayer, John B. Hay, Pierre B. Cornyer, Francis Bourron, Joseph Ducharme, Moses Henry, Garmel Roland, John B. Willarty, Louis Lunnayon, hiers of A. Burkhead, heirs of Jacob Noy, Joseph Laphunt, Pierre Craumacher,

Louis Ramulet, Francois Petler, John Savage, John Creely, Thomas B. Dugout, William Spencer, Archibald George, George Manure, Isaac Law, Richardson Spencer.

---

## Capt. William C. Ralls' Company
### Black Hawk War, June 15, 1832
### Illinois Adjutant General's Records

Note: These mounted volunteers are from the counties of Schuyler, Monroe, Adams, St. Louis, Mo., and Shelby.

Capt. William C. Ralls, First Lt. Radford M. Wyatt, Sgts. John M. Jones, Samuel M. Pierce, Stephen A. St. Cyr, S.G. Bond, Pvts. John Briscoe, Stephen Brooks, Erastes Beebe, John D. Crawford, Jefferson Coonrod, Johnston Chapman, Joel Eves, James W. Johnston, Thomas Johnston, Ezra Kirkland, Ruthford Lane, Daniel Moore, William Morris, Andrew Melvan, Luke Owens, Jacob Richardson, Aaron Richardson, Xerxes F. Trail, Eben Turner, Jacob Wilkerson.

---

## Perry County, Illinois
### Delinquent Taxes for the year 1838
### Vandalia Free Press and Illinois Whig, Saturday, Dec. 27, 1828
### Newspaper Microfilm, Illinois State Historical Library

Alexander Andeson, John Edgar, James H. Franklin, I. Price, Alexander Durham, Robert Woodside, Charles Garner, Maniblmus Lavaglacer, Hugh Brown, William G. Brown.

---

## Fayette County, Illinois
### Delinquent Taxes for the year 1838
### Vandalia Free Press and Illinois Whig, Jan. 3, 1839
### Newspaper Microfilm, Illinois State Historical Library

Nathaniel Pope, Heirs of John McKee, John Stallings, John Dement, J. Wilson and G. Ashley, R.K. McLaughlin, James Mason, Ferdinand Erst, Mose K. Buttford, Joseph Chaffin, Henry Glager, Zephan Case, John Lawler, Robert M. Peebles, Henry Reuman, Abram Dunker, Zephtha Hardin, Silas Bankson.

---

ATTENTION ---- ATTENTION ----- ATTENTION ---- ATTENTION ----

TO ALL SUBSCRIBERS

SAVE, SAVE, SAVE $3.00 on next subscription by

paying now. Beginning with November December 1987,

Volume IV Number 1 issue, subscription

price will be $15.00. Renew now and save for another

year. Send payment to the editor before

December 1987.

Shelby County, Illinois
Obituary Abstracts
Date of newspaper following from newspaper microfilm
Illinois State Historical Library

Stansberry, Henry Ed.   Died 14 July 1895
    Born 9 March 1863 Fairfield Co., Ohio; died of paralysis; mother ill and unable to attend.
        Shelbyville Democrat, 18 July 1895

Stebbins, Hester   Died 1 March 1879
    From Ohio; died at Shelbyville at home of J.P. Davis; body sent back to Ohio for burial.
        Shelbyville Democrat, 6 March 1879

Stiveson, Jacob   Died 18 April 1877 Flat Branch Twp.
    Born or moved from Ohio; died at age 58 of congestive chills; sick only 36 hours; surviving, widow and 7 children; funeral at Locust Grove Church; burial there.
        Shelbyville Democrat, 26 April 1877

Storm, William   Died 7 May 1894
    Born 10 Aug. 1829 Pulaski Co., KY; son of John and Sarah Storm; came with parents family to Ash Grove in 1831; his mother called "Grandma Good" in later years; married 15 Dec. 1847 Elizabeth Rankin; 9 children, two sons deceased; surviving, widow and 7 children, one of which is Mrs. Elnora Lawton of Kansas; burial Ash Grove Cemetery.
        Shelbyville Democrat, 17 May 1894

Stout, John   Died Jan./Feb. 1877
    Died a young man; found dead in bed; an invalid.
        Shelbyville Democrat, 8 Feb. 1877

Strohl, Samuel   Died 24 Oct. 1877
    "We learn this morning that Samuel Strohl died very suddenly last night." Burial, Washington Graveyard.
        Shelbyville Democrat, 25 Oct. 1877

Strohl, William   Died 25 Dec. 1885
    Died at home near Strasburg; came to Shelby County from Hocking Co., Ohio 1865; died at age 72; member of Lutheran Church 25 years; burial, Elm Grove Cemetery, Prairie Twp.
        Shelbyville Democrat, 31 Dec. 1885

Sullivan, Wm. B. and Jennie   61st Anniversary
    Celebrated 26 July 1887 at Cowden, Ill.; William B. born 22 Nov. 1799 Blount Co., TN; lived there 8 years then moved to Ray Co., TN; married wife there who was born 30 April 1809 Sparkenburg Dist., TN; moved to Cowden, Ill. area 56 years ago; 13 children.
        Shelbyville Democrat, 4 Aug. 1887

Sullivan, Jennie S.   Died 21 Sept. 1890
    Born 20 April 1809 Sparkeyburg Dist., TN; moved with parents to McMahone Co., TN; married Wm. B. Sullivan, TN; 12 children, 4 deceased; surviving, husband and children: Mrs. D.A. Banning, Mrs. Henry Blakey, William, James, Robert, George, Mrs. Nathan Hall, Frank.
        Shelbyville Democrat, 2 Oct. 1890
        Our Best Words Weekly, 27 Sept. 1890

Sullivan, William B.      Died 30 March 1891
    Born 22 Nov. 1790/9 Blount Co., TN; married 20 July 1826 Jennie Wilson at Ray Co., TN who died 1890; came to Dry Point Twp., Shelby Co., Ill. after marriage; 12 children; surviving, 5 sons and 3 daughters.
        Shelbyville Democrat, 10 April 1891

Syfert, Infant      Died 17 Sept. 1878
    Child of Nathan Syfert; burial, Hubbart Cemetery.
        Shelbyville Democrat, 3 Oct. 1878

Syfert, Isaac      Died 15 July 1877
    Aged 65 years; died near Sylvan; congestion of the ?; services and burial at Mt. Carmel the 18th; Rev. Brown of Mode, speaker.
        Shelbyville Democrat, 2 Aug. 1877

Swartz, Mr.      Died April 1882
    Father of Mrs. Jennie Wagner.
        Shelbyville Democrat, 20 April 1882

Tallman, Benjamin      Died Feb. 1877
    Died last Saturday of pneumonia; of Dry Point twp. but lived in Shelbyville.
        Shelbyville Democrat, 1 March 1877

Tandy, Martha M. Reid      Died 28 Oct. 1886
    Born 3 Oct. 1805 Lexington, KY; married 31 Oct. 1822 Willis Tandy; 12 children, 4 deceased; surviving, D.R. Tandy of Helena, MT, H.C. Tandy of Visalia, CA, A.J. and G.W. Tandy of Harristown, Ill., W.S. Tandy of Lincoln, Ill., Mrs. S.J. Shrock of Covington, KY, Mrs. Elias Smith of Shelbyville, Ill.; also three brothers and 1 sister; burial, Jacksonville, Ill.
        Shelbyville Democrat, 18 Nov. 1886

Tennery, Samantha      Died 1 March 1880
    Born circa 1857; died with lung fever at father's home near Beecher City.
        Shelbyville Democrat, 11 March 1880

Thompson, George M.      Died 13 Jan. 1887
    Born 17 Sept. 1831 Sheffield, Eng.; surviving, 5 orphan children, all minors; mother died two weeks before.
        Shelbyville Democrat, 20 Jan. 1887

Thornton, Lucy B.      Died 12 April 1876
    Born 25 Sept. 1803 Essex Co., VA; married 2 May 1821 Charles T. Thornton, brother of W.F. Thornton, who died of cholera in summer of 1855 Shelbyville; moved to state of Georgia until 1831, then Tennessee for 21 years; came to Shelby Co., Ill. 1853; surviving, daughter Mrs. S.B. Hickman and other children; burial, city cemetery.
        Shelbyville Democrat, 27 April 1876

Tolly, James      Died 7 Nov. 1889 Moweaqua, Ill.
    Born 7 June 1801 Mercer Co., KY; moved with parents at age 2 to Madison Co., Ill.; 1831 moved to Shelby Co., Ill.; married first, April 1821 Winnie Davis of KY at Troy, Ill.; ten children, 7 deceased; surviving, Daniel, Neal, John; married 2nd, Sept. 1871 Mrs. Margaret Shaw, Shelbyville; one son, Benjamin; burial, Tolly Cemetery.
        Moweaqua Call Mail, 14 Nov. 1889

## SHELBY COUNTY, ILLINOIS
### Cholera era victims of June, July 1855
### Deaths entered in probate court

John Merriman, died 25 June 1855
Phillip Purcell, died 21 June 1855
Nicholas Brooks, died 29 July 1855
Abram H. Dutton, died 16 July 1855
John D. Bruster, died 14 July 1855
Samuel F. Cook, died 2 July 1855
Jesse Kennedy, died 29 June 1855
John Getz, died 9 July 1855
Elijah Parkhurst, died 8 July 1855
James P. Divins, died 26 July 1855
William Inman, died 22 July 1855
Samuel A. Clesson, died 3 July 1855
John H. Drennen, died 31 July 1855
Amon Butter, died 1 July 1855
Francis Wonnenburg, died 9 July 1855
John Clark, died 11 June 1855

---

### War of 1812 Regiment
### Capt. Daniel Boultinghouse
### Sept. 8 to Dec. 8, 1814 Service
### Illinois Adjutant General's Records

Capt. Daniel Boultinghouse; First Lt. John Graves; 2nd Lt. Robert Tavery; 3rd Lt. John Morris; Ensign Thomas Tavery; Sgts. William Nash, Stephen Stanley, James Boyd, James Hopkins, Tira Robinson; Corps. John Wilson, Robert Boyd, David Haney, William Cummings, Asa Ross, Robert Clark; Pvts. Real Porter, Edward Potter, James Dunlap, William Trask, Rolen Lane, Benjamin Kirkendall, Hiram Jones, Daniel McHenry, John Dover, James Hencely, Jesse Kirkendall, George Sturm, John Morris, George Martin, John Burney, Needham Stanley, Charles Hencely, James Paton, Jonathon Steward, John Brown, Eli Selph, James Boultinghouse, Charles Burney, Daniel Boultinghouse, George Morris, David Daniel, John Daniel, David Brown, Irvan Wilson, Charles Steward, William Vaughn, John Dennis, Philip Steward, John Buckels, James Corn, Archibald Clayton, Nathan Young, Nathan Harris, Thomas Pool, William Meriday, John Moor, John Lucas, William Burney, Joseph Daniels, Jesse Donan, Jarrard Trawell, Seth Hargrave, Daniel Snodgrass, Joseph Lawry, William Adkins, James Davenport, James Wilson, Robert Stafford, John Martin, Robert D. Cates, Henry Coley, John Beck, Moses Sweeton, Charles Dickerson, Hugh Collins, Edward Meloy, James Hix, Willis Chambers, Jesse Adkins, Wyatt Adkins, Thomas Chambers, Joseph Culbertson, Arvin Wilson, William Read, William Chambers, John Ferret, Edward Michel, John Poley, Thomas McAllister, Alden Henry, James Martin, Archibald Rowan, Joel Metcalf, Elijah Reece, Henry Wheeler, Samuel Davidson, Moses Lamb, William McCormick, Ezekial Hide, John Gastin, Charles Lezeenby, James Morris, Robert Gastin, Merritt Taylor, Nimrod Taylor, Edmond Starks, William McGehee, Thomas Gastin, John McGahan, William Clark, Jonathon Hampton, John Walls, William McCoy, John Perry, Elias Chaffin, Brice Hannah, Thomas Wilson, John McCallister, Reuben Walden, James Gastin

John Heart, Henry Stumm, John Whitaker, George McCann, James Haynes.

---

WILLIAMSON COUNTY, ILLINOIS
Biographies listed in
History of Gallatin, Saline, Hamilton, Franklin
& Williamson Counties, Illinois
Chicago: Goodspeed Pub. Co., 1887

Willis Allen, J.E. Allen, J.E. Bainbridge, David Barth, Dr. A.P. Baker, Dr. M.D. Baker, M.L. Baker, Dr. G.J. Baker, A.J. Benson, S.C. Boles, Thos. Bones, Reuben Borton, J.M. Brandon, M.J. Brewer, Frank Brown, Dr. Curtis Brown, Capt. John Brown, F.H. Bulliner, J.M. Burkhart, J.H. Burnett, M.C. Campbell, Laban Carter, Geo. B. Chamness, A.L. Cline, J.F. Connell, E.G. Creal, T.N. Cripps, E.L. Darrow, Josiah Davis, G.W. Davis, H.M. Davis, B.F. Davis, A.J. Davis, E.L. Denison, C.H. Denison, Thos. Dunaway, Samuel Dunaway, W.W. Duncan, John H. Duncan, A.J. Duncan, J.W. Erwin, W.H. Eubanks, D.R. Felts, Leander Ferrell, Levi Ferrell, Dr. J.J. Fly, E. Peter Follis, J.M. Fowler, L.A. Goddard, Goodall & Tippy, F.M. Goodall, John Goodall, J.J. Graham, Isaac Hammer, D.K. Harrison, Dr. James Hayton, Jesse Hendrickson, H. Hendrickson, G.A. Henshaw, Ephraim Herrin, W.H. Hinchcliff, Brice Holland, R.D. Holland, John Huddeston, Lt. Z. Huggens, Rev. A. Hunter, G.W. Ingram, J.C. Jackson, Thomas H. Keeler, C. Kennedy, C.M. Kern, Rev. G.W. LaMaster, John C. Lee, R.M. Lupfer, W.R. McCall, W.C. McCormick, M.M. McDonald, W.J. McNiel, W.H. Mann, W.J. Martin, G.O. Mitchell, E.B. Mitchell, J.C. Mitchell, W.H. Moren, H.C. Murrah, Giles Nelson, John G. Newton, A.H. North, Rev. Martin Odum, Henry Ogden, A.N. Owen, A.M. Palmer, Charles Parks, W.A. Perrine, Dr. W.H. Perry, J.H. Perry, Henry Phillips, Scott Prindle, A. Luke Ralls, A.P. Reeves, Hugh M. Richart, W.J. Ridgway, P.L. Roberts, J.W. Roberts, J.L. Roberts, M.W. Robertson, J.L. Russell, W.E. Sizemore, James W. Smith, Mrs. E.N. Sprague, Jacob Stein, J.H. Stewart, Dr. G.W. Thomas, S.D. Thompson, James Thompson, J.F. Tidwell, W. Tregoning, Elijah Turner, Irvin M. Walker, W.S. Washburn, Dr. A.D. Watson, C.A. White, Azzi F. White, N.S. White, R. Winning, J.L. Wolfe M.D., Judge G. W. Young, F.C. and W.H. Zimmerman.

---

SPECIAL HALF PRICE SALE FOR THOSE CHRISTMAS PEOPLE

People and Rural Schools of Shelby County, Ill. Over 3000 people in index. On sale now for $12.50. Regularly $25. Postage paid.

The Shelby County Book. Biographies, and reunions from 1937. On sale now for $5. Regularly $10 postage paid.

Remember to renew now and save on another year of SEARCHING ILLINOIS ANCESTORS at the old rate of $12.00 for six issues. Beginning December 1987, subscription price will be $15.00.

The Illinois State Historical Library will no longer search newspaper microfilm unless a fee of $5 plus is paid in advance. The editor of this magazine will still search newspaper microfilm.

SPECIAL NOTICE For those very difficult genealogical problems, this editor will search the Newberry Library in Chicago--21 miles of records including genealogy. $100 deposit with clear detailed outline of problem and area to search. Contact the editor.

## PAID ADVERTISING

Seek information on John J. Haydon, b. 1821 Kentucky, son of William and Elizabeth Haydon of Moultrie & Shelby County, Ill. 1/wife Clary Munson, 2/w Mary Elizabeth Wright. 1860 and 1870 living Shelbyville, Ill. Occupation: merchant/banker. Possibly left 1870-1880 Shelbyville. Children: Frances M. Haydon, Rachel E. Haydon m. Henry M. Peden.

Diane L. Webb, 1320 Cedar Ridge Lane, Colorado Spgs, CO 80919

EDITOR'S NOTE: From this magazine, Jan. Feb. 1985 issue, page 43, appeared the following obituary abstracts.

Haydon, Elizabeth, died 21 April 1876, born 5 April 1796 Franklin County, Kentucky; married circa 1815 William Haydon; couple came to Coles County, Ill. 1831; 1853 moved to Sullivan, Ill. Surviving, sons, John and W.L. Haydon of Shelbyville. [4 May 1876 Shelby County Democrat, Shelbyville, IL.]

Haydon, John James, died 4 May 1877, born 9 Sept. 1820 Franklin County, Kentucky; married first, 1845 Clarissa Munson who died 1849; married second, 8 Aug. 1852 Lizzie Wright; one son drowned in Okaw River 3 July 1858; one daughter, Mrs. H.M. Peden died 4 May 1872; surviving, grandson ? Peden. [10 May 1877 Shelby County Democrat, Shelbyville, IL.]

---

## MORE QUERIES

SANGAMON, MONTGOMERY: Westbrook, Dunn

Emilie Fowler, 808 Carob St., Brea, CA 92621

EDITOR'S NOTE: From Jan. Feb. 1987 issue of this magazine, page 30:

Briton Harris and Nancy Westbrook, Christian County, Ill. marriage, book 1, page 58.

From page 42 of magazine, same issue, David Westbrook and Richard Westbrook of Saline County, Ill. have biographies in 1887 History of Gallatin, Saline, Hamilton, Franklin and Williamson County, Ill.

SHELBY: Sickles, Wood, Black

Glenda Velon, 6700 Butler Road, Penryn, CA 95663

---

TO ALL CURRENT SUBSCRIBERS:

Please update your Illinois county and Illinois ancestor interests by sending it on a postcard to the Editor, Box 392, Shelbyville, IL 62565. Many subscribers have NOT indicated any county preference or surname. Simply spell out the county and the ancestor's full name you are searching. Send it before Dec. 1, 1987 so it will be included in the next issue of Searching Illinois Ancestors. Also remember to save money now by taking out another year at the old price before Dec. 1, 1987.

---

## INDEX TO SEARCHING ILLINOIS ANCESTORS
### VOLUME 3 NUMBER 6

| | | | |
|---|---|---|---|
| Abbott, 124,125 | Abernathy, 122 | Accault, 125 | Ackerman, 125 |
| Adams, 122,125 | Addams, 125 | Adkins, 131 | Ains, 124 |
| Akers, 125 | Akin, 125 | Alcorn, 125 | Aldrich, 125 |
| Alexander, 125 | Allen, 125,132 | Allinson, 127 | Anderson, 120 |
| Andeson, 128 | Apple, 122 | Ashley, 128 | Ashmore, 123 |

Austin, 120        Baber, 121         Bainbridge, 132
Baker, 122,124,126,127,132            Baldridge, 120   Bankson, 128
Banning, 126,129   Barker, 127        Barnes, 122,123  Barron, 127
Barrow, 126        Barth, 132         Basye, 126       Beck, 131
Beebe, 128         Behan, 124         Benson, 132      Bingerman, 124
Bishop, 122        Bivins, 131        Blackburn, 124   Blair, 127
Blakey, 129        Boles, 132         Boman, 131       Bond, 128
Bones, 132         Borton, 132        Boultinghouse, 131
Bourron, 127       Boyd, 131          Bowman, 122      Bowman, 121
Bradley, 122       Bradford, 122      Brandon, 132     Brewer, 132
Brewers, 127       Bridges, 124       Briscoe, 128     Brockett, 124
Brookman, 124      Brooks, 128,131    Brown, 123,124,127,128,130,131,132
Bruster, 131       Bryant, 127        Buck, 127        Buckels, 131
Bulliner, 132      Bunnayon, 127      Burkhart, 132    Burkhead, 127
Burnett, 132       Burney, 131        Butter, 131      Buttford, 128
Calbert, 122       Campbell, 122,124,132               Carlin, 124
Carman, 121        Carns, 127         Carpenter, 121   Carr, 127
Carter, 127,132    Cartwright, 124    Casad, 123       Case, 128
Cash, 121          Cates, 131         Cauchran, 127    Celton, 122
Chaffin, 128,131   Chambers, 131      Chamness, 132    Chaplin, 126
Chapman, 128       Chatterton, 128    Cheadis, 121     Cheeks, 123
Cherry, 122        Chesney, 123       Childers, 122    Clark, 123,124,131
Clayton, 131       Clesson, 131       Cline, 132       Cocannour, 126
Cole, 121          Coley, 131         Collin, 122      Collins, 131
Colman, 122        Combs, 123         Connell, 132     Conter, 122
Conway, 124        Cook, 131          Coonrod, 128     Corayer, 127
Corn, 131          Cornyer, 127       Corrie, 127      Cox, 120
Craumacher, 127    Crawford, 127,128                    Creal, 132
Creely, 128        Cripps, 132        Crocker, 122     Crosthwait, 121
Culbertson, 131    Cummings, 131      Cunningham, 127  Cutler, 123
Cutright, 121      Daniel, 131        Darrow, 132      Davenport, 131
David, 122         Davidson, 131      Davis, 122,129,130,132
Day, 120           Defenbaugh, 124    Delong, 127      Dement, 128
Denison, 132       Dennis, 131        Dickerson, 131   Dorsey, 127
Dover, 131         Drennen, 131       Ducharme, 127    Dudley, 127
Dugout, 128        Dukes, 122         Dunaway, 132     Duncan, 124,132
Dunker, 128        Dunlap, 131        Dunn, 121,123    Durham, 128
Dutton, 131        Eddy, 127          Edgar, 122,128   Edwards, 127
Egbert, 122        Ellington, 123     Ellis, 122       Erst, 128
Erwin, 122,132     Eubanks, 132       Eves, 128        Farmore, 124
Felts, 132         Ferrell, 132       Ferret, 131      Fields, 127
Fiene, 126         Flatt, 124         Fly, 132         Follis, 132
Foor, 121          Foreman, 120       Forman, 127      Forth, 124
Fowler, 127,132    Franch, 127        Franklin, 128    French, 122
Fry, 124           Funkhouser, 124    Gallagher, 127   Garner, 128
Garrison, 124      Garvin, 127        Gastin, 131      Gatewood, 127
George, 121,128    Getz, 131          Gillinwatters, 124
Glager, 128        Goddard, 131       Goforth, 127     Gold, 127
Good, 129          Goodall, 132       Graham, 132      Graves, 131
Gray, 127          Greene, 124        Greer, 127       Griffith, 124
Griswold, 124      Grove, 127         Haines, 122      Hainline, 126
Hall, 127,129      Halstead, 123      Hammer, 132      Hampton, 122,131

| | | | |
|---|---|---|---|
| Haney, 131 | Hannah, 131 | Hanon, 121 | Hardin, 123,127,128 |
| Hargrave, 127,131 | Harris, 122,131 | Harrison, 132 | Hart, 124,126 |
| Hatchett, 121 | Hatsell, 127 | Hay, 127 | Haynes, 132 |
| Hayton, 132 | Heart, 132 | Heddon, 127 | Heinlein, 122 |
| Hencely, 131 | Hendrickson, 132 | Henneman, 126 | Henry, 127,131 |
| Henshaw, 132 | Heralson, 127 | Herrin, 132 | Hewitt, 124 |
| Hick, 127 | Hickman, 130 | Hicks, 121 | Hide, 131 |
| Hill, 122 | Hinchcliff, 132 | Hinklin, 121 | Hish, 126 |
| Hix, 131 | Hobbs, 127 | Hodges, 126 | Hogan, 126,127 |
| Holland, 132 | Hollingsworth, 122 | | Hooper, 126 |
| Hopkins, 131 | How, 126 | Howard, 121 | Huddard, 123 |
| Huddleston, 132 | Hudgens, 132 | Hunter, 132 | Ingram, 132 |
| Inman, 126,131 | Jackson, 132 | Jameson, 127 | Jane, 124 |
| Johnston, 126,128 | Jones, 124,126,127,128,131 | | Journey, 123 |
| Kaldhar, 126 | Keeler, 132 | Kennedy, 131,132 | Kern, 132 |
| Kessler, 121 | Keys, 122 | King, 127 | Kinkade, 127 |
| Kinney, 122 | Kinsey, 122 | Kirkendall, 131 | Kirkland, 128 |
| Kirkpatrick, 127 | Klinefelter, 122 | Knief, 126 | Knight, 123 |
| Ladd, 127 | Lakey, 127 | Lamaster, 132 | Lamb, 131 |
| Lane, 127,128,131 | Langley, 121 | Laphunt, 127 | Lavaglacer, 128 |
| Law, 127,128 | Lawler, 128 | Lawry, 131 | Lawton, 129 |
| Layman, 122 | Lee, 122,132 | Leech, 127 | Leggott, 126 |
| Lemaster, 122 | LePoer, 126 | Lewis, 122,127 | Linn, 122,124 |
| Little, 127 | Lorton, 124 | Loy, 124 | Lucas, 131 |
| Lupfer, 132 | Lytle, 123 | McAllister, 131 | McCall, 132 |
| McCallister, 131 | McCann, 132 | McCaskey, 121 | McClain, 126 |
| McConkey, 121 | McConnall, 121 | McCormick, 131,132 | McCoy, 121,131 |
| McCurdy, 124 | McDaniel, 122 | McDonald, 121,132 | McDonough, 122 |
| McGahan, 131 | McGehee, 131 | McGehen, 127 | McGinnis, 127 |
| McGlone, 127 | McHenry, 131 | McKee, 128 | McKennee, 121 |
| McKinzy, 121 | McLaughlin, 128 | McNiel, 132 | McQuon, 121,122 |
| Maddox, 122,123 | Madox, 122 | Malom, 122 | Mann, 132 |
| Manure, 128 | Marshall, 122 | Martin, 131,132 | Mason, 121,122,128 |
| Masters, 121 | Mathew, 121 | Mathias, 126 | Maxfield, 122,124 |
| May, 121,122 | Meads, 122 | Meloy, 131 | Melvan, 128 |
| Menard, 122 | Meriday, 131 | Merriman, 131 | Metcalf, 131 |
| Michel, 121,131 | Michels, 122 | Middleton, 122 | Milam, 121 |
| Miles, 127 | Miller, 121,123,124 | | Milligan, 121 |
| Minnis, 121 | Misenbarger, 122 | Missen, 121 | Mitchell, 122,123,132 |
| Moderal, 123 | Moffett, 123 | Montel, 121 | Montgomery, 122 |
| Moor, 131 | Moore, 121,122,128 | | Moren, 132 |
| Morgan, 121 | Morgret, 122 | Morris, 121,122,123,127,128,131 | |
| Morrisey, 126 | Morrison, 122,127 | Morton, 123 | Mount, 121 |
| Muchler, 127 | Huer, 122 | Mugin, 122 | Murrah, 132 |
| Murry, 121 | Myer, 122 | Nash, 131 | Nasworthy, 126 |
| Neff, 126 | Nelson, 132 | Newton, 132 | Nichols, 123 |
| Nicholson, 121 | North, 132 | Noy, 127 | O'Brien, 120 |
| Odum, 132 | Ogden, 132 | Oldham, 122 | Owen, 132 |
| Owens, 128 | Page, 127 | Pailee, 124 | Palmer, 132 |
| Parish, 121 | Parker, 122 | Parkhurst, 131 | Parks, 126,132 |
| Pate, 121,122 | Paton, 131 | Patrick, 127 | Patterson, 123 |
| Pearce, 122 | Peebles, 128 | Penren, 122 | Perkins, 127 |

Perrine, 132; Perry, 131,132; Peter, 127; Petler, 128
Phenix, 121; Pherigo, 121; Phillips, 132; Pierce, 123,127,128
Poley, 131; Platt, 126; Pool, 131; Pope, 128
Porter, 131; Post, 124; Potter, 127,131; Potts, 122
Powell, 124; Price, 122,128; Prichett, 121; Prindle, 132
Provine, 122; Pursell, 131; Printy, 127; Radeker, 126
Radfield, 122; Radsittle, 127; Raffity, 122; Ralls, 132
Ramulet, 128; Rankin, 129; Rawlings, 127; Rawls, 128
Read, 131; Record, 126; Reed, 126; Reede, 131
Reeves, 132; Reid, 130; Reuman, 128; Reynolds, 122
Rice, 127; Rich, 120; Richardson, 120,121,124,128
Richart, 132; Ridgway, 132; Riggs, 122; Rittenhouse, 122
Rittmeyer, 121; Roberts, 121,132; Robertson, 132; Robinson, 123,124,131
Rogman, 127; Roland, 127; Ross, 131; Rowan, 131
Rudick, 127; Russell, 132; Saline, 127; St. Cyr, 128
Saunders, 123; Savage, 128; Schmidt, 121; Schneider, 126
Schoenberger, 126; Scriber, 122; Scudmore, 127; Schoon, 126
Seabolt, 127; Seegars, 127; Selph, 131; Sexton, 127
Shaw, 130; Shrock, 130; Silkwood, 122; Sizemore, 132
Slade, 122,123; Slaymaker, 126; Slover, 124
Smith, 121,124,126,127,130,132; Smock, 120; Snodgrass, 131
Southmaid, 127; Spalt, 121; Spencer, 128; Splen, 127
Sprague, 132; Stafford, 131; Stallings, 128; Standish, 126
Stanley, 131; Stansberry, 129; Starks, 131; Stebbins, 129
Steele, 123; Stein, 132; Steward, 131; Stewart, 132
Stiveson, 129; Stockton, 124; Storm, 129; Stout, 129
Strode, 122; Strohl, 129; Stumm, 132; Sullivan, 129,130
Swartz, 130; Swearingen, 123; Sweeton, 131; Sweeman, 127
Syfert, 130; Tallman, 130; Tanant, 124; Tandy, 130
Taurante, 127; Tavery, 131; Taylor, 121,122,127,131
Tennery, 130; Thacker, 127; Thaxton, 124; Thomas, 124,132
Thompson, 124,127,130,132; Thornton, 126,130; Tidwell, 132
Tippy, 132; Tite, 127; Tolly, 130; Trail, 128
Tramell, 131; Trammell, 126; Trask, 131; Tregoning, 132
Trinkle, 122; Trower, 123; Tucker, 123; Turner, 128,132
Turpin, 124; Tutle, 123; Vanarsdale, 122; Vanlandingham, 127
Vincents, 122; Vinciner, 124; Vinson, 127; Vaughn, 131
Wagner, 130; Walden, 131; Walker, 132; Walls, 131
Ward, 123; Warren, 121; Washburn, 122,132; Waters, 122
Watson, 122,132; Webster, 123; Wheeler, 131; Whitaker, 132
White, 127,132; Whiteside, 124; Whitten, 123; Wilkerson, 128
Will, 122; Willarty, 127; Williams, 122,127; Willis, 127
Wilson, 121,122,127,128,130,131; Wilton, 122; Winning, 132
Wise, 127; Wolf, 122; Wolfe, 132; Wonnenburg, 131
Woodside, 128; Wrence, 124; Wyatt, 128; Young, 126,131,132
Zimmerman, 132

---

Advertising rates remain the same. Check with the editor for current information.

www.ingramcontent.com/pod-product-compliance
Lightning Source LLC
Chambersburg PA
CBHW081235170426
43198CB00017B/2762